NOT TOO OLD

college
press
Joplin, Missouri

ENDORSEMENTS

"*Not Too Old* is just terrific! It's the best and most thorough book on aging I've ever read, and it is the best gift you could give to someone who's struggling with aging. It will lift their spirits and challenge them to live every day to the fullest. It's also a great gift for preachers and church leaders (including younger ones) because it reminds us that healthy churches are inter-generational churches. This book is challenging, humorous, practical, helpful, thorough, and biblical. It lifted my spirits and challenged me to keep stretching to make every day count."

BOB RUSSELL
Senior Minister (Retired)
Southeast Christian Church
Louisville, Kentucky

"Throughout this book, Dave Faust serves as a compassionate guide through the realities of growing older. Chocked full of engaging stories, warm wisdom, and practical ideas, *Not Too Old* is a beautiful and empowering traveling companion and equipping tool for anyone desiring to finish the last season of life well, while preparing with great anticipation for the season yet to come."

WENDY HERRBERG
Registered Nurse, Counselor, and Life Coach
with Renewal Counseling, LLC

"I am in the 'Builder' generation of which David writes in this book, and I really benefitted from his enlightening words. In seventeen chapters David touches on such things as fears about aging, the high calling of grandparenthood, and entering the role of a caregiver. Each chapter is worth the price of the book. David writes in a winsome and compassionate manner, and I know this book is going to be a blessing to all who 'take up and read.'"

VICTOR KNOWLES
Founder/President
Peace On Earth Ministries
Joplin, Missouri

"This book answers every question a Christian has about growing old, from both a spiritual and a practical perspective. Who needs to read this book? Those of us who are already old or will one day grow old, which includes you, your children, your parents, and your grandparents. The wisdom imparted here will bless, guide, and encourage not only you and your loved ones, but your church as well. I'm currently in my 70s, yet Dave Faust reminds me that I'm NOT TOO OLD to turn my later years into greater years!"

ED SIMCOX
former Indiana Secretary of State

"This book will be useful for helpers, counselors, or those who are grieving themselves. It has something for everyone, even those of us who are definitely 'not too old.' As a counselor, I see the nuggets of truth and encouragement in these pages as something I can use with clients, supervisees, or peers to help them in their journeys."

NATALIE HUBARTT, LMHC
Director of Counseling, Support & Recovery
East 91st Street Christian Church

"*Not Too Old* is a must-read for those of us in this later season of life. Dave Faust has woven together great advice, humor and biblical promises that will set us up for success. After finishing this book, I'm ready to make adjustments that assure my later years become greater years."

SCOTT SWAN
News Anchor
WRTV, Indianapolis

"*Not Too Old* shows us that age is merely a number when it comes to fulfilling our God-given destiny and achieving victory in life's race. Through engaging storytelling and biblical truths, Dave Faust uplifts, inspires, and turns the tables on age, cheekily suggesting that you're only as old as you feel when sprinting toward your finish line—walker and orthopedic shoes optional."

COLONEL MARCUS H. THOMAS
U.S. Army (Retired)

DEDICATION

This book is written in loving memory of my great-grandparents, Frank and Addie Faust. They died before I was born, so I won't meet them until I get to heaven; but their faith has cascaded down through the generations like a river watering parched soil.

I also dedicate this book to two friends who have served Christ faithfully and fruitfully, not only when they were young, but also during their senior adult years. Bob Russell's practical biblical preaching and John Samples' loving pastoral care continue to help people turn their later years into greater years.

APPRECIATION

Jim Nieman, managing editor of *Christian Standard*, used his editorial skills to help make this book a lot better than it would have been without his sharp eyes and godly wisdom. I am deeply grateful for his assistance. And I am grateful to my wife, Candy, and my friends at East 91st Street Christian Church who understand and encourage my desire to write articles and books that "teach the Bible and love the people."

TABLE OF CONTENTS

1 | You Need to Read This Book— Even if You Are Young

*"Old age is like everything else.
To make a success of it, you've got to start young."*
—Theodore Roosevelt

*"The best time to plant a tree was 20 years ago.
The second-best time is now."*
—Chinese proverb

It's time to take a new look at old age.

On my sixtieth birthday my grandchildren gave me a serviceberry tree to plant in my backyard. Before that day I didn't know serviceberry trees existed, but it turns out, they are common in Indiana where I live. If you manage to keep the birds away, by early June the trees produce delicious red berries that taste like tart cherries. My grandkids said, "Papa, we want you to have a serviceberry tree because serving God is important to you."

I enjoyed my birthday celebration, but some unpleasant questions crossed my mind while we planted the tree. I wondered, *Now that I have reached age 60, how much service do I have left? Is the best part of my life behind me?*

You may have asked questions like these yourself. But notice what it says in the book of Psalms:

> The righteous will flourish like a palm tree, they will grow like a cedar of Lebanon; planted in the house of the Lord, they will flourish in the courts of our God. They will still bear fruit in old age, they will stay fresh and green (Psalm 92:12-14).

I like that description of old age. Who wouldn't want to "flourish like a palm tree" and "grow like a cedar of Lebanon"? I want to "still bear fruit in old age" and "stay fresh and green" as long as possible—not just wither away and wait to die.

The apostle Paul probably was in his sixties when he urged his young friend Timothy to "be prepared in season and out of season" (2 Timothy 4:2). Are you well-prepared for the next season of life? If you live into your seventies, eighties, or nineties, will you keep serving the Lord and bearing fruit for him? Will you be a faithful Christ follower or an old fuddy-duddy? A cheerful soul or a grumpy old grouch? A hope giver or a dream crusher? Will you "be prepared to give an answer to everyone who asks you to give the reason for the hope that you have" (1 Peter 3:15)?

At this point in my life—somewhere between Generation X and Generation X-Ray—I'm still adjusting to viewing myself as a senior adult. I'm not a spring chicken anymore. Apparently, I'm now a fall (or winter) chicken.

A young colleague on my church staff was describing another member of our church. "He's an *old* guy," my friend explained, "in his *sixties.*" To me, 60 doesn't sound old. Another staff member mentioned "classic old hymns" people sing in church, and he was talking about songs from the 1990s.

When my daughter was 10 years old, she asked, "Dad, when you were little, did you dress like the Pilgrims?"

"No," I answered, "but I think Grandpa did."

One time I told my mom, "It's hard to believe my kids are all in their thirties now."

She replied, "How do you think I feel? My boys are all in their sixties!" (She always referred to my two older brothers and me as her "boys," even though we are grandpas ourselves.)

Soon after my sixtieth birthday I was invited to speak to a group of senior adults at a retreat. I entitled my message, "Not Too Old," and afterward I felt a growing desire to write a book on that topic to encourage adults to age well and stay engaged in serving God. I jokingly told my friends, "I want to write a book about aging, but I don't feel qualified because I'm not old enough." Eventually, though, I decided I shouldn't wait any longer to write this book, lest I become too old to accomplish the task!

I am convinced that Scripture has a lot to teach us about aging, and older people have untapped wisdom and ministry potential to be unleashed. No matter how old you are, you are *not too old* to make a difference.

Why Should You Think About Aging?

During nearly 50 years of Christian ministry, I have presided at hundreds of funerals and interacted with thousands of senior adults. I am amazed by the number of people who are in denial about aging. Why should old age and death catch us by surprise? Years ago, Dr. James Dobson wrote a book for parents called *Preparing for Adolescence* to prepare them and their children for the tumultuous transitions of the early teens. Since I am writing about aging, should I call this book *Preparing for Obsolescence?* No! We don't have to become obsolete in our later years.

No matter who you are, this book is for you, because there are compelling reasons you should think about aging.

YOU MIGHT ALREADY BE OLD NOW.

Maybe you picked up this book or someone suggested you should read it because you are already old.

My wife, Candy, asked our granddaughter Kayla, "Do you think Nana and Papa are old?" Kayla thought a moment and replied, "*Medium* old." Candy and I still are trying to figure out when we will cross the line between "medium old" and "extremely old."

The word *senior* comes from the same root as the word *senate* (a gathering of wise, seasoned leaders); but from the same root we also get the unflattering word *senile*. In the workplace, a title like "senior vice president," "senior partner," or "senior minister" earns respect, but some older people bristle at being called "senior citizens" and consider it a patronizing or degrading designation. Some cultures (and many churches) consider it an honor to be called an "elder," but for many of us, "elderly" brings to mind poor health and diminished ability. One church member over age 80 said she didn't want to be part of a "senior citizen" group because it made her feel old!

Oliver Wendell Holmes quipped, "Old age is always 15 years older than I am." The U.S. Social Security Administration defines anyone age 65 or older as "elderly." However, people today tend to live longer than in the past. When Social Security began in 1935, the average life expectancy in the United States was 61 years, but now that number has increased by more than a decade. AARP, originally known as the American Association of Retired Persons, proudly states the organization is "dedicated to people over 50, [but] there is no minimum age to join." Yes, an 18-year-old can be a member of AARP!

How can we turn our later years into greater years? In this book you will find practical Bible-based wisdom designed to help you wrestle with important issues like these:

- **Aging makes me anxious.** *How should I deal with my fears?*

- **I don't want to become a grumpy old grouch!** *How can I cultivate my sense of humor as I grow older?*

- **I'm concerned about the next generation.** *How can I maximize my influence as a grandparent?*

- **I believe God speaks through Scripture.** *What does the Bible say about aging?*

- **I wonder about retirement.** *What should I do when my working career ends? How should I handle my finances before and during my retirement years?*

- **I want to keep growing spiritually.** *How can I enjoy a fruitful relationship with God as I grow older?*

- **I don't want to be irrelevant.** *Where do senior adults fit in the church?*

- **Physical health is important to me.** *How should I take care of my body as I age?*

- **Caregiving worries me.** *What if I need to take care of my spouse or another loved one during my senior years? What if I am the one who needs care?*

- **Widowhood worries me.** *What if my spouse dies? How should I deal with grief when friends and family members pass away?*

- **Death is on my radar.** *What does the Bible say about death and dying? How should I deal with my own mortality and prepare to die well?*

EVEN IF YOU ARE YOUNG NOW, YOU ARE LIKELY (ALTHOUGH NOT GUARANTEED) TO BE OLD YOURSELF SOMEDAY.

Your senior years will arrive faster than you imagine. Time flies like a supersonic jet and a long life isn't guaranteed. James says, "You are a mist that appears for a little while and then vanishes" (James 4:14). Peter compares our lives to grass and flowers that spring up green and beautiful but quickly wither and die (1 Peter 1:24-25).

In January 1842, Scottish preacher Robert M'Cheyne wrote, "Call upon the name of the Lord. Your time may be short." M'Cheyne lived only one more year after penning those words. He died of typhus in March 1843 at age 29.

A study by the Stanford Center on Longevity suggests that in the United States, as many as half of today's 5-year-olds can expect to live to the age of 100.[1] No one but God, however, knows exactly how long anyone will live. In the United States, the average lifespan of a man is 73.2 years and 79.1 for a woman.[2] This data matches well with Psalm 90:10, which says, "Our days may come to seventy years, or eighty, if our strength endures."

If God blesses you with a long life, your later years can be greater years.

YOU KNOW OTHERS WHO ARE OLD.

Are there older people in your circle of family and friends? Do you have aging parents or grandparents? Do senior citizens attend your church or live in your neighborhood? "Love your neighbor" includes the older generation.

The Law of Moses instructed younger people to rise to their feet when an older person entered the room. "Stand up in the presence of the aged, show respect for the elderly and revere your God" (Leviticus 19:32). The apostle Paul told Timothy, "Do not rebuke an older man harshly, but exhort him as if he were your father. Treat younger men as brothers, older women as mothers, and younger women as sisters, with absolute purity" (1 Timothy 5:1-2). It honors God when we respect, value, and care for the aged.

AMERICA'S AGING POPULATION CREATES
NEW CHALLENGES AND OPPORTUNITIES.

The U.S. Census Bureau estimates that by 2030, when the last of the Baby Boomer generation moves into older adulthood, more than 71 million residents over age 65 will live in the United States. That number is expected to rise to more than 85 million by 2050—roughly 22 percent of the overall U.S. population. In other words, more than one in five Americans will be age 65 and older, and about one in three will be over age 50. It's vital for the church to have a robust ministry with children and students as we nurture the next generation, but at the same time, we must not neglect our older neighbors. According to census data, by 2034 older adults will outnumber children for the first time in U.S. history.[3] Other studies indicate that people over 50 control the majority of the financial assets of the U.S.[4]

America is becoming more ethnically diverse, and that includes the senior adult population. People of color currently make up about 25 percent of America's older adults, but by 2060 the percentage will approach 50 percent. Experts observe that "declines in marriage, increases in divorce, and lower fertility mean more Baby Boomers will reach age 65 without a spouse or adult child to rely on for care. This will put new and unique stresses on the health care system and challenge how our society currently cares for older adults."[5] The approaching wave of retiring Baby Boomers will create significant ministry opportunities for the church in the years ahead.

According to the Pew Research Center, only about half of the Builder generation (those born 1945 or before) and one-third of Baby Boomers (born 1946 to 1964) attend church at least once a week, and less than half of senior adults participate regularly in any kind of personal or group Bible study.[6] In other words, the majority of our older neighbors have no meaningful connection to a local church. How can we reach and serve this growing number of senior adults? Jesus said, "Open your eyes and look at the fields! They are ripe for harvest" (John 4:35). Another translation describes those fields filled with ripened grain as "white already to harvest."[7]

White-haired people are part of the Lord's harvest field. They need to be loved in Jesus' name, connected with God's family, and deployed into service.

HEALTHY CHURCHES CARE ABOUT ALL GENERATIONS, INCLUDING THOSE WHO ARE OLDER.

Some churches choose to market themselves with taglines like, "We're not your grandma's church." Oh, really? Personally, I want to be part of a church where Grandma and Grandpa are still involved—mentoring young married couples, loving babies in the church nursery, leading small groups, and helping to raise up the next generation of Christ followers, elders, and missionaries to fulfill the Great Commission.

In biblical times, different generations often lived together in the same house. Grandpa and Grandma lived with their children and grandchildren, or they lived nearby. Shouldn't the church be an intergenerational family, too? Why can't all generations be part of "God's household, which is the church of the living God, the pillar and foundation of the truth" (1 Timothy 3:15)?

I want to be part of a congregation where little kids and older folks interact, share life experiences, learn from each other, worship together, and serve shoulder-to-shoulder across generational lines. Senior adults need the creativity, vision, and enthusiasm of the young, and our younger friends need the experience and wisdom of the old.

We shouldn't pit the up-and-coming generation against the elderly as if they are rivals. It doesn't have to be "either/or." It can be "both/and." God cares about the young, the old, and everyone in between. Jesus said, "Whoever does God's will is my brother and sister and mother" (Mark 3:35). Doesn't that include spiritual grandparents and aunts and uncles as well?

I want to be part of a church where "one generation commends your works to another" (Psalm 145:4) as "young men and women, old men and children" all "praise the name of the Lord" (Psalm 148:12-13). We can reach the younger generation without disrespecting older people and treating them as irrelevant. "Pure and faultless" religion includes caring both for needy children and for vulnerable adults . . . "look[ing] after orphans and widows in their distress" (James 1:27).

Before speaking at a church near Louisville, Kentucky, one Sunday morning, I took a walk near the hotel where I was staying. A big antique car show was in town that weekend. Classic old cars were parked in front of the hotel, right next to late-model cars. Those old and new cars mingled together in the parking lot illustrate what the church should be like: the old and the young, traveling on a journey together.

The Bible envisions all generations praising the Lord together. I want to be part of a church where older people are not "put out to pasture," but they are pastored and shepherded like everyone else . . . where older people are not merely coddled and catered to, but are cared for and called to serve . . . where young and old members—centered on Christ, not self—share a common mission to love and serve the Lord.

GOD CARES ABOUT EVERY STAGE OF YOUR LIFE– INCLUDING YOUR OLDER YEARS.

At first glance, Numbers 33 looks like a boring part of the Bible because it lists all the places the Israelites camped before they moved on. The chapter begins, "Here are the stages in the journey of the Israelites when they came out of Egypt" (Numbers 33:1). Why should we care if the Hebrews camped at a certain place for a while and then moved to another place? But I am glad this chapter is in the Bible, because it shows every stage of our journey matters to God. He knows

- every school you have attended.

- every job you have had.

- every place you have lived.

- every problem you have faced in the past, and every challenge you are facing now.

He knows if you are a kid in elementary school . . . a young adult getting started in your career . . . or a widow living alone. Every stage of your spiritual journey matters, whether you are a new Christian starting to grow in your faith, or you have been walking with the Lord for years. The Lord knows if your soul is tired . . . if you are facing doubts . . . if your faith is being tested.

Just as he did with the ancient Israelites, God knows where you are camped right now. In fact, he is camped right there with you. The Israelites wandered in the wilderness for 40 years, but the Lord kept leading them toward a land of milk and honey. Their job was to keep following. God cares about every stage of your journey, and there are wonderful rewards ahead.

YOUR LATER YEARS CAN BE GREATER YEARS.

Senior adulthood can be a time to grow deeper in your faith.

. . . A time to serve God with joy and delight.

. . . A time of relational richness when you make new friends and enjoy old friends you have known for years.

. . . A time for character development as you discover what it means to "be temperate, worthy of respect, self-controlled, and sound in faith, in love and in endurance" (Titus 2:2).

. . . A time to reflect on the past and prepare for a glorious future.

The serviceberry tree my grandkids helped me plant on my sixtieth birthday has grown in my backyard for nearly a decade. It has endured harsh winters and summer droughts. It displays tender pink blossoms in the spring, and its green leaves turn purplish-brown and drop to the ground in the fall. Through all the different seasons, the tree's roots have kept growing deeper, and the older it gets, the more fruit the tree bears. I want to be like that, too. What about you?

2 | You Are Not Too Old— Unless You Think You Are

"Grow old with me! The best is yet to be."
—Robert Browning

A friend in her eighties calls old age the "used to" phase of life. "I *used to* be pain-free," she says. "I *used to* go wherever I wanted. I *used to* drive my car without anyone worrying about my safety. I miss all the things I *used to* do!"

I understand what she means.

When I was young, I could devour three cheeseburgers and a large order of fries without gaining weight. Now I study the "lite" menu in restaurants and wonder if carrot cake qualifies as a salad.

I used to talk fast, walk fast, drive fast, and get in and out of the car fast. I used to run like the wind (but now it feels like the wind is against me). I grew up on an Ohio farm. I could spend the day baling hay and building fences, then play softball all evening without taking a single pain-relief pill.

I used to be agile. I don't like the prospect of becoming fragile.

I miss my parents. Dad never went to college, but after years of farming and serving as an elder at church, he was a master of homespun wisdom. Mother was a quiet woman with a pure heart and a deep faith. (It sounds old-fashioned, but my brothers and I always called her "Mother.") I miss eating the fried chicken and gravy she concocted in a cast-iron skillet and the casseroles she baked in an old yellow bowl. After Dad died, I phoned Mother every Sunday at 6:45 p.m. She died several years ago, but I still feel a tug in my heart on Sunday evenings around 6:45.

What I *Like* About Getting Older

Despite the negatives, there are positive things I enjoy about senior adulthood.

I like having a long marriage. When our younger friends hear that Candy and I were married in 1975, they look amazed, as if they were beholding a relic in a natural history museum. After all these years, Candy and I are still best friends.

I like having longtime friends. In the community where I live there's a street called Gray Road and a church building with a sign that says, "Gray Friends Church." That sign makes me chuckle, for I have a lot of "gray friends" these days. Some of them I seldom see in person, but when we get together, we immediately settle into a comfortable conversation. Long-lasting friendships are one of God's sweetest gifts.

I like being a grandfather. I enjoy spending time with my four grandchildren and attending their music programs and sporting events. Have you heard about the boy who asked his grandpa how old he was? The old man teasingly replied, "I'm not sure." The little boy advised him, "Look in your underwear, Grandpa. Mine says I'm 4 to 6."

I like experiencing God's faithfulness over the long haul. I have a long list of questions I would like to ask God, but I recognize he has been faithful to me. I see his hand in nature. I hear his voice in Scripture. I see his grace in the kindness of my friends. I have lived long enough to endure some suffering and to receive God's comfort. I have watched him turn short-term pain into long-term good.

Psalm 136 recounts Israel's history and repeats the same phrase over and over again. Twenty-six times in 26 verses, the psalmist writes, "His love endures forever." (*The Message* version paraphrases the repeated refrain, "His love never quits.") At first glance, this repeated phrase might seem boring, but the older I get, the more I realize that no matter what happens, God's love never quits. Martin Luther declared, "I have held many things in my hands, and I have lost them all; but whatever I have placed in God's hands, that I still possess."

There are many positives about growing older. However, aging does have a downside.

What I *Don't* like About Getting Older

I don't like the physical challenges. One older friend observes, "'Head and shoulders, knees and toes' is no longer just a song to me. It's a diagnosis." I'm at the stage in life when, if I tie my shoes, I ask myself, "What else useful can I do while I'm down here?" I heard about an old man who was filling out a form that asked for his name and address. A line on the form said, "Zip." The old fellow wrote, "Normal for my age."

I struggle to keep up with technology. Why do computer programmers and cell phone service providers wait till I finally figure out how everything works, and then update everything to make it different? To me, it feels unnatural to type with my thumbs and print in block letters like my grandkids do. A 12-year-old girl told me that she and her fellow students no longer learn cursive writing in school. She joked, "Cursive is the older generation's 'secret code.' When the next generation takes over the world, you can still communicate with each other secretly by using cursive writing!"

It bothers me that time is passing so quickly. I have lived more of my life on earth than there is ahead of me. Pope Paul VI observed, "In youth, the days are short and the years are long. In old age, the years are short and the days are long."

I don't like having to bite my tongue so often. I don't want to be the old guy who constantly says, "I told you so" or "We tried that before, and it didn't work." But I struggle to be patient when others seem impressed by a "new idea" I heard about long ago. My younger friends don't want to hear me say over and over again, "I remember the time when. . . ."

Which reminds me . . . *I don't like how my aging brain finds it harder to remember things.* I committed a lot of Scripture to memory when I was a kid, but now, memorization (especially remembering names) is more difficult than it used to be. I can remember a friend's phone number from 30 years ago, but after five decades of marriage, I still can't recall my wife's Social Security number.

I dislike changes that are outside my control. Older people can be amazingly flexible. Imagine all the changes a 100-year-old man or woman has experienced over the last century! But as we age, more changes happen "to us" than are initiated "by us." It helps when leaders manage change wisely and give us time to adapt. I advise young leaders, "People trust you with the steering wheel. Just don't forget how it feels when you are riding in the back seat and you can't see where the car is going."

When my wife, Candy, and I were in our twenties, we developed a puppet ministry for kids. Candy decided to write a puppet play and a song for adults called "Growing Older" featuring two puppets called Grandpa and Grandma Gray. She included in the song several stereotypes about older people, and we chuckle now because we have reached the age when we face these challenges ourselves. The song includes these lines:

> Grandma: Although my hair is turning gray,
> Grandpa: My bones begin to creak—
> Grandma: I've lost my girlish figure,
> Grandpa: And my back is getting weak,
> Grandma: My walk is getting slower,
> Grandpa: And I have to wear false teeth;
> Both: Just knowing God is with us brings us sweet relief!
>
> Grandma: We're blessed with grandchildren
> Grandpa: Who sit upon my lap,
> Grandma: And when they all go home,
> Grandpa: I need to take my nap!
> Grandma: Our lives are rich and full—
> Grandpa: We've been blessed in many ways;
> Both: We have fond memories of the good old days!
> Growing old, growing older—
> When it comes to growing old,
> We're getting bolder.
> And as long as we have God to see us through,
> Growing old can be a beautiful thing to do.[1]

You are *not too old* to turn your later years into greater years! Here are eight reasons this is true.

1. You are not too old to be *useful*.

Abraham and Sarah were in their nineties when they became parents of God's covenant people. Moses was 80 years old when he led the Israelites out of Egypt, and the veteran warriors Joshua and Caleb were senior adults when they led the Israelites to conquer Canaan. The aging King Solomon wrote books of wisdom and observed, "Gray hair is a crown of splendor" (Proverbs 16:31). Many Bible scholars think Daniel may have been in his eighties when he survived a scary night in the lion's den. You don't have to be youthful to be useful.

Zechariah and Elizabeth were old when their son John the Baptist was born (Luke 1:5-25, 57-66). Simeon and Anna were old when they praised baby Jesus (Luke 2:25-38). John probably was in his nineties when he wrote the Gospel of John, his three letters (1, 2, and 3 John), and Revelation.

If senior adults could serve God in Bible times, what can the Lord accomplish through you? In front of the European United Nations headquarters in Geneva, Switzerland, a beautiful nearly 200-foot long mural covers the fence; it was painted by artist Hans Enri when he was 100 years old. You are not too old to be useful.

2. **You are not too old to be** *cheerful.*

I often voice this simple prayer: "Lord, keep me from being a crotchety old man." I want to be kind, not crabby; friendly, not frowning. I want to encourage the next generation, not discourage them. I want to empathize more than I criticize and listen more than I lecture.

"Rejoice in the Lord always," wrote the apostle Paul, who was probably in his sixties at the time. Then, as if he anticipated we would struggle to be joyful, Paul repeated, "I will say it again: Rejoice!" (Philippians 4:4). Please note, he offers no exemption for the elderly. "Rejoice in the Lord *always.*" That includes your later years. You are not too old to have joy in your heart.

3. **You are not too old to be** *grateful.*

My grandmother used to plant flowers called gladiolas in her garden. I remember her heading out to the garden to "plant some glads."

Has God "planted some glads" (reasons for gladness) in your life? Is your heart "overflowing with thankfulness" (Colossians 2:7)? You are never too old to "worship the Lord with gladness" and "come before him with joyful songs" (Psalm 100:2).

Are you grateful for your memories? For your friends? For your church? Are you glad to have a roof over your head? Are you thankful for nourishing food and clean water? Can you still appreciate beautiful music and the warm hug of a child? Are you thankful for your health—and for those who care for you when you are sick?

The older you grow, the more blessings you have to count. "Give thanks in all circumstances, for this is God's will for you in Christ Jesus" (1 Thessalonians 5:18).

4. **You are not too old to be *prayerful.***

Jesus said to "always pray and not give up" (Luke 18:1). The apostle Paul urged Christians to be "faithful in prayer" (Romans 12:12), and James insisted, "The prayer of a righteous person is powerful and effective" (James 5:16).

Some of the most effective prayer warriors I know are senior adults. Older people usually have more time to invest in prayer. And with advancing age, we realize how much we need to rely on the Lord.

Anna, while in her eighties, "worshiped night and day, fasting and praying" (Luke 2:37). She was the kind of widow who "puts her hope in God and continues night and day to pray and to ask God for help" (1 Timothy 5:5).

Prayer isn't about us informing God; it's about God forming us. Senior adulthood is a time to deepen your relationship with God and pray for your grandchildren, your neighbors, and your church. It's a time to obey the biblical command "that petitions, prayers, intercession and thanksgiving be made for all people—for kings and all those in authority, that we may live peaceful and quiet lives in all godliness and holiness" (1 Timothy 2:1-2).

5. **You are not too old to be *careful.***

Satan doesn't back away just because you are older.

We need to stay alert because "the devil prowls around like a roaring lion looking for someone to devour" (1 Peter 5:8). Regardless of our age, Scripture warns, "Put on the full armor of God, so that you can take your stand against the devil's schemes" (Ephesians 6:11).

It's disappointing when people old enough to know better give in to temptation, drift into moral failure, and squander their later years in foolish behavior. Bernie Madoff pleaded guilty to theft and fraud in his seventies. Bill Cosby went to jail for sex crimes in his eighties. The number of senior citizens incarcerated in the United States is growing at a rapid rate. According to the Federal Bureau of Prisons, over 10 percent of the U.S. prison population is age 55 or older, and from 1999 to 2016, the population of prisoners 55 or older increased by 280 percent despite a reduction in the overall prison population during those years.[2]

Uzziah became king of Judah when he was 16 years old. "As long as he sought the Lord, God gave him success" (2 Chronicles 26:5). Indeed, "his fame spread far and wide" (v. 15). As time passed, though, Uzziah neglected his walk with God and "after Uzziah became powerful, his pride led to his downfall. He was unfaithful to the Lord his God" (v. 16). After he contracted leprosy, Uzziah was driven away from the palace and "banned from the temple of the Lord" (v. 21), and he died in disgrace.

"Pride goes before destruction, a haughty spirit before a fall" (Proverbs 16:18). As we age, we need to be humble and vigilant. We must "resist the devil" and "come near to God" (James 4:7-8).

You are not too old to be careful.

6. **You are not too old to be *fruitful.***

The prayer of every older Christian should be, "Even when I am old and gray, do not forsake me, my God, till I declare your power to the next generation, your mighty acts to all who are to come" (Psalm 71:18). If God grants you a long life, these extra years aren't meant merely for watching TV and playing golf. God is giving you opportunities for extended influence and fruit-bearing.

The Bible says, "When Joshua had grown old, the Lord said to him, 'You are now very old, and there are still very large areas of land to be taken" (Joshua 13:1). Joshua was old, but there was still more work for him to do. Near the end of his life, Joshua challenged the Israelites, "Choose for yourselves this day whom you will serve . . . but as for me and my household, we will serve the Lord" (Joshua 24:15)—and that is a choice we need to make in every season of life.

Bruce is a senior adult. I often see him working around the church building, shampooing the carpets or picking up trash. I asked him, "Why do you help out so much?" He replied, "I took one of those spiritual gifts tests, and it said I have the gift of service, so I thought I'd better use it!" He is bearing fruit for the Lord.

Tom, another older man in our church, volunteered with the middle school boys until he was in his eighties.

When my mom grew physically weaker, she was no longer able to teach Sunday school or play the organ at church, so she found new ways to serve the Lord. She began mentoring younger women and met with a group of volunteers every week to handwrite encouraging notes to shut-ins.

For several years, I served as editor of *The Lookout,* a magazine for Christian families. One of our columnists, Orrin Root, wrote a Bible study column for the magazine every week for 56 years. He was still writing his weekly columns when he was 98 years old. When he was dying, I visited him in the hospital. As I walked into the room, he smiled at me and joked, "Don't worry, Dave, I won't miss my deadline." After Mr. Root died, we found he had written his columns four months ahead so we would have time to find another writer to replace him.

Jesus said, "I am the vine; you are the branches. If you remain in me and I in you, you will bear much fruit; apart from me you can do nothing" (John 15:5). As long as we live, we can bear fruit for the Lord.

7. **You are not too old to be *hopeful.***

Proverbs 23:18 assures us, "There is surely a future hope for you, and your hope will not be cut off." As someone has said, Christians are not moving from the land of the living to the land of the dying. We are moving from the land of the dying to the land of the living. Even when we die, "to be away from the body" means being "at home with the Lord" (2 Corinthians 5:8).

The resurrection of Jesus Christ not only changed history; it changes our present and future, too. God "has given us new birth into a living hope through the resurrection of Jesus Christ from the dead" (1 Peter 1:3).

The older we grow, the more we should hold onto "hope as an anchor for the soul, firm and secure" (Hebrews 6:19).

8. **You are not too old to be** *faithful.*

In 2 Samuel 19, the Bible tells about Barzillai, a wealthy friend of King David. David invited Barzillai to join the king's men. "But Barzillai answered the king, 'How many more years will I live, that I should go up to Jerusalem with the king? I am now eighty years old. Can I tell the difference between what is enjoyable and what is not? Can your servant taste what he eats and drinks? Can I still hear the voices of male and female singers? Why should your servant be an added burden to my lord the king?'" (2 Samuel 19:34-35).

Many senior adults can relate to Barzillai. When invited to serve, he said basically, "Look, I'm 80 years old. I can't hear very well or taste my food anymore. I'm tired. I have done my part in the past. I don't want to be a burden. Ask someone else."

It's OK to be honest about our physical limitations, but we should never resign from serving our King. Serving the Lord may take a different form as we age, but we should never stop fighting the good fight of faith.

You are not too old . . . unless you *think* you are. Henry Ford said, "Whether you think you can or you think you can't, you're right." Your mindset determines your outlook. You are not too old to be *useful, cheerful, grateful, prayerful, careful, fruitful, hopeful,* and *faithful.*

Did you notice? Each of those words ends with the suffix "ful." As we grow older, it looks like we are becoming emptier, not fuller. We often view life as an hourglass, with the grains of sand dropping down quickly. Soon there won't be any time left. But what if you flip the hourglass over and view it from the other direction? What if, from God's eternal perspective, your life is becoming fuller, not emptier, with the passing of time? "In Christ you have been brought to fullness" (Colossians 2:10).

You are *not too old!* With God's help, your later years can be greater years.

QUESTIONS FOR PERSONAL REFLECTION AND GROUP DISCUSSION

1. What do you *like* about growing older (or think you will like about growing older in the future)? What do you *dislike* about growing older (or think you will dislike as you age)? *[Explain.]*

2. Who is an older person you consider a good example of a faithful, fruitful, cheerful follower of Christ? What qualities do you see in them that you want to cultivate in your own life?

3. Which Bible character(s) do you relate to most?

   - *Abraham and Sarah*—because in my older years, God has brought me unexpected blessings and a new sense of purpose that stretches my faith.

   - *Moses*—because my later years are turning out to be a significant time for me to serve the Lord.

   - *Anna*—because as I grow older, I'm learning more about how to pray.

   - *Barzillai* (2 Samuel 19:31-39)—because I'm tired and I don't feel up to serving the Lord anymore.

   - *Uzziah* (2 Chronicles 26:3-23)—because as I grow older, I'm tempted to be prideful and neglect my walk with God.

3 | Scared of the Dark—
Facing Your Fears About Aging

"You are as young as your faith, as old as your doubt;
as young as your self-confidence, as old as your fear;
as young as your hope, as old as your despair."
—General Douglas MacArthur

"Courage is about doing what you're afraid to do.
There can be no courage unless you're scared."
—Eddie Rickenbacker, Medal of Honor recipient
fighter pilot, and race car driver

"A ship is safe in the harbor, but that's not what a ship is for."
—Unknown

When I was a boy, everyone in my rural community left their cars and houses unlocked. Dad left his keys in the car's ignition so he wouldn't have to carry them around. The doors of the local church building remained unlocked 24 hours a day, seven days a week.

Back in the good old days (the twentieth century), alarm systems were for jewelry stores and banks, not private homes. Airport security checks were quick and easy. Hardly anyone worried about identity theft or credit card fraud. Medicine bottles didn't need plastic strips around their lids to assure us they were "sealed for our protection."

Schools had no metal detectors or security guards. Kids didn't need chains and padlocks to lash their bicycles to a steel pole when they bought candy at the neighborhood store. The church nursery didn't need a formal check-in system, because Aunt Bessie had safely rocked babies in the nursery since the Eisenhower administration.

That was then. This is now.

Today, there is a lot to be afraid of—including old age. At least, many of us seem to think so.

Movies and fairy tales often portray older people as frightening figures. Little Red Riding Hood's grandmother isn't just helpless and bedridden; she's a wolf in disguise. A nasty queen tries to poison Snow White, a wicked witch frightens Dorothy in *The Wizard of Oz*, and an evil old woman tries to use a gingerbread house to capture Hansel and Gretel.

Movies like *On Golden Pond* and *Driving Miss Daisy* portray older people in positive ways, but others like *Grumpy Old Men* reinforce negative stereotypes about the elderly. Remember the strange old man with a snow shovel in *Home Alone* and the eccentric woman who fed the birds in Central Park in *Home Alone 2*? (Both of those scary characters turned out to be friendly in the end.) And what about Mr. Burns, Homer Simpson's greedy, devious boss in *The Simpsons*? In various episodes of the animated comedy series, Mr. Burns is said to be between 81 and 104 years old.[1]

Fiction aside, old age can be scary. It's true: "Old age isn't for sissies." Senior adults need *courage* and *strength*—words often reserved for muscular athletes, brave soldiers, and healthy young adults. Old-age stereotypes bring to mind words like *frail* and *feeble*, *weak* and *washed-up*. It's no wonder aging makes us anxious.

Our Four Biggest Fears

To overcome our fears, first we need to name them. After interacting with many senior adults over the years, here are what I call our Four Biggest Fears about aging: (1) the possibility of mental decline, (2) the likelihood of physical suffering, (3) the reality of death, and (4) the loss of things we value.

WE'RE SCARED OF MENTAL DECLINE.

Early in our marriage, Candy worked as a nurse's aide in a residence facility for the elderly. One of the residents there muttered nonsense syllables all day. "He used to be a bank president," one of Candy's coworkers told her. Another resident—a sweet grandmotherly woman—imagined that water was rising like a flooded river in the hallway outside her room. Their once-keen minds had slipped into dementia.

It's frightening to imagine losing our mental acuity. We don't want family and friends to say, "He's not as sharp as he used to be," or "She barely remembers our names anymore."

WE'RE SCARED OF PHYSICAL SUFFERING.

Healthy, once-attractive bodies decline with age. Muscles shrivel. Eyesight weakens. Smooth skin wrinkles. Nerves misfire and fill the body with pain.

A famous Bible verse urges, "Remember your Creator in the days of your youth, before the days of trouble come and the years approach when you will say, 'I find no pleasure in them'" (Ecclesiastes 12:1). The chapter then launches into a vivid description of the consequences of aging, using poetic language that compares the human body to a worn-out old house that is falling apart. The text highlights one problem after another that older people face.

- "The sun and the light and the moon and the stars grow dark, and the clouds return after the rain" (Ecclesiastes 12:2). Life loses its zest and things look gloomy.

- "The keepers of the house tremble, and the strong men stoop" (v. 3a). "The house" evidently refers to the body and the "keepers of the house" are your arms and hands, which tremble in old age. Even "strong men" stoop when their aging legs are no longer as steady and stable as they used to be.

- "The grinders cease because they are few" (v. 3b). Dental problems make your "grinders" stop working so well. Aging teeth require fillings, root canals, extractions, bridges, and implants.

- "Those looking through the windows grow dim" (v. 3c). Your eyesight worsens. Cataract laser surgery, anyone?

- "The doors to the street are closed" (v. 4a). As you age, you may find it harder to go outside and accomplish what in the past you did with ease. It's possible the "doors to the street" refer to the lips or mouth, through which we communicate with the outside world.

- "The sound of grinding fades" (v. 4b). Your hearing isn't as keen as it used to be.

- "When people rise up at the sound of birds, but all their songs grow faint" (v. 4c). Ironically, retirees finally have the luxury to sleep later in the morning, only to discover they wake up early anyway—when the birds start chirping at dawn.

- "When people are afraid of heights" (v. 5a). Fear of falling increases with age. Canes and walkers become our allies. Problems with vision, balance, and stamina make it more difficult to climb stairs or hike up hills. In recent years Candy has advised me to stay away from ladders. I was fixing the roof of my house not all that long ago when I remembered my parents talking about my grandfather. They said, "Grandpa shouldn't be standing on the roof. He's in his sixties!" I remembered their words . . . while I was in my sixties, standing on the roof!

- "When people are afraid . . . of dangers in the streets" (v. 5a). With advanced age come increased safety concerns. Travel is more difficult, and senior adults feel more vulnerable to crime.

- "When the almond tree blossoms" (v. 5b). This is a poetic way of describing white hair! My "almond tree" started to "blossom" when I was in my fifties. While at the Motor Vehicle Bureau to renew my driver's license, I filled out sections of the form that asked for my height, weight, and eye color. When I came to the question about hair color, I paused, and without hesitation, the government employee on the other side of the counter blurted out, "Gray." It was the first time I realized my hair was conspicuously showing my age!

- "The grasshopper drags itself along" (v. 5b). This is an unflattering image, but as you grow older there may be days when you feel like a grasshopper dragging yourself out of bed to face another day.

- "And desire no longer is stirred" (v. 5b). This may refer to sexual desire, the appetite for food, or to other passions and interests. Aging often drains away some of the enthusiasm and zest that energized us when we were young.

This ancient description of old age sounds scary, doesn't it? And physical suffering is only the precursor of an even bigger fear.

WE'RE SCARED TO DIE.

Ecclesiastes 12 goes on to say, "Then people go to their eternal home and mourners go about the streets" (Ecclesiastes 12:5c). Notice how the text uses poetry to describe death.

- "Remember him—before the silver cord is severed, and the golden bowl is broken" (v. 6a). In the ancient Middle East, some wealthier homes contained a lamp made of a golden bowl filled with oil, suspended from the ceiling by a cord interwoven with silver. If the cord broke, the bowl would crash to the ground and the oil would spill. The biblical writer uses this vivid image to illustrate both the high value of life (silver and gold) and the sadness of death when the lamp of life comes crashing down.

- "Before the pitcher is shattered at the spring and the wheel broken at the well" (v. 6b). In ancient times, people would draw water by lowering a clay pitcher or jar into the well, pulling it up by using a rope wound around a wheel. The water stopped flowing if the pitcher or the wheel broke—another symbolic way to describe death.

- "And the dust returns to the ground it came from, and the spirit returns to God who gave it" (v. 7). At death our bodies stop functioning, but our spirits live on and return to the Creator who gave us life, awaiting the final resurrection when, as Jesus said, "Those who have done what is good will rise to live, and those who have done what is evil will rise to be condemned" (John 5:29).

It's scary but true: "Death is the destiny of everyone; and the living should take this to heart" (Ecclesiastes 7:2). But remember: Christ came to "free those who all their lives were held in slavery by their fear of death" (Hebrews 2:15).

This brings us to the last of our Four Biggest Fears about aging.

WE'RE AFRAID TO LOSE THINGS WE CONSIDER IMPORTANT.

Everyone loses things now and then. It's annoying if you misplace your keys or you can't find a favorite tool in the garage. But often, old age means losing other valuables that matter deeply.

- *Loss of freedom.* When you were young, you were free to do what you wanted and go wherever you pleased. But with age, you start to wonder, "Am I too old to travel? Can I still take care of my lawn? How long should I live in my own house? What if I must quit driving?"

- *Loss of identity and significance.* In the past, you were a person with influence and clout. Others consulted with you and sought your advice. You were respected at work and may even have been the boss; but when you retire, will you become irrelevant? You used to be a leader at church, but as you age, will anyone seek your input or care about your ideas?

- *Loss of loved ones.* With advancing age, you attend more funerals. Death takes away familiar friends, former coworkers, trusted church leaders, and familiar mentors you turned to for advice and wise counsel. For some of us, the prospect of losing our spouse creates more fear in our hearts than the thought of dying ourselves. The downside of having a good marriage or good friends is the pain that comes when they are gone. We fear losing our loved ones and being alone.

- *Loss of control.* Jesus told Simon Peter, "When you were younger you dressed yourself and went where you wanted; but when you are old you will stretch out your hands, and someone else will dress you and lead you where you do not want to go" (John 21:18). According to tradition, Peter was nailed to a cross—but he insisted on being crucified upside down, for he considered himself unworthy to die in the exact same manner as the Lord Jesus. Most of us won't face such a painful demise, but with advancing age, the time may come when caregivers decide what we eat (and when). Perhaps our adult children will manage our finances and decide where we live. It's normal to want to remain in control of our own lives, so old age can be scary indeed.

In addition to our Four Biggest Fears about aging (mental decline, physical suffering, death and dying, and losing things we value), there are still . . .

More Reasons to Worry

I don't want to depress you, but I need to mention two more troublesome issues that cause anxiety for senior adults: (1) concerns about financial security and (2) pessimism about the future of the nation, the world, and the church.

CONCERNS ABOUT FINANCIAL SECURITY.

Money alone can't make us secure. The Bible warns, "Cast but a glance at riches, and they are gone, for they will surely sprout wings and fly off to the sky like an eagle" (Proverbs 23:5). Valuable as they are, even silver and gold are called "perishable things" in the Bible (1 Peter 1:18). John wrote, "The world and its desires pass away" (1 John 2:17). We could summarize this truth by saying . . .

> "By and by,
> Everything we buy and buy
> Goes bye-bye!"

Nevertheless, finances are important to senior adults. Do thoughts like these cross your mind as you grow older?

- "I don't want to be a financial burden to my children."

- "The cost of living keeps rising. How can I keep up with inflation?"

- "Will I outlive my savings? Do I have enough funds in my retirement accounts to pay for my daily needs, medical expenses, and possible long-term care?"

- "How reliable is the Social Security system?"

- "How long should I keep working?" Or, "I'm retired, but should I go back to work?"

CONCERNS ABOUT THE FUTURE OF THE WORLD, THE NATION, AND THE CHURCH.

The daily news fans the flames of fear. Will America retain its shared cultural values, or will political turmoil and diverging worldviews create even more polarization and disorder? Will the economy worsen—or even collapse? Do our national and global leaders have the wisdom and character to lead us in the right direction? What about the rise of AI (Artificial Intelligence)? Will it serve us well, or will it distort reality and make it even harder to discern what is real and right? Will tensions in Asia, Europe, and the Middle East boil over into a devastating world war?

Jesus promised to build his church "and the gates of Hades will not overcome it" (Matthew 16:18), so the Lord's church will ultimately prevail. But if you love the church, you can't help but feel concerned about declining worship attendance and the trend for young adults to identify as "Nones" who claim no religious faith. According to a recent Gallup poll, only 31 percent of Americans say they attend services weekly or nearly weekly (down from 67 percent who attended when they were children) and most nonreligious Americans are uninterested in exploring religion.[2] A study conducted by the Barna research organization found that 82 percent of the American adult population falls into the "World Citizen" category, described as people "who may embrace a few biblical principles but generally believe and behave in ways that are distinct from biblical teaching."[3] Senior adults can't help but wonder, *What kind of world will our children, grandchildren, and great-grandchildren inherit from us?*

Old age? It's definitely not for sissies. Jesus predicted, "In this world you will have trouble." But after warning about the troubles ahead, the Lord went on to say, "But take heart! I have overcome the world" (John 16:33).

Two Keys to Overcoming Fear

Even though aging can be scary, you are not too old to be bold! God's "perfect love drives out fear" (1 John 4:18). To deal with our fears about aging, we need to cultivate two important qualities: gutsy faith and crazy joy.

GUTSY FAITH

Old age isn't for wimps. Our later years are a time to display authentic, mature, well-thought-out, heartfelt faith in God. I call this "gutsy faith," because according to the dictionary, *gutsy* means "showing courage, pluck, grit, and determination." Shallow religiosity and a vague belief in God won't cut it. The challenges of senior adulthood require a faith that is bold, courageous, and adventurous.

Gutsy faith is more than a vague belief. Simplistic answers won't suffice when darkness closes in. It's not enough merely to rely on the faith of your minister or your friends. As you age, it's important to ask yourself, "What do I really believe—and why do I believe it?" Martin Luther wrote, "Faith is a living, well-founded confidence in the grace of God, so perfectly certain that it would die a thousand times rather than surrender its conviction."

A friend I'll call Nelly was enjoying retirement in her early seventies when her husband slipped into dementia. Nelly cared for him faithfully until he died, and then as a widow she managed her household for the next eight years until she was diagnosed with late-stage pancreatic cancer. Even then, she continued coming to church each week.

SOME RECOMMENDED RESOURCES FOR DEEPENING YOUR FAITH

To address common questions about God and the Bible, I wrote a book called *Honest Questions, Honest Answers: How to Have Compelling Conversations About Your Christian Faith* (Standard Publishing, 2012), but there are many other helpful resources available. Here are a few suggestions.

BOOKS TO READ:
C. S. Lewis, *Mere Christianity* • Josh McDowell, *More Than a Carpenter*
Lee Strobel, *The Case for Christ* • Philip Yancey, *Where Is God When It Hurts?*

ONLINE RESOURCES:
The website roomfordoubt.com exists for those who want to ask questions, address doubts, and strengthen their faith. It provides resources for churches, classes, small groups, high school youth groups, campus ministries, and Christian camps.

I visited her in the hospital a few days before she died. "Are you scared?" I asked.

"I'm not afraid," Nelly replied, "but I'm apprehensive. I wonder exactly what it's going to be like." Leaning forward in her bed, she managed a smile and whispered, "I've received so many blessings in my life, and I'm grateful for all the Lord has done for me. But I'm a little nervous because I have never died before!" Despite her apprehensions, it was obvious that Nelly had gutsy faith. Like the apostle Paul, she could say, "For to me, to live is Christ and to die is gain" (Philippians 1:21).

Gutsy faith is based on solid evidence. Senior adulthood is a good time to learn more about Christian apologetics—not only for your own sake, but so you can "always be prepared to give an answer to everyone who asks you to give the reason for the hope that you have. But do this with gentleness and respect" (1 Peter 3:15). J. Warner Wallace was a detective who specialized in solving cold cases that baffled investigators. Today he is a respected proponent of the Christian faith and the author of the book, *Cold-Case Christianity*. According to Wallace, "Christians in all disciplines of inquiry and discovery have used their reasoning power to investigate the evidence. Christians are *not* irrational, and Christian faith is *not* blind. The rich intellectual history of Christianity calls each of us to have a reasonable, examined, evidential, case-making faith. This kind of faith honors God and withstands skeptical criticism and personal doubt."[4]

Gutsy faith means relying on the rock-solid, never-changing God, not on the shifting sands of human wisdom. Some say, "As long as you have your health, all is well." But you won't always have your health! Since your body

---

SENIOR ADULT HEROES OF FAITH

Hebrews 11 is often called God's Honor Roll of Faith. The chapter begins by asserting, "Now faith is confidence in what we hope for and assurance about what we do not see" (v. 1). Look closely and you'll find that several heroes of faith mentioned in this chapter were people of advanced age.

"In holy fear," Noah "built an ark to save his family" (v. 7), and Noah was 600 years old when the floods came (Genesis 7:11). Abraham and Sarah obeyed God, moved to an unfamiliar land, and had a baby when they were long past the normal age for childbearing (Hebrews 11:8-12). When Jacob was approaching death, he blessed his grandchildren "and worshiped as he leaned on the top of his staff" (v. 21). As Joseph grew old and death drew near, he "spoke about the exodus of the Israelites from Egypt and gave instructions concerning the burial of his bones" (v. 22). Moses lived by faith during the last third of his life and he "persevered because he saw him who is invisible" (v. 27).

and brain eventually will succumb to death, how can your own physical health and mental ingenuity resolve your fears without God's help?

Gutsy faith isn't passive belief; it's an active way of life. "Faith without deeds is dead" (James 2:26). Dale Carnegie said, "Inaction breeds doubt and fear. Action breeds confidence and courage. If you want to conquer fear, do not sit home and think about it. Go out and get busy."

People with gutsy faith find security in God. They agree with David, who told God, "When I am afraid [and yes, sometimes we will be], I put my trust in you" (Psalm 56:3).

According to information technology experts, there are three main ways to prevent thieves from stealing information from your computer. First, electronic security can come from *something you have*—an object such as a key or a photo ID. Second, security can come from *something you know*—a password or a PIN code (which can be stolen or guessed by an experienced or lucky hacker). Third, security can come from *something you are*—your physical identity (a fingerprint, voice recognition, or a retinal scan) used to verify access.

Securing the information on a laptop computer is one thing, but how can our souls be secure? John wrote, "I write these things to you who believe in the name of the Son of God so that you may know that you have eternal life" (1 John 5:13). *There is security in something we have: eternal life. There is security in Someone we know—Jesus Christ. There is security in something we are.* "See what great love the Father has lavished on us, that we should be called children of God!" (1 John 3:1).

People with gutsy faith say, "God's promises give me courage." The Christian faith doesn't depend on made-up stories and religious platitudes. Jesus' own integrity is on the line. He promised that we can trust him (John 14:1-3).

People with gutsy faith say, "Jesus' resurrection gives me hope." The Lord told his friend Martha, "I am the resurrection and the life. The one who believes in me will live, even though they die" (John 11:25). Then he asked her, "Do you believe this?" (v. 26). To overcome fear, you must answer that same question. Do you believe Jesus is the resurrection and the life? Without Christ, death looks scary indeed; but if you trust him to give you eternal life, what is left to worry about?

People with gutsy faith say, "The Holy Spirit gives me strength." They embrace the promise of Romans 8:11: "And if the Spirit of him who raised Jesus from the dead is living in you, he who raised Christ from the dead will also give life to your mortal bodies because of his Spirit who lives in you."

As we age, we should lean into our faith, not drift away from it. God is strong enough to handle our Four Biggest Fears and our lesser worries. If our minds decline, the Lord remains all-knowing and infinitely wise. If our bodies suffer, he will be our strength—and he promises to give us new bodies in the future when we are resurrected (1 Corinthians 15:42-45). Even death cannot separate us from God's love. Whatever we lose is nothing compared with the surpassing worth of knowing Christ. Money isn't our ultimate security if we have stored up treasures in heaven, "where moths and vermin do not destroy, and where thieves do not break in and steal" (Matthew 6:20). Instead of worrying about the future, we can let tomorrow "worry about itself," knowing that each day "has enough trouble of its own" (Matthew 6:34).

Old age isn't for wimps, and neither is faith in God. It takes guts to live by faith, but if we choose to trust the Lord, it leads to what I call . . .

CRAZY JOY

The farm where I grew up had a big old barn that was over 100 years old. By day it was just an ordinary barn—a place where my brothers and I fed calves and Dad milked cows. There was a basketball hoop in the barn, and by day I loved playing there. But at night that old barn was a scary place full of dark shadows and strange creaks as the wind whistled through cracks in the old wooden walls. When the cows mooed at night, I didn't like walking into that dark, scary barn to see what was going on.

But if Dad was with me, I wasn't scared of the dark. Walking into the barn at night didn't bother me at all if my father was with me. His presence made all the difference.

We don't need to be afraid of the dark when our heavenly Father is with us. Fear fades away in the light of his presence. Remember the 23rd Psalm? "Even though I walk through the darkest valley, I will fear no evil, for you are with me" (Psalm 23:4). In fact, if you walk with the Lord as you grow older, it's likely you will experience a crazy kind of joy.

Of course, by "crazy" I don't mean mentally unhinged or foolish. I don't want to be considered a crazy old man. But the word *crazy* also can refer to unbridled enthusiasm ("He's crazy about football"), being unusually smart, capable, or gifted ("She's crazy enough to take on the job no one else would tackle"), or uninhibited fun ("We had such a good time, we laughed like crazy.") I don't mind being known as someone who is "crazy about Jesus" or "crazy about my wife and kids" and "crazy enough to take big steps of faith." Those kinds of craziness aren't bad! One fruit of the Spirit is joy (Galatians 5:22). Even if others consider me a little crazy, I want the joy of the Lord to fill my heart and overflow from my life as I grow older.

First-century believers were persecuted for preaching Christ, but the Bible describes them as "rejoicing because they had been counted worthy of suffering disgrace for the Name" of Christ (Acts 5:41). That's crazy joy!

During one eventful night, a jailer in the Greek city of Philippi went from suicidal to saved, and after he and his household were baptized, "he was filled with joy because he had come to believe in God" (Acts 16:34). What a crazy story—but it happened!

The longer we live, the more we discover there is no time limit on the joy of the Lord. So please keep reading. In this chapter we have focused on the scary side of aging. But now it's time to think about the lighter side.

QUESTIONS FOR PERSONAL REFLECTION AND GROUP DISCUSSION

1. When you think about growing old, which of the following makes you feel afraid? *(Explain.)*
   a. Mental decline
   b. Physical suffering
   c. Death
   d. Losing things that are important to you
   e. Financial uncertainty
   f. Worries about the future of our nation, world, and church
   g. Other:

2. Which of the following helps you to face your fears? *(Explain.)*
   a. Your faith in the Lord
   b. Promises found in the Scriptures
   c. Supportive friends and family
   d. Other:

3. Which of these passages from the Bible do you find most helpful in facing your fears about aging? *(Explain.)*

   "Be strong and courageous. Do not be afraid; do not be discouraged, for the Lord your God will be with you wherever you go" (Joshua 1:9).

   "The Lord is my light and my salvation—whom shall I fear? The Lord is the stronghold of my life—of whom shall I be afraid?" (Psalm 27:1).

   "When you lie down, you will not be afraid; when you lie down, your sleep will be sweet. Have no fear of sudden disaster or of the ruin that overtakes the wicked, for the Lord will be at your side and will keep your foot from being snared" (Proverbs 3:24-26).

CONTINUED ON NEXT PAGE

"Even to your old age and gray hairs I am he, I am he who will sustain you. I have made you and I will carry you; I will sustain you and I will rescue you" (Isaiah 46:4).

"Do not be afraid of those who kill the body but cannot kill the soul. Rather, be afraid of the One who can destroy both soul and body in hell. Are not two sparrows sold for a penny? Yet not one of them will fall to the ground outside your Father's care. And even the very hairs of your head are all numbered. So don't be afraid; you are worth more than many sparrows" (Matthew 10:28-31).

"Who shall separate us from the love of Christ? Shall trouble or hardship or persecution or famine or nakedness or danger or sword? As it is written: 'For your sake we face death all day long; we are considered as sheep to be slaughtered.' No, in all these things we are more than conquerors through him who loved us. For I am convinced that neither death nor life, neither angels nor demons, neither the present nor the future, nor any powers, neither height nor depth, nor anything else in all creation, will be able to separate us from the love of God that is in Christ Jesus our Lord" (Romans 8:35-39).

"Do not be anxious about anything, but in every situation, by prayer and petition, with thanksgiving, present your requests to God. And the peace of God, which transcends all understanding, will guard your heart and your minds in Christ Jesus" (Philippians 4:6-7).

"Who is going to harm you if you are eager to do good? But even if you should suffer for what is right, you are blessed. 'Do not fear their threats; do not be frightened.' But in your hearts revere Christ as Lord. Always be prepared to give an answer to everyone who asks you to give the reason for the hope that you have. But do this with gentleness and respect" (1 Peter 3:13-15).

4 | The Levity in Your Longevity—Enjoying the Lighter Side of Aging

"Humor is the shock absorber of life;
it helps us take the blows."
—Peggy Noonan

"You don't stop laughing when you grow old.
You grow old when you stop laughing."
—George Bernard Shaw

You are not too old to have fun.

How many of the wrinkles on your face are laugh lines? Do you smile more than you frown? Life is serious business, and many aspects of aging are no fun, but are you able to chuckle at a lighthearted observation like this one?

> If you fall down the stairs and everyone laughs, you're young. If you fall down the stairs and others rush to help you, you're old. But you're *really* old if you fall down the stairs and instead of being upset, you're happy because it's the fastest you've moved in years!

Joy in God's Presence

A friend of mine, Bob Tinsky, had a keen sense of humor. In his ninetieth year, Bob wrote a book called *I'm Not Old, I've Just Lived a Long Time.* The book's chapters had lighthearted titles like "Hair Today and

Gone Tomorrow," "How to Keep Your Car Keys (Longer)," and "How NOT to Dress Like an Old Person." A year later he wrote another book called *Jump for Joy* in which he asked, "Where do we get the idea that Christianity is something dull, lackluster, lifeless and dopey? It is not supposed to be that way."[1] Bob's final volume was called *94 and Still Going*. He joked that if the Lord granted him another year, he might write a book called *95 and Still Alive*.

I visited Bob a few days before he died. He was at peace and his faith was strong. Before I left, he looked me in the eye and said, "I love you." There were tears at his funeral (he died at 95), but there were also a lot of smiles. Bob knew the Lord welcomes faithful servants into his eternal presence by saying, "Come and share your master's happiness!" (Matthew 25:21, 23).

One of the funniest people I have ever met was Wayne Smith, who served for 40 years as the senior minister of Southland Christian Church in Lexington, Kentucky. Wayne had the heart of a pastor, cared intensely for people, preached the gospel without compromise, and took courageous stands about moral issues. But he was known for his sense of humor. Here is how one friend described Wayne:

> His laugh is memorable, a fun-filled guffaw that shakes all over. Smith's laugh, washed by his own tears, lifts entire congregations.
>
> Smith's laugh renews auditoriums, arenas, hearts, and homes. He visits hospitals after hours, is welcomed past locked doors in nursing homes. And when he enters, everyone and anyone are targets. He ministers to the sick and to the staff. He offers hope to the students as well as teachers. He is easy to locate; just listen. You can hear that laugh.
>
> It begins as a chuckle. The whole body shakes. The laugh starts deep within, [and] comes rolling out. He laughs at everything, including, and most of all, himself.[2]

What a wonderful way to be remembered!

The Bible says, "There is a time for everything, and a season for every activity under the heavens," and that includes "a time to weep and a time to laugh, a time to mourn and a time to dance" (Ecclesiastes 3:1, 4). Your senior adult years will likely include some weeping, but they should also be "a time to laugh."

The usually austere journal of the Biblical Archaeology Society published an article called "Laughter in the Bible? Absolutely!" The author states:

> Jesus must have been a compelling personality to keep the attention of crowds for days and the steadfast loyalty of at least twelve disciples for three years. In addition to being a riveting teacher whose words brought life, he was likely the kind of personality that was just fun to be around.
>
> . . . . In his classic work *The Humor of Christ*, Elton Trueblood lists 30 humorous passages in the Synoptic Gospels. . . . [They include] one liners, parables or stories Jesus told. Trueblood thinks Jesus' audience would have laughed at the image of those who loudly proclaim their righteous actions to others (Matt. 6:2) because it was all too prevalent. An audience would have found the idea of rulers calling themselves benefactors ludicrous (Luke 22:25)—because the working folks knew all too well it wasn't so. No doubt the audience chuckled when Jesus commended the vociferous, obstreperous widow for her persistent pestering of the unjust judge and cited her as a successful model of prayer (Luke 18:1-8).[3]

Jesus said there is joy "in the presence of the angels of God over one sinner who repents" (Luke 15:10). Joy *in the presence* of the angels? That makes me wonder if the Lord himself joins their rejoicing. I think he does.

Do others find joy in your presence? Humor helps to put people at ease. Pianist and humorist Victor Borge said, "Laughter is the shortest distance between two people."

A sign printed in English was posted in an international hotel: "The elevator is being fixed for the next day. During that time, we regret that you will be unbearable."[4] No one wants to be someone others find unbearable. If you don't want to be a grumpy old grouch—a surly old man or woman who yells and tells neighborhood kids, "Get off my lawn!"—then it's time to . . .

Take Your Medicine

The Bible says, "A cheerful heart is good medicine, but a crushed spirit dries up the bones" (Proverbs 17:22). People tend to take more medicine as we grow older, but one of the most important "meds" is a cheerful heart. Scientific studies link laughter to a variety of positive benefits including decreased blood pressure, relief of stress and pain, decreased anxiety, and strengthening of the immune system. At funerals, mourners often eulogize deceased loved ones by saying they "had a good sense of humor." Why not develop your sense of humor and put it to use now?

If you want to have a positive, lighthearted attitude as you age, here are four suggestions: (1) Don't take yourself too seriously. (2) Embrace the joy of the Lord. (3) Take advantage of every opportunity to smile and laugh. (4) Learn to lighten up.

DON'T TAKE YOURSELF TOO SERIOUSLY.

During my five decades of preaching and teaching, I have noticed that a bit of self-deprecating humor helps audiences connect to my messages. Listeners seem to relate more to my struggles and failures than to stories about the times I got it right. And I have lots of material to draw from, because I have made a lot of mistakes and done a lot of funny things.

Once, in a grocery store parking lot, I was too impatient to get out of my car and push a shopping cart out of the way, so I inched my car forward and nudged the cart with my front bumper. Unfortunately, the parking lot was located on a slight incline, so I watched helplessly while the shopping cart turned and headed down the hill, picking up speed until it smacked into the side of a parked car. After telling that story, I asked the congregation, "Have you ever done something you regret because you were too impatient and lazy to do the right thing?"

In another message, I told the congregation about the time I was driving in a crowded parking lot when a car headed toward me in my lane. I moved over so the young woman driving the other car could get past me, but I gave her a look that said, "What is wrong with you?" I wanted to make sure she knew I was irritated. To make matters worse, she didn't look the least bit sorry or repentant for what she had done. That's when I noticed the one-way sign and realized I was the one going in the wrong direction! I used that story to show how easy it is to criticize others while overlooking our own faults.

As we grow older, it's tempting to become harsh, impatient, and demanding. But Christ calls us to be humble, gentle, and patient with one another. It helps if we can chuckle at our own goof-ups and silly mistakes.

Don't misunderstand. We should take God seriously and worship him with reverence and awe. We should take others seriously and never belittle or minimize their problems. And we should take life seriously, because our time on this earth is precious and it shouldn't be wasted. But we shouldn't be so serious that we miss the fun and overlook the funny moments.

God gives you laughter to lighten your burdens, ease your pain, and make you more enjoyable to be around. If you want your later years to be greater years, don't take yourself too seriously.

EMBRACE THE JOY OF THE LORD.

A minister friend once told me, "Joy is what you have when your biggest problem in life has been solved." Our biggest problem is death; and because Christ has solved that problem for us, joy is the result.

Joy isn't just a positive feeling we conjure up to make ourselves feel better. The Bible calls it "the joy *of the Lord*" because we can't manufacture it on our own. Real joy—what I call "crazy joy"—comes from God. Tim Keller said, "Christianity offers a contentment and joy not based on changing circumstances. Our bad things will turn out for good (Romans 8:28), our good things can't be taken from us (Ephesians 1:3), and the best things are yet to come (1 John 3:1-3)."

WHAT IS JOY?

- Joy is a gift—a gracious blessing to be received from God. After an Ethiopian government official received God's gift of salvation, he may have still been wet from his baptism when he "went on his way rejoicing" (Acts 8:39). God gives us the ability to go on our way rejoicing, too.

- Joy is a fruit—the result of the Holy Spirit's presence and influence in our lives. "The fruit of the Spirit is . . . joy" (Galatians 5:22).

- Joy is a choice—a decision we make to have a positive outlook because we are convinced God has our best interests at heart.

- Joy is a shareable commodity—not something we should keep to ourselves. The Bible says, "Rejoice with those who rejoice" (Romans 12:15). Strangely, joy multiplies and grows when we share it with others.

Crazy joy is the deep, abiding sense of well-being that comes from trusting that God is good, his love never fails, and his purpose will prevail. Crazy joy comes from helping others succeed and be honored, not from pursuing success and recognition for yourself. Crazy joy means tithing and giving extravagantly, learning to be a "cheerful giver" (2 Corinthians 9:7). This unselfish, crazy kind of joy moved the apostle Paul to tell Christians he loved, "For what is our hope, our joy, or the crown in which we will glory in the presence of our Lord Jesus when he comes? Is it not you? Indeed, you are our glory and joy" (1 Thessalonians 2:19-20).

In his book, *A Good Old Age*, Derek Prime identifies these hallmarks of Christian joy:

> Its distinctive feature is that it is joy in God himself through our Lord Jesus. He has been the anticipated joy of the ages—Abraham and others rejoiced at the thought of seeing his day (John 8:56; 1 Peter 1:10-12). God the Holy Spirit delights to convey this joy in the Lord Jesus to a believer's soul, a glorious joy that is a foretaste of heaven (1 Peter 4:13; Jude 24). It is inexpressible since it is incapable of adequate explanation in words (1 Peter 1:8). It is an everlasting joy to be experienced in all its perfection in heaven (Isaiah 35:10; 51:11).[5]

If you want the joy of the Lord to flood your soul . . .

- Pray for it. David prayed, "Restore to me the joy of your salvation" (Psalm 51:12). Maybe you need to pray that same prayer.

- Learn about it. Read and reflect on the many biblical texts about joy.

- Soak it up *from* others. Spend time with joyful people, and don't allow the daily news or gloomy people to drain away your joy.

- Spread joy *to* others. Be an uplifter, not a downer. "Therefore encourage one another and build each other up, just as in fact you are doing" (1 Thessalonians 5:11).

TAKE ADVANTAGE OF EVERY OPPORTUNITY TO SMILE AND LAUGH.

Mark Twain said, "Against the assault of laughter nothing can stand," and scientific research supports his contention.

A scholarly article called "The Laughter Prescription" appeared in the *American Journal of Lifestyle Medicine*. "It is commonly accepted that laughter

UPLIFTING BIBLICAL TEXTS ABOUT JOY

"For the Lord your God will bless you in all your harvest and in all the work of your hands, and your joy will be complete" (Deuteronomy 16:15).

"Weeping may stay for the night, but rejoicing comes in the morning" (Psalm 30:5).

"Shout for joy to God, all the earth!" (Psalm 66:1).

"Your statutes are my heritage forever; they are the joy of my heart" (Psalm 119:111).

"Those who promote peace have joy" (Proverbs 12:20).

"You will go out in joy and be led forth in peace; the mountains and hills will burst into song before you, and all the trees of the field will clap their hands" (Isaiah 55:12).

"I delight greatly in the Lord; my soul rejoices in my God. For he has clothed me with garments of salvation and arrayed me in a robe of his righteousness, as a bridegroom adorns his head like a priest, and as a bride adorns herself with her jewels" (Isaiah 61:10).

"But the angel said to them, 'Do not be afraid. I bring you good news that will cause great joy for all the people'" (Luke 2:10).

[Jesus speaking] "Very truly I tell you, you will weep and mourn while the world rejoices. You will grieve, but your grief will turn to joy" (John 16:20).

"For the joy set before him he [Jesus] endured the cross, scorning its shame, and sat down at the right hand of the throne of God" (Hebrews 12:2).

"Rejoice in the Lord always. I will say it again: Rejoice!" (Philippians 4:4).

"Rejoice always" (1 Thessalonians 5:16).

"Consider it pure joy, my brothers and sisters, whenever you face trials of many kinds, because you know that the testing of your faith produces perseverance" (James 1:2-3).

"Though you have not seen him, you love him; and even though you do not see him now, you believe in him and are filled with an inexpressible and glorious joy" (1 Peter 1:8).

"I have no greater joy than to hear that my children are walking in the truth" (3 John 4).

produces *psychological* benefits, such as improving affect, depression, anxiety, and stress," the authors of the article state. "Nevertheless, there is growing evidence that laughter as a physical activity can additionally produce small but quantifiable positive *physiological* benefits." The benefits appear to increase in cases of "group laughter," where funny moments are shared with others. The authors conclude, "Evidence indicates that laughter may . . . help prevent diseases, reduce costs, and ensure a healthier population. . . . [T]here is not much to lose in laughing. With no downsides, side-effects, or risks, perhaps it is time to consider laughter seriously."[6]

Laughter won't make our problems go away, but it makes them more bearable. The Bible reminds us, "Even in laughter the heart may ache" (Proverbs 14:13). Some laughter is little more than a feeble attempt to escape or cover up sadness. Embracing humor doesn't mean living in denial. Life is serious; but that's why we need to laugh whenever we can.

A friend of mine who was fighting cancer kept a life-size cardboard cutout of the Three Stooges in his hospital room—his way of lightening the mood when visitors stopped by.

I encourage you to laugh every chance you get! Share good jokes with your friends and family. Watch funny movies and TV shows. Follow clean comedians on social media. Take in a daily diet of healthy humor that makes you smile.

QUOTES AND QUIPS ABOUT AGING

FROM WELL-KNOWN SOURCES:

"I'm at an age where my back goes out more than I do." —Comedian Phyllis Diller

"I have reached an age when, if someone tells me to wear socks, I don't have to." —Scientist Albert Einstein

"Age is an issue of mind over matter. If you don't mind, it doesn't matter." —Author/humorist Mark Twain

"The older I get, the better I used to be." —Golfer Lee Trevino

"At age 20, we worry about what others think of us. At age 40, we don't care what they think of us. At age 60, we discover they haven't been thinking of us at all." —Advice columnist Ann Landers

"You know you're getting old when the candles cost more than the cake." —Actor/comedian Bob Hope

"There is still no cure for the common birthday." —Astronaut/U.S. Senator John Glenn

FROM WITTY BUT UNKNOWN SOURCES:

"The older I get, the earlier it gets late."

"I'm getting so old, all my friends in heaven will think I didn't make it!"

"He's so old, his Social Security number is 2."

"He's so old, his first watch was a sundial."

"He's so old, when he was a kid, the Dead Sea was only sick."

"Old age is when you still have something on the ball, but you are just too tired to bounce it."

"I'm in the snapdragon phase of life: Part of me has snapped and the rest of me is draggin'."

LEARN TO LIGHTEN UP

Jesus carried a heavy emotional load, and his mission was deadly serious. But his burdens didn't make him surly and mean-spirited toward others. To bear up under the strain, the Master intentionally carved out time to replenish his physical and spiritual strength. He "often withdrew to lonely places and prayed" (Luke 5:16). Your later years will be greater years if you cultivate the habit of spending quiet time alone with God.

When Jesus taught about prayer, he wasn't trying to lay a guilt trip on his disciples. The ways of Jesus contrasted sharply with the ways of the Pharisees, whose approach was to "tie up heavy, cumbersome loads and put them on other people's shoulders" (Matthew 23:4). By contrast, Jesus portrayed prayer as simpler, more personal, and more inviting. Don't view prayer as a way of impressing God and others, Jesus taught. Instead, "go into your room, close the door and pray to your Father. . . . And when you pray, do not keep on babbling like pagans" who think the more they say, the better chance they have of being heard (Matthew 6:5-7). Instead, Jesus said to find a private place for conversation with the Father. The model he gave us in the Lord's Prayer takes only about one minute to recite.

If you are uptight and on edge, the Lord invites you to lighten up. He says, "Come to me, all you who are weary and burdened, and I will give you rest. Take my yoke upon you and learn from me, for I am gentle and humble in heart, and you will find rest for your souls. For my yoke is easy and my burden is light" (Matthew 11:28-30).

In her book *Life Is Too Important to Be Taken Seriously*, Mandy Smith explains how, instead of enjoying today, she was always thinking about "The Mandy of Tomorrow." She says:

> I would work like a dog today, without a break, so that The Mandy of Tomorrow would have everything done. If I was given a nice candle for my birthday, I would save it for The Mandy of Tomorrow. . . . The Mandy of Today never got to enjoy anything! And suddenly it hit me: 'Hey, *I'm* the Mandy of Today!' I realized that I could drop dead today and never enjoy the fruits of my labors!

She continues:

> I had been the kind of hostess who saved the new silverware for guests or holidays. So I was always waiting for special occasions

and special guests. I soon learned that to have real joy on a daily basis, I had to learn to enjoy today. I had to stop thinking that guests were the only special people in the world and start treating my family like *they* were the special guests. I had to stop waiting for parties or outings and start seeing ordinary things like walks with my husband or playtime with my daughter as special. After all, special occasions are nice, but life really takes place on ordinary days. Life is today.[7]

If you want your later years to be greater years, lighten up and discover that "the joy of the Lord is your strength" (Nehemiah 8:10).

QUESTIONS FOR PERSONAL REFLECTION
AND GROUP DISCUSSION

1. What do you enjoy (or think you will enjoy) about growing old?

2. Think of older persons you know who seem to consistently have "the joy of the Lord" in their hearts. Suggestion: interview a couple of senior adults who exemplify joy and ask them to tell you the secret of their cheerful attitude.

3. Do you think it is realistic to be joyful even in difficult circumstances? Why, or why not?

4. This chapter contains a list of Scriptures labeled "Uplifting Biblical Texts About Joy." Which of these passages do you find most encouraging as you grow older?

5. Can you think of any older people who need some cheering up? Why not visit them, phone them, invite them to lunch, or send them a card of encouragement?

5 | Crowned with Gray— What the Bible Says About Old Age

"Do not cast me away when I am old;
do not forsake me when my strength is gone."
—Psalm 71:9

"Gray hair is a crown of splendor."
—Proverbs 16:31

"Even to your old age and gray hairs I am he,
I am he who will sustain you and I will carry you;
I will sustain you and I will rescue you."
—Isaiah 46:4

After years of handling, my old Bible looks worn and torn. Layers of duct tape hold the leather cover together. Several times I have reattached pages to the spine with glue. Some sections of my Bible are so tattered and yellow, they're starting to resemble those ancient manuscripts copied and handed down by medieval monks. Jesus said his words will never pass away, but what should you do when your personal copy of God's Word starts to wear out?

Should I trade it in for a new model? My old Bible doesn't contain any fancy study guides and commentaries. Small, faded letters on the cover read simply, *Holy Bible.* Should I replace it with one of those nifty new ones niche-marketed for people like me? Surely there's a *New Revised Devotional Spirit-Filled Study Bible for Aging Left-Handed Guys* out there somewhere.

No. I like my beat-up Bible the way a baseball player prefers his broken-in ball glove. The way a chef savors her favorite recipe. The way a carpenter favors his most-trusted hammer. It feels comfortable in my hand. I know where my favorite Scriptures appear on the page.

This Bible has been with me hundreds of times when I've stood up to preach. It's been on my desk in the early mornings when I have needed wisdom and strength from the Lord. Several pages contain scribbled notes and verses I have underlined. This Bible has gone with me on mission trips where interpreters translated it while I taught in English. I pulled it from my backpack on top of Mount Sinai and read the Ten Commandments. I carried it up the slippery stone surface of the Areopagus on a windy day in Athens and read Paul's sermon from Acts 17. Sailing on the Sea of Galilee, I turned to the Gospels and read the story of Jesus walking on the water.

No, I won't discard this Bible. I will use it as long as I can, and someday pass it along to my children.

You can't judge a book by its cover, anyway—or a person. "Everything is uncovered and laid bare before the eyes of him to whom we must give account" (Hebrews 4:13). Some senior adults appear stress-free. They appear to have all the bells and whistles life could offer; but underneath those impressive covers, their hearts are burdened by worry, insecurity, and fear. Some worriers even read a lot of Scripture, but somehow it brings them no peace. Is it possible to have both a worn-out Bible and a shriveled-up soul?

On the other hand, some older adults look weary and worn on the outside, but underneath those tattered covers they possess amazing strength and peace. What is their secret? Inwardly, they are "being renewed day by day" (2 Corinthians 4:16). They are learning to live by gutsy faith that believes the Lord intellectually, trusts him emotionally, and follows him obediently. They have nothing to cover up, for God has already covered and erased their shame. "Blessed is the one whose transgressions are forgiven, whose sins are covered" (Psalm 32:1).

Considering all it has been through, my Bible has stood the test of time quite well. And this time-honored old book has a lot to say about how to turn our later years into greater years. In this chapter, let's take a broad look at the Word of God and consider what the Bible says about aging.

REMEMBER WHEN YOU WERE IN YOUR PRIME?
(Lessons from Job 29)

Job not only lost his health and his wealth; with age, he faced the loss of significance. The weary patriarch pined for the good old days and reflected, "How I long for the months gone by, for the days when God watched over me. . . . Oh, for the days when I was in my prime, . . . when the Almighty was still with me and my children were around me" (Job 29:2, 4-5, emphasis added). Do you ever feel that way? Senior adults can relate to Job's words because as we age, it dawns on us that we are no longer in our prime.

No one wants to fade into irrelevance like a yellowed old newspaper—yesterday's news. A woman who used to turn heads when she walked into a room now looks at herself in the mirror and wonders if anyone still finds her attractive. A man once admired for his physical skills realizes he can't compete with younger athletes anymore. A retiree misses the rhythm of daily work. An older church member discovers her opinions are rarely solicited.

Job missed the respect he used to receive. "When I went to the gate of the city and took my seat in the public square, the young men saw me and stepped aside and the old men rose to their feet. . . . Whoever heard me spoke well of me, and those who saw me commended me" (Job 29:7-8, 11).

He reminisced about the ways he used to serve others. "I rescued the poor who cried for help, and the fatherless who had none to assist them. The one who was dying blessed me; I made the widow's heart sing. . . . I was eyes to the blind and feet to the lame. I was a father to the needy; I took up the case of the stranger" (vv. 12-13, 15-16).

He realized that his dreams of a happy old age were likely to go unrealized. "I thought, 'I will die in my own house, my days as numerous as the grains of sand'" (v. 18).

He missed how, in the past, others sought his advice. "People listened to me expectantly, waiting in silence for my counsel. After I had spoken, they spoke no more; my words fell gently on their ears. They . . . drank in my words as the spring rain" (vv. 21-23).

He remembered the positions of responsibility he used to hold. "I chose the way for them and sat as their chief; I dwelt as a king among his troops" (v. 25).

Job 29 shows the folly of relying too much on our past accomplishments. Job was a good man, but his comments contain a tinge of self-righteousness. The words I, my, and me appear 52 times in this chapter's 25 verses. As we age, we shouldn't be preoccupied with our own importance. We don't have to make sure everyone knows the things we have done, the places we have been, the jobs we have held, and the honors we have received. And we should spare others from hearing us drone on about our experiences.

We can't live in the past. It's fine to relish past victories, but not at the expense of serving God in the present and pressing on toward the future. Our value isn't determined by our personal accomplishments, but by our relationship with God—and he is always in his prime.

Aging in the Old Testament

The primary purpose of the Hebrew Scriptures, of course, is not to give us a roadmap for growing old. The Bible states its own purpose: The Holy Scriptures "are able to make you wise for salvation through faith in Christ Jesus" (2 Timothy 3:15). Written over a time span of about 1,000 years, the 39 books of the Old Testament cover a variety of important topics, including:

- *Creation.* God designed a universe so vast and complex it's beyond our comprehension, and he created us in his image, giving dignity and value to every human life.

- *Covenant.* God established a covenant relationship with Abraham and his descendants, through whom he would bless the whole world. The historical account of God's chosen people, with all their ups and downs, winds its way throughout the Old Testament.

- *Commands and Ceremonies.* God provided moral guidance and religious observances for his covenant people to observe. The Law of Moses instructed the Israelites about practical lifestyle issues (such as what to eat, how to treat family members and neighbors, and how to handle criminal justice issues). And it established a rhythm of daily sacrifices, weekly sabbaths, and annual feasts to weave reverent worship for God into their fabric of life.

- *Christ.* "Prophets, though human, spoke from God as they were carried along by the Holy Spirit" (2 Peter 1:21). These inspired prophets called God's people to repentance and offered hope by pointing toward the coming Messiah. Jesus summed up the Hebrew Scriptures by saying, "Everything must be fulfilled that is written about me in the Law of Moses, the Prophets and the Psalms" (Luke 24:44).

According to theologian Norman Geisler, the first five books of the Old Testament (Genesis through Deuteronomy) establish the *ethical* code that governed the Israelite nation. The historical books from Joshua to Esther explain the nation's *political* life. The books of poetry highlight the *spiritual* experiences of the people. The Law lays the *foundation* for Christ; history is the *preparation* for Christ; poetry represents the *aspiration* for Christ; and prophecy reveals the *expectation* of Christ.[1]

"All Scripture is God-breathed and is useful for teaching, rebuking, correcting and training in righteousness, so that the servant of God may be thoroughly equipped for every good work" (2 Timothy 3:16-17). The

Lord gave us the Bible to equip and guide us in every season of life, so let's examine what the Old Covenant Scriptures tell us about being faithful to God as we age.

PATRIARCHS AND MATRIARCHS

Do you ever picture humanity's first parents, Adam and Eve, as senior citizens? According to Genesis 5:5, "Altogether, Adam lived a total of 930 years, and then he died."

That's a lot of birthday candles! Another senior adult named Methuselah holds the record for attaining the oldest age mentioned in the Bible. He died at 969 (Genesis 5:27), so he didn't need to have a midlife crisis till around the age of 500! How could anyone live more than 900 years? In the beginning, God's perfect creation meant humans lived in a clean, untainted environment. Nothing polluted the Garden of Eden's water and air. No harmful bacteria caused disease. It took a while for death to take hold. By the time Moses wrote Psalm 90:10, however, he observed that most people live to be about 70 or 80 years old, just as they do today. (Moses himself was an exception to the rule, for he lived to be 120, but according to Deuteronomy 34:7, God granted him unusual physical strength and keen eyesight for a man of such advanced age.)

During the early patriarchal period, Enoch lived to be 365 years old—the equivalent of one year for every day in the calendar. Enoch was unique because "he did not experience death" (Hebrews 11:5). Instead, he "walked faithfully with God; then he was no more, because God took him away" (Genesis 5:23-24). Someone has said it's as if Enoch simply walked into the sunset with his best Friend. "Walking with God" is a noble aspiration for all of us. At the end of your life, wouldn't it be great to be remembered as someone who "walked faithfully with God"?

Despite living in a world overwhelmed by wickedness, "Noah found favor in the eyes of the Lord" (Genesis 6:8). He was "a righteous man, blameless among the people of his time, and he walked faithfully with God" (Genesis 6:9). Noah was old when the flood came, but he demonstrated gutsy faith because "in holy fear [he] built an ark to save his family" (Hebrews 11:7). Altogether Noah lived to the ripe old age of 950 years (Genesis 9:29).

Abraham and Sarah lived by faith when they were senior adults. If your senior years require downsizing or moving to a different home, you can relate to this ancient patriarch and matriarch. When Abraham was 75, God called him to move to a distant land, and Abraham "obeyed and went, even though he did not know where he was going" (Hebrews 11:8). He and his wife "were already very old, and Sarah was past the age of childbearing," when the Lord promised to give them a son (Genesis 18:10-11). You don't see a lot of 90-year-olds in the maternity ward, but Abraham was 100 and Sarah was 90 when Isaac was born. Sarah died at age 127 (Genesis 23:1). The Bible devotes an entire chapter to her death, Abraham's mourning, and his acquisition of a gravesite for his beloved wife (Genesis 23). Abraham himself "died at a good old age [175], an old man and full of years," and he was buried next to Sarah (Genesis 25:7-10).

As with all of us today, the individuals and families we read about in Genesis were imperfect; they led complicated lives and faced external threats and internal conflicts. Before Isaac died at the age of 180 (Genesis 35:28), he repeated his father Abraham's ruse by lying and telling people his wife was his sister (Genesis 26:1-11). Jacob tricked his brother Esau out of his blessing (Genesis 27:1-41), dreamed about a stairway that reached to heaven (Genesis 28:10-22), and spent a night in a wrestling match with God that left him limping for the rest of his life (Genesis 32:22-32). Before dying at age 147, Jacob gave instructions to his sons, "giving each the blessing appropriate to him" (Genesis 49:28). The book of Genesis ends with the death of Jacob's beloved son Joseph at the age of 110 (Genesis 50:26).

A PARTICULARLY PATIENT PATRIARCH

The patriarch Job considered old age an advantage. He asked, "Is not wisdom found among the aged? Does not long life bring understanding?" (Job 12:12). Yet, Job is best-known for his suffering and the losses he endured. He lost his possessions (1:13-17). He lost his children (1:18-22). He lost his health (2:1-8). And he lost the confidence of his wife (2:9-10).

He suffered physically when boils covered his body. He suffered socially when his former admirers found him repulsive. He suffered emotionally when his children died. He suffered financially when his possessions were stolen and destroyed. He suffered spiritually when God seemed unresponsive. He suffered intellectually when his friends' attempted explanations failed to satisfy his mind.

Perhaps as you grow older, you puzzle over the mystery of suffering. If so, you can relate to Job. He wished he hadn't been born (Job 3:1-3, 11, 16; 10:18). He wondered why his life should continue when he felt so miserable (3:20-26). He complained bitterly (6:1-4; 7:11; 10:1). He felt too weak to carry the burdens that were upon him (6:11-13). He had trouble sleeping (7:4). He suffered nonstop physical agony (7:5). He felt unfairly treated by God (7:20; 10:8-9). He was frustrated because he couldn't confront God as he might face someone else (9:32-35; 23:1-5, 8-9). He felt embarrassed and abandoned by his friends—and even his wife found him loathsome (12:4; 19:13-21). At times he felt hopeless (14:7-10; 17:1).

It's natural to ask tough questions as we grow older—especially when suffering comes. But ultimately we must learn to say, as Job told God, "I am unworthy—how can I reply to you?" (40:4). Author Philip Yancey rightly observes in his book, *Where Is God When It Hurts*, "Our arms aren't long enough to box with God."

In the book of Job, suffering is providentially allowed, but it is not fully explained. Yet, the book has a happy ending. After wrestling with the mystery of unanswered prayer, the book ends by emphasizing how God *answered* Job's prayers. Throughout the book, Job was preoccupied with his own suffering, but things took a positive turn when he prayed for his friends. "After Job had prayed for his friends, the Lord restored his fortunes and gave him twice as much as he had before" (Job 42:10).

In fact, "The Lord blessed the latter part of Job's life more than the former part" (Job 42:12). Once again, Job had thousands of sheep, camels, oxen, and donkeys. God blessed him with a family again, "seven sons and three daughters," and Job "saw his children and their children to the fourth generation" (vv. 13, 16). The book concludes, "And so Job died, an old man and full of years" (v. 17).

Job lost a lot of things, but he didn't lose his faith. He found that human logic is inadequate to fully explain evil and suffering. We often ask, "Why?" But rather than explaining everything about the "why," the Bible emphasizes the "how"—how will we *respond* when suffering comes? If your house is on fire, it's not the time to sit down and study a book called *The Origin of Fires in Private Homes*. You try to put out the fire! As someone pointed out, the Bible doesn't tell us everything about the "genesis" of suffering, but it assures us there is an "exodus" (a way out).

LAWGIVERS AND LEADERS, KINGS AND QUEENS

Moving on from the patriarchal period, we come to the lawgiver Moses and his older siblings, Miriam and Aaron. Moses' life can be divided into three sections of 40 years each. From birth to age 40, he lived as a prince in Pharaoh's palace. In the middle third of his life, from age 40 to 80, he was an obscure shepherd in the land of Midian. Then the Lord appeared to him at the burning bush and called him to lead the Israelites out of Egypt. Moses was 80 years old, and his brother Aaron was 83, when they confronted Pharaoh (Exodus 7:7). It's been said that Moses spent the first 40 years thinking he was somebody, the next 40 years thinking he was nobody, and the last 40 years learning what God can do with a nobody.

Moses showed gutsy faith when he "chose to be mistreated along with the people of God rather than to enjoy the fleeting pleasures of sin. He regarded disgrace for the sake of Christ as of greater value than the treasures of Egypt, because he was looking ahead to his reward. By faith he left Egypt, not fearing the king's anger; he persevered because he saw him who is invisible" (Hebrews 11:25-27).

Moses was an old man when he climbed up Mount Sinai and received God's laws engraved on stone tablets. The first four of the Ten Commandments deal with love for God: don't worship other gods, make no graven images, don't misuse God's name, honor the Sabbath day. The final six commandments deal with love for our neighbors, and the fifth commandment starts with our closest neighbors—members of our own households. "Honor your father and your mother" (Exodus 20:12) lays a foundation of respect for the older generation reflected in other Old Testament verses like this one: "A wise son brings joy to his father, but a foolish son brings grief to his mother" (Proverbs 10:1).

The Law of Moses includes this admonition: "Stand up in the presence of the aged, show respect for the elderly and revere your God. I am the Lord" (Leviticus 19:32). Commenting on this text, authors Bill and Judy Norris pointed out, "Years ago children were taught to rise when an elderly person entered a room, offering our chairs, our undivided attention, but most of all our respect to anyone older. Calling an old person by his or her first name was frowned upon and never permitted unless the older person asked for it."[2] Centuries later, the prophet Jeremiah saw it as an indication of social decline when "elders are shown no respect" (Lamentations 5:12).

Respect for the elderly wasn't based on age alone, however; people assumed the older generation had valuable insights to share. Deuteronomy 32:7 says, "Remember the days of old; consider the generations long past. Ask your father and he will tell you, your elders, and they will explain to you."

Moses died at age 120 (Deuteronomy 34:1-12). His brother Aaron, who served as a priest and as Moses' spokesman, died at age 123 (Numbers 33:39). Their older sister Miriam, who was a prophet, singer, and worship leader (Exodus 15:20-21), died and was buried in the desert during the Hebrews' 40-year trek across the wilderness (Numbers 20:1).

When it was time for the Israelites to conquer the land of Canaan, Caleb bravely stepped up and declared, "So here I am today, eighty-five years old! I am still as strong today as the day Moses sent me out; I'm just as vigorous to go out to battle now as I was then. Now give me this hill country that the Lord promised me that day" (Joshua 14:10-12). In his mid-80s, Caleb still wanted to tackle a mountain-sized challenge! So did Moses' successor, Joshua, who challenged the people to "fear the Lord and serve him with all faithfulness. Throw away the gods your ancestors worshiped . . . and serve the Lord." Joshua was an old man when he famously said, "Choose for yourselves this day whom you will serve. . . . But as for me and my household, we will serve the Lord" (Joshua 24:14-15). He died at the age of 110 (Joshua 24:29).

The book of Judges chronicles a stormy period of war, conflict, and social chaos in Israel. Moses had died, Joshua had died, and it wasn't clear who was in charge. Judges 2:10 paints a grim picture of cultural decline: "After that whole generation had been gathered to their ancestors, another generation grew up who knew neither the Lord nor what he had done for Israel." The inspired writer twice sums up the situation by explaining, "In those days Israel had no king; everyone did as they saw fit" (Judges 17:6; 21:25).

To fill the void, God raised up people commonly known as "judges," although they didn't sit in a courtroom wearing black robes. These judges were civil rulers and military generals. Others looked to them for leadership in a culture that was falling apart. We don't know her exact age, but it's clear Deborah was respected as a mature prophet who led Israel for a season of peace that lasted 40 years (Judges 4:1–5:31). Gideon, another notable leader during this time, showed flashes of faith-filled devotion to God; but as an old man, he drifted into idolatry that weakened his witness for God (Judges 8:22-27). The era of the Judges also includes the story of the aging widow Naomi and her daughter-in-law Ruth, who played important roles in God's redemption story.

The books of 1 and 2 Samuel, 1 and 2 Kings, and 1 and 2 Chronicles describe a series of good and bad kings and queens who reigned over Israel and Judah. Some of these rulers give us a lot to think about as we grow older. For example:

- Solomon's later years weren't greater years, because he became unfaithful to the Lord. "As Solomon grew old, his wives turned his heart after other gods, and his heart was not fully devoted to the Lord his God, as the heart of David his father had been" (1 Kings 11:4).

- King Rehoboam refused to listen to the advice of the elders, choosing instead to heed the young friends who had grown up with him. After rejecting the wise counsel of the older generation, the king presided over bitter rebellion and moral depravity within his own nation, and eventually the king of Egypt attacked Jerusalem and carried off many of its treasures (1 Kings 12–14).

- The Spirit-led transfer of the prophetic role from Elijah to Elisha provides an illustration of how healthy succession can work as older leaders relinquish responsibility to the next generation (1 Kings 19; 2 Kings 1–2).

- Israel's kings and queens illustrate valuable principles about how to die well. King David, for example, lived only to age 70, but he "died at a good old age, having enjoyed long life, wealth and honor" (1 Chronicles 29:28).

POETS AND PROPHETS

As we continue this overview of what the Old Testament says about aging, let's consider the section of the Hebrew Scriptures filled with poetry, proverbs, and songs of praise. Several of the Psalms allude to the aging process. Here are some examples:

- "I was young and now I am old, yet I have never seen the righteous forsaken or their children begging bread" (Psalm 37:25).

- "Do not cast me away when I am old; do not forsake me when my strength is gone" (Psalm 71:9).

- "They will still bear fruit in old age, they will stay fresh and green" (Psalm 92:14).

I agree with authors Bill and Judy Norris, who observed, "Most believers appreciate the Psalms more when they grow older. So many of the Psalms appear aimed at quiet meditation, praise and thanksgiving. We also find poignant cries for God's help in trying circumstances. Aging prepares us for calm introspection. The hectic days of youth and middle age leave little time for quiet activity. Older folk usually have suffered enough to recognize their deep need for a sustaining arm. The faithful find that sustenance in God."[3]

And what about these observations from the book of Proverbs?

- "Gray hair is a crown of splendor; it is attained in the way of righteousness" (Proverbs 16:31). Don't be dismayed by your gray hair. It's "a crown of splendor"!

- "The glory of young men is their strength, gray hair the splendor of the old" (Proverbs 20:29).

- "Listen to your father, who gave you life, and do not despise your mother when she is old" (Proverbs 23:22).

The Old Testament prophets refer to the aging process, as well. Scholars believe Isaiah lived to be at least 80 years old, for his prophetic ministry spanned the reigns of several different kings. Isaiah quotes these encouraging words from the Lord: "Even to your old age and gray hairs I am he, I am he who will sustain you. I have made you and I will carry you; I will sustain you and I will rescue you" (Isaiah 46:4). The prophet's vision of the new heavens and new earth include a prediction that there will never again be "an old man who does not live out his years" (65:20).

The prophet Daniel served as a statesman in the administrations of four non-Hebrew kings (Nebuchadnezzar, Belshazzar, Darius, and Cyrus). As an old man (probably in his eighties or nineties), Daniel didn't retire from his career as a prophet. At one point late in Daniel's life, God revealed such a disturbing message that Daniel went on a partial fast for three weeks. According to Daniel 10, God sent a heavenly ambassador to speak with him face-to-face, and Daniel's friends fled, leaving the old prophet to confront the divine messenger all by himself. Overwhelmed, Daniel admitted, "I had no strength left, my face turned deathly pale and I was helpless" (Daniel 10:8). He passed out and fell to the ground (v. 9). As the conversation continued, Daniel staggered to his feet "trembling" (v. 11) and "speechless" (v. 15), barely managing to sputter, "My strength is gone and I can hardly breathe" (v. 17). We rightly consider Daniel a hero, but at this point, by his own description, he was old, weak, exhausted, scared, speechless, and alone—which doesn't sound very heroic.

Daniel is known for trusting God to rescue him from the lions, but he continued to exercise gutsy faith as a much older man. God's message to the old prophet in Daniel 10 remains relevant to us in every stage of life. We must humble ourselves before God. He will answer our prayers and renew our strength. His Book of Truth (Daniel 10:21) remains in force. If the Lord is with us, even when we feel overwhelmed, we are not overmatched.

In this brief overview, we have not exhausted what the Old Testament says about the aging process. Centuries later, the Day of Pentecost brought the fulfillment of the prophet Joel's prediction that God would pour out his Spirit and "your old men will dream dreams, your young men will see visions" (Joel 2:28). And in his brilliant description of the messianic kingdom, another prophet foretells, "Once again men and women of ripe old age will sit in the streets of Jerusalem, each of them with cane in hand because of their age. The city streets will be filled with boys and girls playing there" (Zechariah 8:4-5).

Aging in the New Testament

Young adults dominate the pages of the New Testament. Mary was a young woman when God chose her to give birth to his Son. Jesus completed his earthly ministry by the time he was 33, and when he called his 12 apostles, they apparently all were young adults. Yet, the Gospels and the rest of the New Testament have valuable things to tell us about aging.

The physician and historian Dr. Luke sets the stage for Jesus' birth with the story of Zechariah and Elizabeth, an older couple who remind us of Abraham and Sarah. Zechariah and Elizabeth were childless and beyond the age of child-bearing when told they would have a son, the individual we know as John the Baptist. Zechariah asked the angel Gabriel, "How can I be sure of this? I am an old man and my wife is well along in years" (Luke 1:18). Wouldn't we have had doubts about this, too? In time, though, God's promise was fulfilled. The boy John, born to these stunned senior citizens, not only served as the forerunner to Messiah Jesus, he also was "a joy and delight" to his aging parents (Luke 1:14).

Two more older adults played a role in the story of Jesus' infancy. A few days after Jesus' birth, an old man named Simeon took the baby in what likely were arthritic arms and praised the Lord, for the Spirit had revealed to him "that he would not die before he had seen the Lord's Messiah" (Luke 2:25-35). Simeon wouldn't exit the world until he saw Christ enter it; we won't see Christ with our own eyes until we exit it! Aren't you glad you have lived long enough to learn about the Savior, Jesus Christ? Anna, another senior adult in her eighties, "never left the temple but worshiped night and day, fasting and praying," and she thanked the Lord and told others about the baby Jesus (Luke 2:36-38).

In some instances, we can only speculate about the ages of the men and women we read about in the Gospels. Historians calculate that the powerful ruler Herod the Great was around 70 years old at the time of Jesus' birth. It's likely that Zebedee, the father of the fishermen James and John, was in midlife or older when Jesus called his sons to leave their fishing nets and follow him. Jesus engaged in a famous interaction with a fellow known as the "rich young ruler," but he also had a famous appointment with an influential older ruler named Nicodemus who met with him by night. Jesus interacted with several widows during his ministry, and it's likely some of them were senior adults.

It appears that the apostle Paul was born within a few years of the birth of Christ, and the timetable of his life falls into two main segments. During the first half of his life, he was known as Saul of Tarsus, a hard-driving

Pharisee who violently opposed Christ and the church. After his dramatic conversion, however, Saul's name was changed to Paul, and he lived the second half of his life as a sold-out follower of the Messiah he had viciously opposed. Paul was likely in his fifties and early sixties when he wrote his New Testament letters, and he died as a martyr for the faith, apparently before reaching the age of 70.

In his short letter to his friend Philemon, Paul leveraged his senior adult status to strengthen his appeal for reconciliation on behalf of Onesimus, the runaway slave. How could Philemon resist Paul's request when the aging apostle appealed to him "on the basis of love" and identified himself as "none other than Paul—an old man and now also a prisoner of Christ Jesus" (Philemon 9)?

Paul stressed the importance of treating older people with respect in his letters to Timothy and Titus, both of them young leaders. Paul wrote, "Do not rebuke an older man harshly, but exhort him as if he were your father. Treat younger men as brothers, older women as mothers, and younger women as sisters, with absolute purity" (1 Timothy 5:1-2). Paul told Titus, "Teach the older men to be temperate, worthy of respect, self-controlled, and sound in faith, in love and in endurance. Likewise, teach the older women to be reverent in the way they live, not to be slanderers or addicted to much wine, but to teach what is good" (Titus 2:2-3).

As Paul prepared to die, he looked back and saw God at work in his life, and he looked ahead with gutsy faith. He wrote, "I have fought the good fight, I have finished the race, I have kept the faith. Now there is in store for me the crown of righteousness, which the Lord, the righteous Judge, will award to me on that day—and not only to me, but also to all who have longed for his appearing" (2 Timothy 4:7-8).

Without specifically mentioning senior adults, Hebrews 13:7 brings the older generation to mind when it says, "Remember your leaders, who spoke the word of God to you. Consider the outcome of their way of life and imitate their faith."

Simon Peter had some things to say about aging, too. Calling himself "a fellow elder and a witness of Christ's sufferings," Peter urged the elders of the church to shepherd God's flock with willing hearts, be eager to serve, and set a positive example for others (1 Peter 5:1-4). In his second and final letter, knowing that his death was approaching, the aging apostle reminded his readers to stay "firmly established in the truth" so that after he departed, the generations to follow would "always be able to remember these things" (2 Peter 1:12-15).

And what about the apostle John? Longstanding tradition suggests John was the youngest of the 12 apostles and he outlived all of them. Jesus had referred to John by saying, "If I want him to remain alive until I return, what is that to you?" (John 21:22), and based on a misunderstanding of those words, a rumor spread among the early Christians that John would never die (v. 23).

John was exiled to the island of Patmos "because of the word of God and the testimony of Jesus" (Revelation 1:9). There on Patmos, John received the great visions recorded in the book of Revelation, which include references to "twenty-four elders" who worship the Lord in heaven (Revelation 4:4, 10; 5:8-14; 19:4). According to the historian Eusebius, John was in exile for 18 months. It's widely believed that John returned to his home in Ephesus after the death of the Roman emperor Domitian in AD 96, and tradition says John died there near the end of the first century.

As an old man, John bore witness to what he had seen and heard during his close personal interactions with Jesus. He wanted to make sure the generations to come would know about the Living Word "we have seen with our eyes, which we have looked at and our hands have touched." Like John, don't you want to help others make sure their joy is complete (1 John 1:1-4)? As I age, I can relate to John's sentiment, "I have no greater joy than to hear that my children are walking in the truth" (3 John 4).

In Summary

We can sum up what the Bible says about aging with four words that all start with the letter *W.*

Wisdom. Like Moses who heard God's voice and Solomon who shared practical bits of godly common sense, older people need to gain wisdom and impart it humbly to the next generation.

Work. Like Abraham and Sarah, Joshua and Caleb, Deborah and Daniel, older people have important contributions to make to the Lord's work.

Worship. Like Miriam and Anna, older people should set an example by being devoted to prayer and worshipping God.

Witness. Like Peter, Paul, Simeon, and John, older people can bear witness to the truth of the gospel.

No matter how old or young we are, we can be confident of this: "He who began a good work in you will carry it on to completion until the day of Christ Jesus" (Philippians 1:6).

QUESTIONS FOR PERSONAL REFLECTION
AND GROUP DISCUSSION

1. After reading this chapter, how would you summarize the biblical perspective on aging? What stands out most as you consider what the Bible says about the aging process?

2. Which Bible character(s) do you relate to most, and why?

    —— Abraham and Sarah, whose faith was stretched as God put them to work in surprising ways.

    —— Moses, whose capacity as a leader was greater in his later years than in his younger years.

    —— Solomon, whose life took a disappointing turn in his later years.

    —— Anna, who devoted herself to prayer as she grew older.

    ——John, whose love for Christ moved him to bear witness for the Lord as the years went by.

    —— Other:

3. Which of the four Ws (Wisdom, Work, Worship, Witness) do you find most challenging as you grow older? Why?

6 | Your Children's Children— The High Calling of Grandparenthood

"Nobody can do for little children what grandparents do.
Grandparents sort of sprinkle stardust over the lives of little children."
—Alex Haley

"But from everlasting to everlasting the Lord's love is with those who fear him,
and his righteousness with their children's children."
—Psalm 103:17

"Since my youth, God, you have taught me,
and to this day I declare your marvelous deeds.
Even when I am old and gray, do not forsake me, my God,
till I declare your power to the next generation,
your mighty acts to all who are to come."
—Psalm 71:17-18

You are not too old to have a positive influence on the generations that follow you. In fact, one of the most significant things you do in your entire life might be the way you shape the hearts and minds of a few individuals half a century younger than you.

You don't often see grandparents and killer whales mentioned in the same sentence, but an article in *Science* magazine compares the two. According to the article, "Only female humans, pilot whales, and killer whales are known to go through menopause: At a certain age, they stop reproducing, but continue to lead long, productive lives. Like humans, female killer whales stop giving birth by about 40, but can live into their

90s." As the author puts it, "Killer whales wouldn't get far without their old ladies." Researchers speculate that these older whales share their wisdom and lead their families to find food in times of famine. Young whales depend on the old—especially their mothers and grandmothers—to help them find the salmon they must eat to survive.[1]

We grandparents have our work cut out for us if we want upcoming generations to survive and thrive. Grandparents have been referred to as people who "have silver in their hair and gold in their hearts." Someone observed, "Grandchildren are a grandparent's link to the future. Grandparents are the child's link to the past." Or maybe you resonate more with the person who joked, "Grandchildren are God's reward for putting up with your own children when they were teenagers."

I heard about a grandma who was telling her granddaughter what her childhood was like. She said, "We used to skate outside on a frozen pond. We made a swing out of a tire and hung it from a tree in our yard. We rode a pony. We picked wild blackberries in the woods." Wide-eyed, the little girl remarked, "Grandma, I sure wish I'd gotten to know you sooner!"

The connection with grandparents can be one of the most important relationships in a child's life. When researchers studied spiritual influences in the lives of teenagers, they found parents and grandparents, not youth workers at church, topped the list. According to an article in *U. S. News & World Report*, when grandparents spend quality time with their grandkids, it leads to better mental health for everyone involved. The author states, "For kids, grandparents provide stability, safety, wisdom and fun. In return, caring for grandchildren can help stave off depression, boost social connections, and keep older adults mentally sharp."[2]

DID YOU KNOW . . . ?

- In 1978, the U.S. Congress passed legislation designating the first Sunday after Labor Day as National Grandparents Day. It was signed into law by President Jimmy Carter on August 3, 1978.

- The word *grandparent* is fairly new in human history. The word, as we use it, first appeared in the early 1800s, although the prefixes "grand" and "great" date from the 1200s.

- According to AARP, today there are approximately 70 million grandparents in the United States—more than at any other time in American history. Of all adults over age 30, more than one out of three are grandparents, with an average of five to six grandchildren per grandparent.

My wife, Candy, and I have an unusual marriage because her last name was Faust before she married me. That's right: her maiden name was Faust, so now her full name is Candy Faust Faust! When our children were growing up, they had two sets of grandparents named Grandpa and Grandma Faust. One set of grandparents lived in New York and the other set lived in Ohio—city grandparents and country grandparents.

What impact did your grandparents have on your life? Some of us had grandparents who practically raised us; they lived nearby and we saw them almost every day or every Sunday at church. Others had grandparents we barely knew. Perhaps you viewed your grandparents as respected patriarchs and matriarchs like Abraham and Sarah in the Bible—venerable old leaders respected for their wisdom and experience. Unfortunately, it's possible you may have had a different experience. Maybe your grandparents died before you were born, or they lived so far away you rarely saw them. Or perhaps your grandparents were physically ill, emotionally unavailable, or simply had personalities that made them difficult to be around.

In the rural area where I grew up, I was blessed to have all four of my grandparents living nearby. Grandpa and Grandma Faust lived within walking distance up the road from my house, while Grandpa and Grandma Orebaugh lived a few miles away (close enough that I could ride there on my bicycle). Two of my grandparents were very active in the church, while the others almost never attended—but all four of them loved me.

I have fond memories of playing horseshoes in their yards, sleeping overnight at their houses, and going fishing with my grandpas. The thought of Grandma Orebaugh's delicious fried chicken still makes my mouth water. She patiently hovered over a cast-iron skillet adding the leftover crispy pieces to the gravy we ladled over our mashed potatoes. For dessert, she made chocolate cake from scratch, topped with homemade chocolate frosting.

Of course, not all senior adults have children and grandchildren of their own, but all of us can serve as spiritual parents and grandparents for kids in our churches and neighborhoods. When Candy and I lived on Long Island, New York, we were 800 miles from my parents, but an older married couple nicknamed Corky and Grammy gave special attention to our three young children. The kids loved seeing them at church on Sundays, and this friendly couple would occasionally surprise them with a birthday gift or another special treat.

In this chapter, let's explore what the Bible says about grandparenting so we can better understand how we can help the generations that follow after us.

Bad Grandpas and Grandmas (and Some Good Ones, Too)

Honoring "your parents' parents" was strongly implied in ancient Hebrew culture, for "Honor your father and your mother" was imbedded in the Ten Commandments (Exodus 20:12). When grandparents entered the room, children were expected to stand up as a sign of respect (Leviticus 19:32).

The Hebrew Scriptures refer to multiple generations by using the phrase "your children's children." For example, Psalm 103:17 says, "But from everlasting to everlasting the Lord's love is with those who fear him, and his righteousness with their children's children." Another passage in the Psalms pronounces a blessing on the family that loves God by saying, "Your wife will be like a fruitful vine within your house; your children will be like olive shoots around your table. . . . May you live to see your children's children" (Psalm 128:3, 6).

According to Proverbs 17:6, "Children's children are a crown to the aged, and parents are the pride of their children." (A crown symbolized royalty and honor.) The statement "parents are the pride of their children" motivates us to be the kind of parents and grandparents who make our offspring proud.

Many of the multigenerational families we meet in the Bible were terribly flawed. Adam and Eve were everyone's parents and grandparents—and their firstborn son, Cain, murdered their second son, Abel. The extended families of Abraham, Isaac, and Jacob had all kinds of problems! There was rotten fruit on their family trees, and that rotten fruit produced violence, drunkenness, deception, and favoritism. Jacob's family was so dysfunctional that his sons hated their brother Joseph and sold him into slavery. But in time, Joseph rose to a high government position in Egypt and eventually he reconciled with his brothers, telling them, "You intended to harm me, but God intended it for good" (Genesis 50:20). Evidently, God can even use messy families to accomplish his good purposes.

Later, the Israelite nation suffered under terrible leaders who, instead of making things better for their descendants, passed down problems from generation to generation. For example, a wicked leader named Jehoram reigned in Jerusalem for eight years. When Jehoram died, the biblical writer wryly notes, "He passed away, to no one's regret" (2 Chronicles 21:20). What a sad legacy to leave behind!

Second Kings 11 tells about a bad grandma. Athaliah was the mother of King Ahaziah of Judah. When her son the king died, she had the whole royal family executed so she could reign as queen. It's sad to read about a grandmother so wicked she would order the slaughter of her own family members to solidify her own power. However, one of Ahaziah's sisters, a woman named Jehosheba, was able to preserve the life of one of the princes. This baby—Athaliah's grandson—was named Joash. He remained hidden in a bedroom in the temple, so he wasn't killed. He and a nurse who took care of him lived there in hiding for six years, while Athaliah the wicked queen reigned. When Joash was 7 years old, the high priest brought him out in public and anointed him, put the crown on his head, and proclaimed him king. Queen Athaliah was enraged, but she was soon executed. King Joash went on to rule for 40 years.

Fortunately, the Bible also tells about older men and women who exerted positive influences on succeeding generations.

Naomi was a good grandma. Her daughter-in-law Ruth had a baby named Obed, who became the grandfather of King David. Naomi celebrated the birth of her little grandson Obed and held him in her arms while her friends rejoiced with her. They predicted, "He will renew your life and sustain you in your old age. For your daughter-in-law, who loves you and who is better to you than seven sons, has given him birth" (Ruth 4:14-17).

Another good grandma was Lois, who had a positive influence on a young man who became a significant leader in the early church. The apostle Paul told the young preacher Timothy, "I am reminded of your sincere faith, which first lived in your grandmother Lois and in your mother Eunice and, I am persuaded, now lives in you also" (2 Timothy 1:5). Don't you imagine Lois frequently prayed for her grandson and encouraged him in his ministry? Perhaps Paul had women like Lois in mind when he wrote about older widows who pray night and day, asking God for help (1 Timothy 5:5).

GRANDPARENT NAMES

There are hundreds of different names children use for their grandparents. An eye-opening (and amusing) list of these names appears at the end of this chapter.

---

10 Roles a Grandparent Can Play

Like kids, grandparents are all unique and different, and no grandparents are perfect. But Scripture and common sense show us several positive roles grandparents can have in the life of a child. Here are 10 roles to consider.

1. Steady Presence

Grandparents don't have to do a lot to play a significant part in our grandkids' lives. One of the best ways we show love to our grandchildren is by giving them the gift of undistracted time and attention. Children need someone who will just "be there" and be present for them—someone who is always in their corner, caring for them and pulling for them.

In the book of Genesis, Joseph sent a message to his dad, Jacob, that included these words: "You shall live in the region of Goshen *and be near me—you, your children and grandchildren,* your flocks and herds, and all you have" (Genesis 45:10, emphasis added).

Sometimes the most important thing grandparents can do is simply "be near" their children and grandchildren.

2. Memory Maker

The Lord instructed the Hebrew people, "Remember the days of old; consider the generations long past. Ask your father and he will tell you, your elders, and they will explain to you" (Deuteronomy 32:7). Senior adults need to help the next generations "remember the days of old."

Memory making is a serious responsibility, but it also can be fun! I still have fond memories from more than a half century ago of making hamburgers with my Grandpa Orebaugh and eating ice cream cones in his front yard. I remember how Grandma Faust let me stay up late when I slept overnight at her house, and she made me 7-Up floats before bedtime. I remember working on a school science project in Grandpa Faust's garage. We built a little telegraph machine, using batteries and pieces of metal nailed to strips of wood.

My own adult children still talk about how good the bacon and coffee smelled when my mother made breakfast for them early in the morning. They fondly remember fishing with my dad in the pond on his farm, and how their other grandfather let them scoop their hands into "Pop's Penny Bowl" every Christmas. (The kids got to keep as many pennies as their hands could hold.)

Grandparents can cheerfully embrace our role as memory makers.

3. Storyteller

Grandparents are repositories of family history. My parents passed down a lot of stories about our family, but I wish I had asked them to tell me more.

My mom's collection of antique dishes meant a lot to her. She proudly displayed the punch bowl that sat on the reception table on the day she married Dad. She had a shelf full of pretty vases, "Depression glass" cream and sugar bowls, and dishes for serving ice cream. After Mother died, I wished I had asked her to write down the background stories about her favorite dishes and glassware.

The most important story we can share is the story of Jesus. In the Psalms, God's people made a solemn promise: "We will tell the next generation the praiseworthy deeds of the Lord, his power, and the wonders he has done. He decreed statutes for Jacob and established the law in Israel, which he commanded our ancestors to teach their children, so the next generation would know them, even the children yet to be born, and they in turn would tell their children" (Psalm 78:4-6). That's how the Lord's story gets passed along. "One generation commends your works to another; they tell of your mighty acts" (Psalm 145:4).

Grandparents don't need to be wordy and overbearing. But we can find fun, creative ways to share our personal testimonies about the difference the Lord has made in our lives. We should make sure our grandkids know God has been faithful, he has kept his promises, and he has provided for us in the past. Maybe years later, someone will say to our grandkids what Paul told Timothy: "But as for you, continue in what you have learned and have become convinced of, because you know those from whom you learned it, and how from infancy you have known the Holy Scriptures, which are able to make you wise for salvation through faith in Christ Jesus" (2 Timothy 3:14-15).

4. Values Reinforcer

Unless grandparents are their grandchildren's primary caregivers, they should defer to the parents as the primary influencers who shape the character of those young ones. However, grandparents can play a vital role in supporting, modeling, and reinforcing godly values. During a time in my own adolescence when I rebelled against my parents, my grandparents' influence pulled me back in the right direction. Because of the affection and respect I had for my grandparents, I didn't want to disappoint them.

What core values can you help to instill in your grandchildren? Honesty, courage, kindness, faith? Are you doing your best to model these values in your own life?

Moses told the Hebrews, "Only be careful, and watch yourselves closely so that you do not forget the things your eyes have seen or let them fade from your heart as long as you live. *Teach them to your children and to their children after them*" (Deuteronomy 4:9, emphasis added). Paul told Timothy, "Teach the older men to be temperate, worthy of respect, self-controlled, and sound in faith, in love and in endurance. Likewise, teach the older women to be reverent in the way they live, not to be slanderers or addicted to much wine, but to teach what is good" (Titus 2:1-3).

5. Financial Booster

Grandparents usually don't have to be the primary financial providers for grandchildren, but it's good if we can provide supplemental support. According to Proverbs 13:22, "A good person leaves an inheritance for their children's children, but a sinner's wealth is stored up for the righteous."

Candy and I paid $35,000 for our first house—a tiny but lovely home where we lived for 10 years on Long Island. That price may not sound very expensive by today's standards, but in those days we lived on a very slim minister's salary. We wouldn't have been able to make the purchase without a $5,000 "nonrepayable loan" provided by a generous grandparent.

Maybe you can't afford the down payment for a house, but could you put a few dollars in your grandchild's birthday card? Could you take them with you on a fun vacation? Could you provide gift cards to help your college-bound grandchild buy clothes or pay for gas? Modest gifts can mean a lot.

Grandparents shouldn't use money to spoil our grandkids, but to encourage them—not to replace what they should earn through work, but to help them over the hump when they face legitimate financial needs.

6. Cheerleader

You may be a literal cheerleader if you have the opportunity to attend your grandchildren's ball games. I didn't know much about the rules of volleyball until my granddaughter Kayla began playing. Then I found myself leaving work early so I could drive two hours to a distant school gym to watch her play.

But whether your grandkids are involved in sports or not, they could use a cheerleader—someone who consistently conveys the message, "I love you. I am proud of you. I am here for you, whether you succeed or fail." This is the kind of family atmosphere the apostle Paul urged Christians to have when he wrote, "For you know that we dealt with each of you as a father deals with his own children, encouraging, comforting and urging you to live lives worthy of God, who calls you into his kingdom and glory" (1 Thessalonians 2:11-12). Later, Paul added some more words that apply to any of us grandparents who want to cheer on our grandkids: "And we urge you, brothers and sisters, warn those who are idle and disruptive, encourage the disheartened, help the weak, be patient with everyone" (1 Thessalonians 5:14).

7. Prayer Partner

Even when we are very old and our physical health declines, there remains an important ministry we can offer our grandchildren (and others as well). We can pray for them.

Years ago, as I prayed for God's blessings on my children and grandchildren, I noticed that many of my requests start with the letter *S*. The Lord has heard me say these prayers so often that he knows exactly what I mean when I mention "The S Prayer." I pray for my children and grandchildren's:

- *Salvation* . . . that they will embrace Jesus Christ as their personal Savior and Lord and give their hearts to him in faith and obedience.

- *Spiritual growth* . . . that they will be fully devoted followers of Jesus, loving and serving him throughout their lives.

- *Safety* . . . that the Lord will protect them from physical, emotional, and spiritual harm.

- *Social life* . . . that the Lord will give them positive friendships and bring trustworthy advisors and influencers into their lives.

- *Schoolwork* . . . that they will get a good education and be influenced by wise teachers.

- *Sexual purity and health* . . . that the Lord will give them discretion, wisdom, protection, and self-control.

- *Stewardship* . . . that they will handle their time, money, and talents wisely.

- *Singleness or Spouse* . . . that the Lord will guide them as they decide whether or not (and whom) to marry.

- *Service* . . . that they will learn to live not only for themselves, but also to honor God and show his love to others.

Grandparents can say a prayer like the following for our grandchildren, using words taken directly from Scripture:

> For this reason, since the day we heard about you, we have not stopped praying for you. We continually ask God to fill you with the

knowledge of his will through all the wisdom and understanding that the Spirit gives, so that you may live a life worthy of the Lord and please him in every way: bearing fruit in every good work, growing in the knowledge of God, being strengthened with all power according to his glorious might so that you may have great endurance and patience . . . (Colossians 1:9-11).

8. Blessing Giver

The Hebrew patriarchs offered prayers of blessing for their children and grandchildren. For example, "Early the next morning Laban kissed his grandchildren and his daughters and blessed them" (Genesis 31:55). Jacob (then known as Israel) blessed his grandsons: "When Israel saw the sons of Joseph, he asked, 'Who are these?' 'They are the sons God has given me here,' Joseph said to his father. Then Israel said, 'Bring them to me so I may bless them'" (Genesis 48:8-9).

Jesus took little children in his arms and "blessed them" (Mark 10:13-16). How wonderful it is when grandparents get to do the same for the little ones we love!

In *The Blessing*, authors Gary Smalley and John Trent identify five characteristics of the family blessing as it was bestowed in biblical times:

• Meaningful touch (like a hug, kiss, or hand on the shoulder);

• Spoken words of affirmation/encouragement;

• Expressing high value for the one being blessed;

• Picturing a special future for the one being blessed;

• An active commitment to fulfill the blessing.[3]

Although some aspects of these blessings were unique to ancient biblical culture, it remains true today: Your grandkids need to receive your blessing!

9. Blessing Receiver

Yes, grandparents can be blessing givers. But we also can be blessing receivers! What blessings have you received from being a grandparent?

GRANDPARENT QUOTES

"The simplest toy, one which even the youngest child can operate, is called a grandparent." —Sam Levenson

"When grandparents enter the door, discipline flies out the window." —Ogden Nash

"The best baby-sitters, of course, are the baby's grandparents. You feel completely comfortable entrusting your baby to them for long periods, which is why most grandparents flee to Florida." —Dave Barry

"I phoned my grandparents and my grandfather said, 'We saw your movie.' 'Which one?' I said. He shouted 'Betty, what was the name of that movie I didn't like?'" —Brad Pitt

"Grandparents can be very special resources. Just being close to them reassures a child, without words, about change and continuity, about what went before and what will come after." —Fred Rogers

"The very old and the very young have something in common that makes it right that they should be left alone together. Dawn and sunset see stars shining in a blue sky; but morning and midday and afternoon do not, poor things." —Elizabeth Goudge

"Grandfathers are just antique little boys."—Unknown

"Have children while your parents are still young enough to take care of them." —Rita Rudner

"Elephants and grandchildren never forget." —Andy Rooney

"If nothing is going well, call your grandmother." —Italian proverb

"The reason grandchildren and grandparents get along so well is that they have a common enemy." —Sam Levenson

"The greatest legacy one can pass on to one's children and grandchildren is not money or other material things accumulated in one's life, but rather a legacy of character and faith." —Billy Graham

For Candy and me, our list includes:

- Enjoying the unconditional love of little ones once again.

- Revisiting some of the things we liked about parenting. (While watching our grandchildren, we often say, "Remember when their mom used to do that?")

- Beholding once again the astonishing process of development as our grandchildren grow, express their unique personalities and gifts, learn to read, and interact with others.

- Enjoying our grandchildren without bearing the full weight of responsibility for their upbringing. (We enjoy their visits, but then we get to send them home!)

- Keeping in touch with the next generation's perspectives, questions, dreams, and concerns. (Our young-adult granddaughters also help us keep up with technology changes on our phones and computers.)

In biblical times, children and grandchildren had a God-given responsibility to care for their aging parents and grandparents. The fifth of the Ten Commandments said to honor the preceding generation, and that command was repeated in Deuteronomy 5:16: "Honor your father and your mother, as the Lord your God commanded you, so that you may live long and that it may go well with you in the land that the Lord your God is giving you." The apostle Paul instructed New Testament believers, "But if a widow has children or grandchildren, these should learn first of all to put their religion into practice by caring for their own family and so repaying their parents and grandparents, for this is pleasing to God" (1 Timothy 5:4).

10. Hope Giver

Our grandkids need hope! Growing up has never been easy, but kids today face new (and in some ways, unprecedented) forms of pressure, anxiety, and stress. Now more than ever, a grandparent needs to be a hope giver—a voice of calm, stability, and encouragement—offering reassurance that things are going to be OK after all.

By the time we become grandparents, most of us have lived through a messy mix of tragedy, trauma, and triumph—but somehow by God's grace, we made it through childhood, adolescence, and young adulthood. While the clamoring crowd cries out in fear and despair, our grandchildren need people in their lives like Joshua and Caleb who will stand up in faith and say, "There is still a land of milk and honey ahead! God is leading. The future is in his strong hands. You don't have to be afraid" (see Numbers 14:1-9).

Remember this Scripture: "Always be prepared to give an answer to everyone who asks you to *give the reason for the hope that you have*. But do this with gentleness and respect" (1 Peter 3:15, emphasis added). We can help our grandkids understand that "the Lord is good and his love endures forever; his faithfulness continues through all generations" (Psalm 100:5).

My oldest granddaughter, Abbie, taught me a lesson about hope. In her late teens, she started teaching pottery classes for young children. Abbie's skillful hands can turn a nondescript lump of clay into a beautiful mug, bowl, teapot, sculpture, vase, or candle holder.

I reminded her that the Lord compared himself to a skillful potter. He said, "Like clay in the hand of the potter, so are you in my hand, Israel" (Jeremiah 18:6). While Jeremiah watched, the potter found an imperfection in the clay, so "the potter formed it into another pot, shaping it as seemed best to him" (v. 4). The artist had a particular design in mind and wouldn't be satisfied until the plan was fulfilled, so he squashed the clay back into a shapeless blob and started over again.

"Clay is a medium that is meant to be re-created," my granddaughter told me. "Even if it's completely hardened, you can make it new with a bit of time, water, and knowledge." In fact, Abbie says clay that has been properly "reclaimed" is some of her favorite material to work with.

What a lesson in hope! Whether we belong to the older generation or the younger generation, we can be re-created. Even when life has been rough with us and smashed us down, the Lord can make something beautiful out of the mess. If we invite him to shape our thinking, guide our decisions, and mold our attitudes, we can be a blessing to "our children's children."

QUESTIONS FOR PERSONAL REFLECTION AND GROUP DISCUSSION

1. Think about your grandparents. What kind of relationship did you have with them while you were growing up? What did you learn from them? What did you like/dislike about them? What impact did they have on your life?

2. Which of the "10 Roles a Grandparent Can Play" mentioned in this chapter stand out most to you? Why?

3. It has been said, "There is no distance that can lessen a grandparent's love." What are your thoughts about long-distance grandparenting? What can grandparents do to build strong connections if your grandkids live far away, or if you have limited access to them?

4. What should you do if your grandchildren are not being brought up in the Christian faith, or if they are being taught a value system different from your own?

5. Suggested resources for further reading:

   "7 Essentials for Grandparenting Your Grandkids," by Larry Fowler, Focus on the Family, September 28, 2020, https://www.focusonthefamily.com/parenting/7-essentials-for-grandparenting-your-grandkids/

   "What Does the Bible Say About Grandparents?" by Sylvia Schroeder, Bible Study Tools (website), August 18, 2023, https://www.biblestudytools.com/bible-study/topical-studies/what-does-the-bible-say-about-grandparents-and-how-they-are-blessings.html

   "What Is the Role of a Christian Grandfather or Grandmother?" by Jack Wellman, What Christians Want to Know (website), https://www.whatchristianswanttoknow.com/what-is-the-role-of-a-christian-grandfather-or-grandmother-a-bible-study/

GRANDMOTHER NAMES

Abuela	Grams	Mommaw
Ady ("lady")	Gran	Mom-Mom
Auld Gen Bedstemor	Grandjoy	Mom Mommy
Ba Ba	Grand-Mom	Mom's Mom
Bema	Grandma	Mommy
Bomma	Grandmommy	Momsie
Bone Rainy	Grandmother	Monie
Damma	Granna	Mother
Denda	Granny	Mother-Too
Dobbye	Granny-Bob	Mother-Two
Doddy	Granny-Great	Mu-Mu
Doo-Dah-Day	Granny-Faddle	Mugger
Doody	Honey Di-Di	Mum
Duck Mama	La La	Mumma
Ga-Ga	Ma	Muner
Gabby	Mae-Mae	Munna
Gaggy	Maime (may-me) Big	Munna Mary
Gammoo	Mam	Muzzie
Gamoo	Mama	My-My
Gammy	MamaLillian	Nan
Gangy	Mamalou	Nana
G-C	Mame	Nani
Geema	Mamo	Nanna
G-G	Mammaw	Nanna Kat
Gi-Gi	Mammy	Na-Naw
Giga	Maw	Nannie
Gingo	Maw-Maw	Nanno
Ginny	Mawzy	Nanny
G Mama	Memaw	Nini
Go-Go	Memere	Ninna
Gram	Mi Mi	Ninnie
Gramma	Mina	Nu Nu
Grammuvver	Mo	Nonie
Grammy	Mom	Oldemor

Oma	Tatay	UhaWool
Other Mother	Tiani	Ya-Ya
Pink Mama	Two-Mom	Zaydeh
Po Po	U (Uh)	
Ranny	Uddy-Muddy	

GRANDFATHER NAMES

Abuelo	Doddy	Grand Dude
BaBa	Doody	Grand Pap
Ba-Du	Doo-Day	Grand Papa
Bantaw	Fa-Fa	Grandy
Bedstefar	Fajue	Granky
Big Daddy	Foppy	Grump
Big Jim	Fu-Fu	Grumpa
Biggy	G-P	Grumps
Bobalou	G-Pa	Grumpsey
Bo-Bo	G-PaPa	Gogie
Bop	Ga-Ga	Gups
Bopop	Gamp	Hi Ho
Buck	Gampy	Huggy
Bompa	Gawgy	Jida
Bubba	Gramp	Jo-Jo
Bubbie	Grampapa	Luh-luh-luh
Bumpa	Grampa	Nee-Nee
Bup-Bup	Gramps	Opa
Ca-Ca	Grampy	Pa
Caw-Caw	Gran	Pap
Da	Gran-Gran	Papa
Dad	Grand Dad	Papaw
Dad-Dad	Grand Daddy	Pappa John
Dad's Dad	Grand Datts	Papo
Daddle	Grandfather	Pap-Pap
Dado	Grandjohn	Pappy
Dapado	Grandpa	Papanaw

Papu	Poppaw	Punky-Papa
Paw	Popo	Randaddy
Pawzy	Pop	Sandy
Peepaw	Poppo	Ta-Ta
Peeps	Pop-Pop	Tatay
Pepere	Poppy	YPa
Pobey	Pops	
Po-Po	Popsie	

NOTE: My brother John Faust served for many years as the Senior Adults Minister at Southeast Christian Church in Louisville, Kentucky. For fun, he began collecting names people use for their grandparents, and the list (with some additions I have heard) is reproduced here with his permission.

7 | Temple Maintenance— Staying Fit When Your Body Wants to Quit

"Time may be a great healer, but it is a lousy beautician."
—Unknown

*"If I had known I was going to live this long,
I would have taken better care of myself."*
—George Burns (when he turned 90)

I hadn't seen my friend Matt for several years, so we texted each other and set up a time to meet for lunch. When I walked into the restaurant, he burst into lighthearted laughter.

"What's so funny?" I asked.

Matt answered, "I'm not used to seeing you with gray hair!"

His laughter didn't offend me, although it made me reflect on how my body is changing as I grow older. I try to eat right and take regular walks, but in recent years my body has resembled a used car that needs extra maintenance. During my sixties, I had cataract surgery on my eyes, a basal cell carcinoma surgically removed from my face, and a stage-zero melanoma removed from my neck. I had my gallbladder taken out, an umbilical hernia repaired, and a few teeth extracted and remodeled. I'm beginning to understand the guy who said, "Some days you feel like you can move mountains. Other days, it's all you can do to move from the chair to the couch."

The years take a toll on our physical health, but it helps if we refuse to take ourselves too seriously. Comedian Jim Gaffigan jokes, "When I buy shoes, I don't want cross-trainers and running shoes. I just ask where the 'slipper' section is located, because all I need is something to get me from one place where I sit to another place where I sit!" Here are a few other quips and quotes that help me see the lighter side of the physical decline that comes with age.

- "My favorite childhood memory is my back not hurting." —@ LloydLegalist (posted at X, formerly Twitter)

- "I had hoped by this stage of life, I'd have greatness and splendor. Instead, it's Grape Nuts and Splenda." —@ChrchCurmudgeon

- "There's a change that takes place somewhere in your late thirties or early forties when you stop being motivated to work out because you're vain and start doing it because you're scared." —Drew Dyck (@drewdyck)

- "I named my dog 'Five Miles' so I can tell people I walk five miles every day."

- "As you get older, you begin to suffer the occasional series of increasingly humiliating micro-injuries. 'How did you hurt yourself?' I slept wrong. While I was driving, I happened to yawn while checking my blind spot. I drank water too hard." —Jared Wilson (@ JaredWilson)

- "When we're young, we sneak out of bed to go to parties. When we're old, we sneak out of parties to go to bed." —Richard V. Reeves (from his book *Of Boys and Men*)

- "I hear about people my age climbing mountains. Personally, I feel good about getting my leg through my underwear without losing my balance."

- "Did you hear about the guy whose grandchildren bought him an iPad, but he traded it in for a heating pad?"

- "Did you hear about the guy who donated his body to science, and science contested the will?"

In his book, *I'm Not Old, I've Just Lived a Long Time,* Bob Tinsky reflected on how physical changes as we grow older impact our fashion choices. He made a list "to help us old codgers know what items do not go together." The list includes:

- a nose ring and bifocals
- spiked hair and bald spots
- a pierced tongue and dentures
- short skirts and varicose veins
- a belly-button ring and a gallbladder surgery scar[1]

All joking aside, though, your physical health matters to you, to your friends and family, and to God. According to Jesus, the greatest commandment is to love the Lord your God with all your heart, soul, mind, and strength (Mark 12:30), and "all your strength" includes your physical body. One author explains:

> The word "strength" in the Hebrew from which Jesus quoted is probably best understood as "ability." It's a gritty, functionary word, meant to refer to things we do. Hearing it, the Hebrews would have thought of the physical actions that made up their lives—farming, traveling, war—which is why so much of the Old Testament asks God to bless the harvest, set one's feet on the right path, and grant victory in battle. The early Hebrews lived hard, physical lives. Loving God with their strength was second nature.
>
> In the twenty-first century, it's a bit more of a stretch. . . .
>
> Modern strength is judged by web savvy, Facebook friend counts or Twitter [now called X] followers. Our "ability" and our "body" have become increasingly separated. And the concept of loving God with all our might becomes increasingly strange.[2]

Perhaps you managed to stay fit with minimal effort when you were young, but your body is demanding more attention as you age. If you want your later years to be greater years, you can't ignore your physical health.

Viewing Your Body from a Biblical Perspective

One scholar summed up the biblical view by saying, "The human body has a dignity, originally conferred upon us by the Creator, who shaped it out of earth and glorified it by the incarnation of Christ, the sinless One."[3]

The Lord thought highly enough of the human body that he chose to inhabit one for 33 years. The Word "became flesh and made his dwelling among us" (John 1:14). Christ was "made in human likeness" and became "fully human in every way" (Philippians 2:7; Hebrews 2:17). His physical body was subject to hunger, thirst, and weariness just as our bodies are. He faced the same kinds of hurts and aggravations we deal with, such as mosquito bites, stubbed toes, upset stomachs, sore muscles, toothaches, and sprained ankles.

Jesus' body played a significant role in our redemption. John, an eyewitness of Jesus' ministry, vividly recalled the Lord's physical presence, "which we have heard, which we have seen with our eyes, which we have looked at and our hands have touched" (1 John 1:1). The Lord endured horrible abuse when he was nailed to the cross, but in that profound sacrificial act he "'bore our sins' in his body on the cross" (1 Peter 2:24). Paul used the human body as an analogy for "the church, which is his [Christ's] body" (Ephesians 1:22-23), and he highlighted the importance of Christ's physical body when he wrote, "Beyond all question, the mystery from which true godliness springs is great: He appeared in the flesh, was vindicated by the Spirit, was seen by angels, was preached among the nations, was believed on in the world, was taken up in glory" (1 Timothy 3:16).

Our English word *human* is related to the Latin *humus*, which means "earth" or "soil." Notice the similarity between the Hebrew *adam* ("man") and *adamah* ("ground"). It's humbling to be human. God used common elements of the earth ("the dust of the ground") to form Adam and "breathed into his nostrils the breath of life" (Genesis 2:7). Our bodies ground us in the physical environment where we live and thrive. Have you heard it said, "From dust we came and to dust we shall return"? Roughly 96 percent of the human body consists of four common earthly elements: oxygen, carbon, hydrogen, and nitrogen. The remaining 4 percent is made of small amounts of elements found on the periodic table (even though we don't see them on the dinner table); these include calcium, phosphorus, potassium, sulfur, sodium, chlorine, magnesium, iron, fluorine, zinc, copper, iodine, selenium, chromium, manganese, and other trace minerals.[4] So in a sense, our bodies are as common as the ground on which we walk. Yet, there is something holy and noble about our bodies. What the psalmist David said about his own body is true of us all: we are "fearfully and wonderfully made" (Psalm 139:14), for the Creator has woven amazing complexity into every cell of our bodies.

This chapter will briefly explore three factors that can help you view your physical body from a biblical perspective: (1) Your body is a gift, (2) Your body is a responsibility, and (3) Your body is vulnerable and temporary.

YOUR BODY IS A GIFT

If you're like me, you sometimes complain about your aches and pains, and you're quite aware of your body's flaws. Maybe you wish you were taller, stronger, thinner, quicker, and more attractive. But if you have managed to live to adulthood (and especially if you are a senior adult), wouldn't you agree that overall, your body has served you well?

Have you ever thanked God for your body? Why not pause for a moment and do that right now?

Thank the Lord for your hair (even if it's thinning) and the way it gives you a distinctive look and protects your head from heat and cold. Thank him for your eyes and for all the interesting sights you have seen over the course of your life. Thank him for your nose and the ability to breathe and smell, for your teeth, and for all those taste buds the Creator saw fit to design so you could enjoy a variety of delicious foods. Thank him for your stomach and its ability to digest the food you consume, and for your legs and feet that enable you to move about.

Thank the Lord for your bones (all 206 of them) that give your body structure, strength, and flexibility. Thank him for your heart. Do you realize your heart started pumping months before you were born, and throughout your lifetime, it has beaten about 100,000 times a day (35 million times a year!)? Do the math and multiply your age times 35 million, and you will be astonished to realize your heart has kept pumping so well for so long. (On average, the human heart beats more than 2.5 billion times over the course of a person's lifetime.)

Think of all the places your body has been—all the cars, trucks, buses, trains, boats, ships, and planes you have ridden over land, sea, and air. My body has taken me to approximately 20 different nations and 49 states (every state but North Dakota).

Think of all the things your body has done. Because God gave me a body, I know what it's like to run like the wind (when I was a kid, not now!) . . . to smack a softball with my bat and hit a long line drive over the right fielder's head . . . to play the piano with my fingers and hear satisfying chords with my ears . . . to pick blackberries in the woods on a hot summer day and eat my mom's fresh-made cobbler that evening . . . to hold my wife in my arms, give piggyback rides to my son and daughters when they were little, and receive warm hugs from my grandchildren.

Even with all its imperfections and its aches and pains, your body is a gift. Aren't you glad God gave you senses so you can experience and enjoy the world he created? Aren't you glad you can taste, touch, smell, hear, and see?

YOUR BODY IS A RESPONSIBILITY

Because the body is God's gift, it is a sacred duty to care for it. The apostle Paul said to "offer your bodies as a living sacrifice, holy and pleasing to God—this is your true and proper worship" (Romans 12:1). He reminded us, "Do you not know that your bodies are temples of the Holy Spirit, who is in you, whom you have received from God? You are not your own; you were bought at a price. Therefore honor God with your bodies" (1 Corinthians 6:19-20).

When reminded that the body is a temple, someone joked, "Yeah, mine is a temple of doom!" But caring for the body is serious business. The Bible teaches that we are stewards of God's creation. We are responsible to manage well whatever the Lord has entrusted to us, including our time, our financial resources, our spiritual gifts, and our physical bodies. The Bible doesn't detach faith from physical reality, as if our bodies are unimportant and spiritual things are all that matter. God owns every part of us, including our bodies. That's why the apostle Paul said, "Let us purify ourselves from everything that contaminates body and spirit, perfecting holiness out of reverence for God" (2 Corinthians 7:1). Paul told his young friend Timothy, "Physical training is of some value, but godliness has value for all things, holding promise for both the present life and the life to come" (1 Timothy 4:8). Yes, spiritual things are of utmost importance. Being physically fit isn't enough if you are spiritually immature; but it doesn't please God if we abuse our bodies with gluttony, neglect, and inactivity.

The Lord cares about every part of you, including your physical well-being. Paul articulates the goal in 1 Thessalonians 5:23: "May your whole spirit, soul and body be kept blameless at the coming of our Lord Jesus Christ." Notice what John prayed for his friend Gaius: "Dear friend, I pray that you may enjoy good health and that all may go well with you, even as your soul is getting along well" (3 John 2).

Your body is a gift and it is a responsibility. But it's also important to remember . . .

YOUR BODY IS VULNERABLE

Unfortunately, our bodies are vulnerable to temptation and sin. Adam and Eve misused their bodies by eating forbidden fruit that was "good for food and pleasing to the eye" (Genesis 3:6). The body can glorify God or it can dishonor him. It can express the holy love of a marriage covenant, or it can engage in casual sex that seems pleasurable in the short-term but is emotionally and spiritually damaging in the long run. The body can be used to love God and love our neighbors, or it can be a tool for indulging "the lust of the flesh, the lust of the eyes, and the pride of life" (1 John 2:16).

The body is vulnerable to weakness and harm. Scripture compares our bodies to jars of clay that contain valuable treasures (2 Corinthians 4:7-10). Clay jars crack and leak with age, and so do our bodies. And to state the obvious, our current physical bodies won't last forever; eventually we will die.

In 2 Corinthians 5:1-4, the apostle Paul compares our bodies to an earthly tent. According to Bob Russell, retired senior minister of Southeast Christian Church in Louisville, Kentucky, two words explain what it's like to live in a tent.

> One is the word *insecure*. A tent is not a very good fortress. You can't bolt the door against intruders. The canvas doesn't seem like good protection against wild animals. If you've ever spent the night in a tent in a storm with lightning and wind, you know that

it can collapse easily. Paul was a tentmaker. When he compared this life to a tent, he knew it was not very secure.

This life is uncertain. . . . We try to develop security through insurance and the accumulation of goods and support groups and people, but no matter how much we have of this world's goods, we're still living in a tent that can be blown over easily. David said, "There is only a step between me and death" (1 Samuel 20:3). . . .

The second word that describes living in a tent is the word *uncomfortable*. When I bed down for the night with a sleeping bag on the ground inside a tent, and it's humid, and the mosquitoes are biting, the ground gets harder the longer I'm there. As I lie there in darkness, I start to think about my queen-size bed, the air conditioning, and my wife at home. And then there's always somebody who breaks the silence and says, "This is the life, isn't it?"

"Yes," I respond. "This is what camping's all about."

The longer I toss and turn, the more uncomfortable it gets. After four or five days, everything smells like socks.[5]

Our bodies are like temporary tents. But the apostle Paul said, "If the earthly tent we live in is destroyed, we have a building from God, an eternal house in heaven, not built by human hands" (2 Corinthians 5:1). When we die in Christ, we will exchange the temporary tents of our mortal bodies for permanent resurrection bodies perfectly suited for eternal life. Elsewhere Paul described our current bodies as perishable, weak, and dishonorable, but the flesh-and-blood tents we inhabit now will be replaced by new "imperishable" spiritual bodies characterized by glory and honor, and we will be clothed with immortality (1 Corinthians 15:42-57). No wonder Paul said he "would prefer to be away from the body and at home with the Lord" (2 Corinthians 5:8).

Caring for Your Body as You Grow Older

A classic book about geriatric health called *Physical Dimensions of Aging*, written by a professor of kinesiology and health education at the

University of Texas at Austin, divides the mature population into the following five levels:

- Physically dependent: individuals who cannot execute some or all basic activities of daily living.

- Physically frail: individuals who can perform basic activities of daily living, but who cannot perform some or all of the activities necessary to live independently, generally due to a debilitating disease or condition that physically challenges them on a daily basis.

- Physically independent: individuals who live independently, usually without debilitating symptoms of major chronic diseases, but who have low health and fitness reserves.

- Physically fit: individuals who exercise at least twice a week for their health, enjoyment, and well-being, and who enjoy high health and fitness reserves.

- Physically elite: individuals who train on an almost daily basis and either compete in seniors' sports tournaments or work in a physically demanding job.[6]

Most of us will not attain the "physically elite" designation as we age, but we want to remain fit and independent as long as possible. What are some practical steps we can take?

KEEP MOVING.

Someone said, "It's wise to choose *exercise*, not *extra fries*." According to athletic trainers, "Without exercise, estimated muscle mass declines 22 percent for women and 23 percent for men between the ages of 30 and 70. Add to this a loss in strength of 50 percent, and it doesn't take long to see how many older adults can lose their ability to function independently. Exercise can slow the rate of loss in all of these."[7]

To keep your body moving, there are many options to choose from. Walk. Garden. Go to the gym. Ride a bike. Swim. Join a pool aerobics class. Mow your own lawn, or volunteer to help take care of the grounds for your church or another nonprofit organization. Play pickleball. Lift weights. Do stretching exercises. Take daily walks in your neighborhood or local parks. Play with your grandkids. Serve in your church's nursery or volunteer with the student ministry. (The kids will keep you moving!)

Make small choices that require exercise. Take the stairs instead of the elevator. When you go shopping, don't choose the closest parking spot; park farther away from the entrance so you have to take more steps. Play golf and walk the course instead of using a cart.

Strengthen your legs, knees, and hips by doing squats. "The squat is the most important exercise for seniors," according to a personal trainer who works with older adults. "When you go to the washroom, that's a squat. When you get in the car, that's a squat. Every time you sit down or stand up, that's a squat. If you don't do them well, it affects the way you live.[8] (Hey, if you're lazy, at least you can do diddly-squats!)

The authors of the book *Younger Next Year* estimate that approximately "70 percent of premature death and aging is lifestyle-related." They recommend that to offset the negative effects of aging, you need to exercise six days a week for the rest of your life. Retirees, they insist, should treat exercise like a new job—not a negotiable option, but something you simply must do on a daily basis. Scientific evidence shows that exercise not only strengthens the body; it boosts energy, optimism, and decisiveness, and improves resistance to stress and to depression. If you fear you are losing your marbles, these experts insist, "you grow new marbles all the time. How many you grow is significantly up to you. . . . The more aerobic exercise you get, the more new brain cells you generate and the smarter you become."[9]

Don't take mobility for granted. Keep moving as long as you can. If you don't move it, you lose it.

EAT AND DRINK WISELY.

God provides daily bread to nourish our bodies, and he gave us taste buds so we can enjoy the flavor of it. The Lord created a diverse array of food items "to be received with thanksgiving by those who believe and who know the truth. For everything God created is good, and nothing is to be rejected if it is received with thanksgiving, because it is consecrated by the word of God and prayer" (1 Timothy 4:3-5). Both the physical and relational aspects of dining are important. That's why in the Law of Moses, God laid down instructions for special meals to be eaten in community with others, even specifying the menu for the Feast of the Passover (Exodus 12:1-20).

Instead of demanding that we observe all of the Old Covenant's dietary restrictions, however, Jesus "declared all foods clean" (Mark 7:17-23). He used mealtimes as teaching opportunities with disciples and potential followers, and he attracted criticism for the way he ate frequently with "tax collectors and sinners" (Matthew 9:10-13; 11:18-19). For followers of Jesus, mealtimes ought to be special moments to thank the Lord for his blessings and, whenever possible, to share conversation with family, friends, and guests. We can enjoy our food knowing that the kingdom of God is not primarily a matter of "eating and drinking, but of righteousness, peace and joy in the Holy Spirit" (Romans 14:17).

Humorist Erma Bombeck quipped, "I am not a glutton; I am an explorer of food." She wrote, "Seize the moment. Remember all those women on the 'Titanic' who waved off the dessert cart." Someone else said, "Forget the health food. I need all the preservatives I can get!" But God's Word cautions us about overeating and excessive, careless drinking. There is a big difference between reasonable self-care and irresponsible self-indulgence. Consider this wisdom found in Proverbs 23:20-21: "Do not join those who drink too much wine or gorge themselves on meat, for drunkards and gluttons become poor, and drowsiness clothes them in rags." The New Testament allows believers considerable freedom, but it insists that some activities aren't beneficial even though we have the right to do them. We shouldn't damage the temple of our bodies through sexual immorality or dietary overindulgence (1 Corinthians 6:12-20).

My friend Jane was a remarkable person who lived to be 104. In her nineties, she was still living at home, mowing her own grass, and seal-coating her driveway. On her 100th birthday, her family and friends gathered to celebrate at our church. During the festivities, I interviewed Jane. I asked, "What is the secret of your longevity?" Without hesitation, she replied, "Bacon! I eat lots of it." Her response made everyone smile, although medical experts might disagree with her advice. According to the U.S. Food and Drug Administration, many older adults do not consume enough dietary fiber, vitamin D, calcium, and potassium. The FDA recommends choosing foods that provide more of these nutrients, while reducing consumption of saturated fat, sodium, and added sugars.[10]

When I was 16, I had a summer job working for a construction company. I spent my days mixing mortar, carrying bricks and concrete blocks, pushing wheelbarrows, and digging ditches. My daily food intake that summer was something like this:

Breakfast: two scrambled eggs, bacon, two pieces of buttered toast, and a large glass of orange juice
Midmorning Snack: a Hostess fruit pie
Lunch: two bologna and cheese sandwiches and a thermos of chocolate milk mixed with ice cream
Midafternoon Snack: another Hostess fruit pie
Dinner: a full Mom-cooked meal shared with my family at home

No exaggeration, it probably added up to 4,000 calories a day, but I didn't gain weight because my high metabolism and lots of hard physical labor burned off all those extra calories. That was a long time ago. Doctors say, "A normal American in his fifties or sixties has to get his caloric intake down to roughly 1,500 calories to lose weight. Up to 2,000 a day is maintenance."[11] Past the age of 60, the number of calories we require shrinks even more. My undisciplined brain and taste buds try to tell me that I can still eat two double-cheeseburgers with supersized fries, but according to common sense and the bathroom scale, I need to consume less pie and fewer doughnuts and opt, instead, for lean protein and more fruits and vegetables.

GET PLENTY OF SLEEP.

Problems like insomnia, sleep apnea, and restless legs syndrome are increasingly common among adults over age 60. Some experts use an expression called "sleep debt." As you deal with day-to-day stress, you make deposits and withdrawals in your body. If you keep depriving yourself of sleep, eventually you will pay for it. Sleep is not only about physical rest; it's a restorative, God-given tool for daily mental and emotional recovery.[12]

Here are some commonsense suggestions that can help you get a better night's sleep:

• Follow a regular sleep schedule, going to bed and getting up at the same time each day.

- Avoid napping in the late afternoon or evening.

- Develop a relaxing bedtime routine and avoid late-night adrenaline-arousal. Don't watch unsettling TV shows or use your computer or cell phone when it's time to go to sleep.

- Lower the lights in the evening and keep your bedroom at a comfortable temperature.

- Exercise during the day, but not close to bedtime—and avoid eating large meals or consuming caffeine late in the day.[13]

And while on the subject of rest . . .

DISCOVER AND ENJOY THE SABBATH PRINCIPLE.

This has been a difficult lesson for me to learn. I grew up on a farm where I internalized a strong work ethic. In my early years as a minister, I discovered there are always things to do and people who need help, so as a young church leader I was constantly "on."

Today's technological tools make it possible to stay connected with others all day and all night, seven days a week. But God didn't design us to function that way. Remember what the Lord told the Hebrews in the Ten Commandments? They had been slaves controlled by their masters, but after freeing them from Egyptian bondage, one of the first things God told them was to take a weekly day off. "Six days you shall labor and do all your work, but the seventh day is a sabbath to the Lord your God. On it you shall not do any work" (Exodus 20:9-10). After they worked under slavery conditions seven days a week, what a gracious gift God gave his people by mandating a weekly day off!

Why would anyone in their right mind want to reject the gift of a Sabbath rest? I don't know, but I have done it myself.

By staying busy 24/7, we allow constant activity to be our master. Years ago, when I was feeling exhausted and burned-out from overwork and burning the candle at both ends, I found it helpful to revisit the words of Jesus: "The Sabbath was made for man, not man for the Sabbath" (Mark 2:27). In other words, God meant the Sabbath to be a blessing, not a burden to his people.

In his helpful book *24/6: A Prescription for a Healthier, Happier Life,* Dr. Matthew Sleeth points out how it used to be that most things in society stopped one day a week. He writes, "Gas stations, banks, and grocery stores locked their doors at night and on Sundays. No more. We are no longer a society that goes to sleep at night or conducts business six days a week. Now we go 24/7." It has a profound impact on our lives if we subtract a day of rest each week. Dr. Sleeth asks, "How could it not? One day a week adds up. Fifty-two days a year times an average life span is equal to more than 11 years. Take away 11 years of anything in a lifetime, and there will be a change."[14]

Sabbath requires restraint—a willingness to let go of the controls, reconnect with God, and experience the peace of the Holy Spirit. The Law of Moses not only mentioned Sabbath days; it also prescribed sabbatical years. Imagine telling a farmer not to plant his crop every seven years! But that's what the Lord required, for the land needed rest and the people needed to trust that God would provide for them. Additionally, according to the Law of Moses (Leviticus 25), after seven sabbatical years (49 years altogether) had passed, the fiftieth year was supposed to be a Year of Jubilee when debts were canceled and people returned to their ancestral homes. It was like a huge family reunion. The timing (every 50 years) meant most people would experience one Year of Jubilee in their lifetimes, while a few older folks would enjoy one Jubilee during their childhood and another during their senior adult years. Ironically, though, instead of enjoying the blessings of time off as the Lord intended, God's covenant people ignored his commands and the land didn't enjoy its Sabbath rest until the people were removed for 70 years of exile (2 Chronicles 36:20-21).

The church where I serve has a sabbatical policy for our ordained staff. We are expected to take extended, intentional time away from ministry every seven years; but over the course of my ministry, I rarely have even taken ordinary vacations and weekly days off, let alone a prolonged sabbatical. (I am not proud of this.) My workaholic tendencies harmed my body and soul and caused me to miss precious time with my family. Finally, after nearly 48 years in ministry, I agreed to take a sabbatical—and it turned out to be one of the most wonderful experiences of my life. The theme of my renewal season was "Quiet Ambition" based on 1 Thessalonians 4:11 which says, "Make it your ambition to lead a quiet life." It sounds strange and countercultural to be ambitious about being quiet, or as one translator suggests, "Seek restlessly to be still." But that verse reminded me to quiet down and be still in God's presence.

For three months (May through July) I focused on doing things that make my heart sing. I spent unhurried time with my wife and my adult children and grandchildren. I took lots of walks outdoors enjoying God's creation. And I spent a lot of time reflecting on my own walk with God as I grow older (which included writing this book).

I put my watch aside during those three months, and I didn't miss it at all. I realized I had been enslaved to two masters: the calendar and the clock. After the three months ended, I found that I needed to build more unhurried space into my daily, weekly, monthly, and yearly schedule. I invented a word to describe my new sabbatical attitude: "sabbatitude"! People of all ages, young and old, need to have a positive "sabbatitude" and to find a healthy, sustainable, God-honoring pace for their lives.

Everyone knows about Sabbath days, but what about "Sabbath hours" (or at least "Sabbath minutes")? If every seventh day should be set apart for worship and rest, why not schedule a few times in each 24-hour day to pause, catch your breath, and pray?

Since this book is focused on senior adults, let me remind you that the Sabbath principle applies even if you are retired. Are you regularly setting aside time in your weekly and daily schedule to worship the Lord and let his *shalom*—his peace—fill your body and soul? "Sabbath is not a day off," Mandy Smith shared on the social-media platform X (@ MandySmithHopes). "Sabbath is about life and death. . . . In Sabbath God invites us to practice for our own death in two ways: to get used to being in God's presence for the sake of it and to learn to trust he can carry the world without us."

FIND A COACH (OR A BUDDY) WHO WILL HELP YOU STAY HEALTHY.

My wife, Candy, is my walking partner. Decades ago, when we were in our thirties, we began the healthy habit of taking walks together on a regular basis. Sometimes while on vacation or mission trips, we have enjoyed scenic hikes on mountain trails or along sandy beaches. More often, we simply walk together for a half-hour or so around our neighborhood or in a local park. Something about fresh air and sunshine is good for the soul—and good for our marriage. Candy is not only my walking partner; she is my talking partner. We treasure our daily walks because they not only strengthen our legs and lungs, they give us the opportunity to talk about our day and keep our emotional and spiritual connection strong.

STAY HYDRATED.

Your body contains about 60 percent water, and your muscles are about 80 percent water. Even a 2 percent drop in your body's water content will have a noticeable effect on your well-being by increasing fatigue, reducing motivation, and making exercise more difficult. Dehydration can impair mood and diminish brain performance, and it contributes to headaches and migraines. Drinking adequate amounts of water improves digestion, aids weight loss, and helps prevent kidney stones and urinary tract infections. The bottom line? "Even mild dehydration can affect you mentally and physically. Make sure that you get enough water each day, whether your personal goal is 64 ounces (1.9 liters) or a different amount. It's one of the best things you can do for your overall health."[15]

AS YOUR BUDGET ALLOWS, BUILD A PERSONAL NETWORK OF HEALTH-CARE PROVIDERS YOU TRUST–AND STAY IN TOUCH WITH THEM.

One of my sons-in-law is an M.D. (He has spent most of his career working in emergency rooms.) My wife (now retired) worked for 20 years as a registered nurse. One of my daughters is an R.N., another daughter is a licensed professional social worker, and my son is a minister. I'm blessed to have relatives who encourage me to take care of my body, soul, and mind.

But my family members don't want to discuss my aches and pains over Thanksgiving dinner. So, over the years, I have developed a trusted team of health-care professionals, including a family physician I see every year for my annual exam . . . a dentist who examines my teeth and gums three times a year . . . a dermatologist who checks me periodically to stave off further problems with skin cancer . . . a chiropractor who helps to reduce my back pain . . . and an ophthalmologist who keeps a careful eye on my eyes. Additionally, a trusted expert on health insurance advises me about my coverage and benefits.

Erma Bombeck's wry advice seems apropos: "Never go to a doctor whose office plants have died."

PAY ATTENTION TO YOUR MENTAL HEALTH.

Your body and your mental/emotional health are intertwined. Your state of mind has a big impact on your physical health, and vice versa. Ben Cachiaras, lead minister with Mountain Christian Church in Joppa, Maryland, identifies five *R*s that can make a difference in the way you approach mental health.

1. *Recognition.* If you are dealing with mental and emotional challenges, you don't have to wallow in shame or suffer in silence. Jesus came to heal the brokenhearted, free the captives, and bring light to those imprisoned in darkness (Isaiah 61:1-3; Luke 4:18-19). The Lord can help you recognize and face your struggles honestly and find the help you need.

2. *Relationships.* Instead of surface-level friendships, we all need a web of genuine spiritual companions. Ben says, "More than ever, the church needs to provide a safe harbor of listening ears and spiritual connection among supportive friends who serve as emotional health first responders."

3. *Resources.* Your church can connect you with resources to help with a wide variety of mental health issues, including depression, stress management, suicide prevention, grief, and addiction recovery.

4. *Referral.* Competent and professional Christian counselors can be a wonderful resource. "Counselors and talk therapy are not a replacement for God, prayer, faith, or the church," Ben says. "But just as God works through surgeons and medical doctors to bring healing to our physical bodies, God can work through counselors to bring healing to our minds and spirits." He adds, "God made us complex beings. A skillful counselor can bring hope through the work of the Holy Spirit to help people untangle emotions, heal from grief, overcome hurtful memories, and process wounds. This kind of healing can free people to experience the peace of Christ and serve with greater gusto."

5. *Real hope.* Ben observes, "Following Jesus doesn't mean we won't have struggles, sorrows, pain, or mental health challenges.

Jesus sweat drops of blood during his anguish in the garden. But his confidence in the joy before him enabled him to endure the cross and its shame. That same hope is also our own key to coping with life."[16]

WHAT IF YOUR BODY DOESN'T WORK WELL ANYMORE?

No matter how much we try to stave off the effects of aging, the years wear down our bodies like the constant pounding of the ocean tide crashing against the shore and eroding the land. Why didn't someone warn me that as I age, it would become more difficult to do simple tasks like getting in and out of a car or clipping my toenails? Why didn't someone let me know that my knees would lose their natural cushioning and it would become painful to kneel down on the ground?

We live in a fallen world cursed by death and decline. Like it or not, we are subject to the unrelenting principle in physics known as the second law of thermodynamics—the law of entropy and disintegration. No matter how well we care for our bodies, eventually they will wear out. What should we do when, despite our best efforts, our bodies let us down? Many senior adults live with the stiffness and gnawing ache of arthritis, the frustration of a slow recovery from surgery, and the bumps and bruises (and unsettling fears) that come from falls. Some have experienced the life-altering effects of a stroke or a heart attack, and others have lost the ability to walk, hear, see, or eat as they did in the past.

I will have more to say about this topic in upcoming chapters, but for now let me offer some words of encouragement to readers whose bodies are letting them down. If you struggle with frustrating limitations, unrelenting pain, and debilitating injuries, the Lord hasn't forgotten you. He cares about you. He is present with you. He sympathizes with your pain and frustration.

God heals through a variety of means. Sometimes he heals through the natural passing of time. (Remarkably, he wired our bodies so that skin, bones, and muscles have the natural ability to repair themselves.) Sometimes he heals through the aid of medicine (1 Timothy 5:23). Sometimes he heals supernaturally in response to prayer (James 5:16). Sometimes, though, instead of healing our "thorns in the flesh," he reminds us, "My grace is sufficient for you, for my power is made perfect in weakness" (2 Corinthians

12:7-9). He helps us to persevere and remain faithful while we wait patiently for the new heaven and the new earth where he will wipe every tear from our eyes and where there "will be no more death or mourning or crying or pain" (Revelation 21:4).

Meanwhile, he says, "Come to me, all you who are weary and burdened, and I will give you rest" (Matthew 11:28). The prophet Isaiah pointed to Jesus when he wrote, "A bruised reed he will not break, and a smoldering wick he will not snuff out" (Isaiah 42:3; Matthew 12:20). When you are bent and bruised, he won't push you to the breaking point. When you feel burned out, he won't snuff you out like a flickering candle. A damaged reed is not irreparable, and a smoldering wick can be reignited. Give the Lord a chance and he will fan your faith into flame again.

Our bodies don't stay the same—but Christ does. That's why it is so important to place our faith and hope in Christ who is the same "yesterday and today and forever" (Hebrews 13:8).

The apostle Paul summed it up this way: "Though outwardly we are wasting away, yet inwardly we are being renewed day by day. For our light and momentary troubles are achieving for us an eternal glory that far outweighs them all" (2 Corinthians 4:16-17).

QUESTIONS FOR PERSONAL REFLECTION AND GROUP DISCUSSION

1. When you think about your current physical condition, what is the biggest challenge or frustration you face?

2. How has your body changed with age—or how do you expect it will change in the future?

3. After reading this chapter, what step(s) could you take to improve your physical health?

   • Exercise more often

   • Eat a healthier diet

   • Get more rest

   • Speak to a counselor or coach who could help me improve my physical, mental, or emotional health

   • Other:

4. What is preventing you from getting healthier? What could your friends do to help you reach your goal of having a stronger, healthier body?

8 | Don't Stay too Close to Where You Got in— Pursuing Spiritual Maturity as an Older Adult

"Anyone who stops learning is old, whether at 20 or 80. Anyone who keeps learning stays young."
—Henry Ford

"Most people die at 25 and aren't buried until 75."
—Benjamin Franklin

When children ask me to guess their age, I guess a little on the high side. Kids generally want to be older than they are, so if the child appears to be about 7 years old, I make sure I say "8." But it doesn't work that way with adults! If a grown-up who I think looks about 80 asks, "How old you do you think I am?" I might guess "70" just to be on the safe side. Most adults don't want to be considered older than they are.

How can we stay spiritually young at heart? When we start following the Lord, everything seems new and fresh. We are brand-new creatures in Christ. As time passes, though, it's tempting to become dull in our discipleship, hard-hearted about holiness, bored with the Bible, and weak in our worship. Growing older doesn't have to mean losing the joy of our salvation. How can we keep pressing on toward maturity in our faith? How can we keep our relationship with God faithful, flexible, and fruitful in our senior adult years?

What Spiritual Maturity *Isn't*

Spiritual maturity isn't guaranteed by chronological age. Some individuals are old in years, but they are spiritually immature. On the other hand, some children and young adults demonstrate impressive wisdom and self-control.

I heard about a little boy who fell out of bed. When his mom asked what happened, he said, "I guess I stayed too close to where I got in." Sometimes Christians stay too close to where we got in. Years after accepting Christ, we are still selfish, stagnant, and stuck.

The devotional writer Oswald Chambers said it's good to ask, "Am I getting nobler, better, more helpful, more humble, as I get older? . . . or am I getting more self-assertive, more deliberately determined to have my own way?"

Spiritual maturity isn't the same as being professionally competent. Have you ever known people who were good at their jobs and respected in the workplace, but their personal lives were a mess?

Spiritual maturity isn't the same as being well-educated. College diplomas can cover your wall, but you might still be emotionally immature and have a relationship with God that remains undeveloped.

Someone joked, "You're only young once, but it's possible to stay immature indefinitely." Spiritual maturity is a matter of the heart, not the calendar. I have been a Christian for over 60 years, but I am often amazed at the immaturity I still find in myself. (My wife isn't shocked; she is used to seeing it!) In fact, there are times when I still act like a kid.

My daughter Michelle once sat on a plane next to a Hall of Fame pitcher, former Major League baseball player Gaylord Perry. For some reason, when *I* travel, I usually sit next to someone who has a very bad cold. But my daughter, who doesn't care about baseball, sits next to the first baseball player to win the Cy Young Award in both the National and American leagues. At least she got his autograph for me.

A few days later I got a phone call. The caller said, "Dave, this is Gaylord Perry. I sat by your daughter on a plane the other day."

I was so excited. Michelle and Candy started laughing at me. I held the phone down and said, "Would you guys please be quiet? I'm talking to *Gaylord Perry!*" I told him how I enjoyed watching him pitch. The conversation ended a little strangely, though, when Gaylord said, "Well, I hope your son-in-law treats you better than mine does."

As I hung up the phone, I remembered the date. It was April 1. My daughter and my wife had played an April Fools' joke on me. Michelle really did sit next to Gaylord Perry on the plane, and she really got his autograph. But the voice on the phone was my father-in-law who was in on the joke. Why was I so gullible? Why did I act so ridiculously? Because I'm still immature, that's why. In certain situations, I revert to acting like a kid.

Immaturity isn't a new problem. God's covenant people have struggled with it for centuries. Describing the ancient Hebrews, one author points out, "Moses descended from the mountain at the exact moment his people were worshipping the golden calf. He was bringing them the law that would make them an adult people at the exact moment they were behaving like children."[1] The Israelites drifted into idolatry, sexual immorality, and grumbling against God, and their examples of immature disobedience "were written down as warnings for us" (1 Corinthians 10:6-11).

Even Jesus' 12 apostles were immature, impatient, and impetuous. They quarreled among themselves and struggled to grasp the deeper significance of Jesus' teachings. But the Lord used that little band of flawed followers to change the world, offering hope for the rest of us who are not yet mature.

What Christian Maturity Looks Like

What is the goal God wants us to pursue? Jesus presented a lofty target in the Sermon on the Mount when he said, "Be perfect, therefore, as your heavenly Father is perfect" (Matthew 5:48). The Greek word translated "perfect" means full-grown, complete, or fully developed. We all fall short of the ideal, but the goal is nothing less than reflecting our heavenly Father's character.

Thankfully, we aren't alone in our journey toward spiritual maturity. The Holy Spirit enables us to go beyond the limits of our own minds and willpower.

I taught in a Christian college that offered a theology course called "The Holy Spirit." So many students signed up for the course, administrators moved the class to a larger room. Someone put a sign on the classroom door that said, "The Holy Spirit is now in Room 251." I wanted to hurry over to Room 251!

Here is exciting news for believers in Christ: You are a room where the Holy Spirit dwells! Peter said, "Repent and be baptized, every one of you, in the name of Jesus Christ for the forgiveness of your sins. And you will receive the gift of the Holy Spirit" (Acts 2:38). Paul affirmed, "The Spirit of God lives in you" (Romans 8:9-11), and he asked, "Do you not know that your bodies are temples of the Holy Spirit, who is in you, whom you have received from God?" (1 Corinthians 6:19).

The Bible says, "Since we live by the Spirit, let us keep in step with the Spirit" (Galatians 5:25). It reminds me of the moving sidewalks at airports that empower you to go faster than you can walk in your own strength. When you become a Christian, the Lord takes up residence in your life. He is there to help you learn and grow. He doesn't just throw you in the pool and expect you to swim!

The Fountain of Youth doesn't exist. But in John 7:37-39, Jesus made a promise with no age restriction attached to it. The Lord said, "'Let anyone who is thirsty come to me and drink. Whoever believes in me, as Scripture has said, rivers of living water will flow from within them.' By this he meant the Spirit, whom those who believed in him were later to receive."

The older I get, the more I recognize my own limitations and God's "unlimitations."

You are not too old to be empowered by the Holy Spirit. Let's take a look at some ways the New Testament describes what it means to grow in our walk with God.

MATURITY LOOKS LIKE THE FRUIT OF THE SPIRIT

If you want a vivid illustration of what it means to grow more like Christ, consider what it says in Galatians 5: "But the fruit of the Spirit is love, joy, peace, forbearance, kindness, goodness, faithfulness, gentleness, and self-control. Against such things there is no law" (Galatians 5:22-23). Those qualities remind us what Jesus was like, and with the Lord's help, they show what we should aspire to be as we grow older. As you age, don't you want to become more loving, joyful, peaceful, patient, kind, good, faithful, gentle, and self-controlled?

The apostle Paul ends the list with a tongue-in-cheek observation: "Against such things there is no law." No reasonable government would ever outlaw love, joy, and peace! No clear-thinking employer would ever fire an employee by saying, "The problem is, you're too joyful, kind, good, and faithful, so we have to let you go."

I keep a plaque on my office wall that contains this quote from Jesus: "I am the vine; you are the branches. If you remain in me and I in you, you will bear much fruit; apart from me you can do nothing" (John 15:5). By staying attached to the true Vine, we will bear the fruit of the Spirit.

MATURITY LOOKS LIKE A REFLECTION OF GOD'S CHARACTER

Another helpful description of the path to Christian maturity appears in 2 Peter 1, which says:

> Make every effort to add to your faith goodness; and to goodness, knowledge; and to knowledge, self-control; and to self-control, perseverance; and to perseverance, godliness; and to godliness, mutual affection; and to mutual affection, love. For if you possess these qualities in increasing measure, they will keep you from being ineffective and unproductive in your knowledge of our Lord Jesus Christ (2 Peter 1:5-8).

Peter's list sounds a lot like Paul's fruit of the Spirit, doesn't it? Yet, the concepts are worded a little differently, for evidently the Lord has more than a mere checklist in mind. These character qualities are not a to-do list; they are a way of life as we walk with God and the Holy Spirit forms us into the image of God's Son.

Earlier in the same chapter, Peter highlighted the role of the Holy Spirit by saying God's "divine power has given us everything we need for a godly life" (v. 3). God provides what we need to grow in our faith.

MATURITY LOOKS LIKE CLINGING TO—
AND PASSING ALONG TO OTHERS—
THE ELEMENTARY TRUTHS OF THE CHRISTIAN FAITH

Another key Scripture about spiritual maturity is Hebrews 5, which extends a powerful challenge to everyone who follows Christ. This passage especially applies to those of us who are advanced in years, for the inspired writer says:

> In fact, though by this time you ought to be teachers, you need someone to teach you the elementary truths of God's word all over again. You need milk, not solid food! Anyone who lives on milk, being still an infant, is not acquainted with the teaching about righteousness. But solid food is for the mature, who by constant use have trained themselves to distinguish good from evil (Hebrews 5:12-14).

This text challenges us to ask ourselves some tough questions:

- Am I acquainted well enough with "the elementary truths of God's word" that I can teach them to someone else?

- Am I expanding my diet of spiritual nourishment and consuming "solid food" (the meat of God's Word), or do I just sip some spiritual milk now and then?

- Am I training myself "to distinguish good from evil" and to make lifestyle choices that honor the Lord, or am I merely drifting along with the cultural tide?

When you read, "by this time you ought to be teachers," you might object, "But I am not a skilled communicator" or "I don't know enough to teach someone else." Don't sell yourself short. Every follower of Christ can *be a student and have a student.* We all need a Paul, a Barnabas, and a Timothy. No matter how long you have been a Christian, there is someone ahead of you in spiritual maturity. That person is your "Paul." A peer or coworker who comes alongside you and encourages you—that is your "Barnabas." (His name meant "son of encouragement.") Someone who follows behind you—who needs to know what you have learned about Jesus—that is your "Timothy."

A century ago, one-room schoolhouses were common in America. My parents attended schools like that in the rural area where they grew up in Ohio. In a one-room schoolhouse, all of the students, from first grade through high school, were in the same classroom—big kids and little kids all in the same place. This educational approach sounds old fashioned, but the system worked well because the older students helped to teach the younger ones. You might have found a 16-year-old girl teaching a 6-year-old boy his ABCs. No matter how old or young you were, everyone learned and grew together. I am not advocating that we go back in time and send our kids to one-room schools, but I believe those schools provide a useful analogy. The church is supposed to be an intergenerational family. Whether you're a brand-new Christian or you have been a believer for 30 years, you can learn from those ahead of you and help those who follow behind you.

MATURITY LOOKS LIKE GROWING IN GRACE AND KNOWLEDGE

Another summary description of Christian maturity appears at the end of Second Peter. At every stage of life, followers of Christ are called to "grow in the grace and knowledge of our Lord and Savior Jesus Christ" (2 Peter 3:18). This short verse makes several important points.

HOLD ON TO THE CENTRAL TRUTHS OF THE FAITH.

"There is one body and one Spirit, just as you were called to one hope when you were called; one Lord, one faith, one baptism; one God and Father of all, who is over all and through all and in all" (Ephesians 4:4-6). These verses mention seven core beliefs of the Christian faith:

- One body . . . the church.
- One Spirit . . . the Holy Spirit who dwells in us.
- One hope . . . based on the resurrection of Jesus Christ.
- One Lord . . . Christ, the Son of God.
- One faith . . . we believe God's Word and trust his promises.
- One baptism . . . uniting us with Christ in the likeness of his death, burial, and resurrection.
- One God . . . our heavenly Father.

You are never too old to believe these basic biblical teachings. Make sure you never outgrow the foundational truths of the gospel!

Grow

God has designed us with the capacity to grow and change. God filled the earth with plants and trees and flowers programmed to grow. Growth is a sign of life and vitality. According to Luke 2:52, as Jesus matured, he increased intellectually (in wisdom), physically (in stature), spiritually (in favor with God) and socially (in favor with other people).

When I was a boy, I hoped to be 6 feet 5 inches tall and play basketball in big arenas. Then reality hit, and I had to settle for being 5 feet 11 inches and playing an occasional game of hoops in the driveway. When my children were growing up, I took a long piece of wood and designated it the "Birthday Board." Each year when we celebrated our kids' birthdays, we marked their height as they grew taller. I still have that board in my garage.

Physical growth comes naturally, but spiritual growth requires intentional effort. If you try to climb a rope, it's easier to fall than it is to climb. Maybe you can relate to this quote from Charlie Brown: "Sometimes I lie awake at night and ask, 'Where have I gone wrong?' Then a voice says to me, 'This is going to take more than one night.'"

Growth is normal and healthy. We either keep growing or we die. Immediately after a baby is born, the parents don't say, "OK, kid, you're on your own now." We make sure our children are fed, protected, and educated until they can stand on their own two feet. A wedding ceremony is only the beginning as a couple grows together in their marriage. When students graduate, that doesn't mean they know everything there is to learn. When a new believer is baptized, the church shouldn't just "dip them and drop them." Continual growth is the norm for a follower of Christ—even when we are old.

Grow in Grace

As we mature, our appreciation for God's grace should increase. Do you ever pause and say, "Thank you, Lord, for loving, saving, and blessing me"? Paul declared, "By the grace of God I am what I am" (1 Corinthians 15:10). Can you look back at your life—including your failures—and say, "By God's grace I am what I am"?

God's grace means more to me as I grow older than it did when I was young. I was baptized into Christ when I was 9 years old, yet after all these years I am amazed how stubborn and self-centered I can be. If my own flawless obedience were necessary for salvation, I would be lost; but thank God, Christ's flawless obedience has been applied to me! Paul celebrated God's amazing grace when he wrote:

> I thank Christ Jesus our Lord, who has given me strength, that
> he considered me trustworthy, appointing me to his service.
> Even though I was once a blasphemer and a persecutor and a
> violent man, I was shown mercy because I acted in ignorance
> and unbelief. The grace of our Lord was poured out on me
> abundantly, along with the faith and love that are in Christ Jesus.
> Here is a trustworthy saying that deserves full acceptance: Christ
> Jesus came into the world to save sinners—of whom I am the
> worst (1 Timothy 1:12-15).

As we grow older, God's grace should make us sweet, not sour—
merciful, not mean—grateful, not grumpy. Even if your *position* is right,
what about your *disposition*?

As we grow older, God's Word reminds us, "Be completely humble and
gentle; be patient, bearing with one another in love. Make every effort to
keep the unity of the Spirit through the bond of peace" (Ephesians 4:2-3).
Immature Christians stir up unnecessary controversy and division. Mature
Christians promote unity because they are growing in grace.

But in addition to growing in grace, we also need to . . .

Grow in Knowledge

Of course, knowledge alone isn't the goal. The Bible warns us not to
be the kind of people who are "always learning but never able to come to a
knowledge of the truth" (2 Timothy 3:7). The goal is not merely to fill our
brains with information, but to grow wise so we know the truth and how to
use it.

Someone pointed out, "*Knowledge* is realizing that a tomato is a fruit.
Wisdom is realizing it doesn't belong in your fruit salad. *Discernment* is
knowing that ketchup isn't a smoothie!" Wisdom (godly common sense)
equips us to understand how God's Word applies to real-world problems.

We must grow in knowledge not only for our own sake, but also so we
can assist others who are asking questions about the Lord. Remember what
the Bible says in 1 Peter 3:15? "But in your hearts revere Christ as Lord.
Always be prepared to give an answer to everyone who asks you to give the
reason for the hope that you have. But do this with gentleness and respect."
Your own grandkids may ask you questions about what you believe. So will
other family members, friends, and neighbors.

The quest for spiritual maturity isn't just a self-improvement course. Peter emphasized that the goal is to "grow in the grace and knowledge *of our Lord and Savior Jesus Christ*" (2 Peter 3:18, emphasis added).

Christ, not self, is the focus of the Christian life. Preacher Wayne Smith used to say, "A cross is the letter 'I' crossed out." The apostle Paul defined his ministry by saying, "He is the one we proclaim, admonishing and teaching everyone with all wisdom, so that we may present everyone fully mature in Christ" (Colossians 1:28).

If we want our later years to be greater years, we should take to heart what it says in Colossians 2:6-7: "So then, just as you received Christ Jesus as Lord, continue to live your lives in him, rooted and built up in him, strengthened in the faith as you were taught, and overflowing with thankfulness."

When you accepted Christ as your Savior, it was the beginning of a new relationship with the Lord that continues to expand over time—but you're not in this alone. Spiritual growth is a team effort. That's where the church comes in.

DON'T OVERCOMPLICATE THINGS!

To drive a car, you don't have to know everything about automotive engineering. You may not know a spark plug from a muffler, but to drive safely, you at least need to know about the steering wheel and the brakes.

Spiritual maturity doesn't mean you know the answer to every Bible question or brag about all the "advanced stuff" you know. "Knowledge puffs up while love builds up" (1 Corinthians 8:1).

The "advanced stuff" is more than just gathering information; it means loving God and others well. All our talents and abilities mean little if we don't have love, for "the greatest of these is love" (1 Corinthians 13:13).

MATURITY LOOKS LIKE A HEALTHY CHURCH IN ACTION

Another New Testament picture of spiritual maturity has to do with the church, the body of Christ. The apostle Paul wrote, "Then we will no longer be infants, tossed back and forth by the waves, and blown here and there by every wind of teaching and by the cunning and craftiness of people in their deceitful scheming. Instead, speaking the truth in love, we will grow to become in every respect the mature body of him who is the head, that is, Christ" (Ephesians 4:14-15).

The phrase, "speaking the truth in love," has been a favorite of mine for many years. Truth and love are like two blades of a pair of scissors. One blade alone doesn't cut it; both "blades" (truth and love) are necessary.

Some people are big on truth, but small on love. When they speak at you, it's like they're hitting you with a brick. Others are big on love, but small on truth. A conversation with them makes you feel like you were hit with a pillow.

My recommendation? Be a brick inside a pillow! Speak the truth. Be faithful to God's Word. Have strong convictions. Be willing to say hard things. But be gracious and loving with people. Jesus was full of "grace and truth" (John 1:14), and you will find big doses of grace and truth in healthy churches, too.

No congregation is perfect, but every congregation has the potential to grow into "the mature body of him who is the head, that is, Christ" (Ephesians 4:15). Maybe you have a negative view of the church. Some see the church as a chain that binds and enslaves, or a box that confines. Others see it as little more than a museum displaying a few dusty relics from the past.

Perhaps we ought to see the church as a trellis—a frame or latticework that helps a plant climb. If you grow roses or flowering vines, you might use a trellis to support the plant while it blooms or bears fruit.

Jesus is the vine; we are the branches. Together, we cling to the Lord. The church is like a trellis that supports the branches so we can grow and bear fruit.

Acts 2 offers a beautiful picture of a healthy church. Jesus' first-century disciples "devoted themselves to the apostles' teaching [learning God's Word] and to fellowship [sharing what they had in common in Christ], to the breaking of bread [communing together in the Lord's Supper] and to prayer [consistently talking with the Lord]" (Acts 2:42). They cultivated positive habits that nourished their spiritual health. And they did this together—because spiritual growth isn't something we pursue on our own in isolation from others.

If I were to ask you a specific lesson you learned in third grade, you probably couldn't tell me. But if I ask you the name of your third-grade teacher, you could remember it. In the Bible, discipleship mainly happened in the context of relationship. While it is good to worship, pray, and study the Bible on our own, we grow best in community with others.

In the first-century church, the power of the gospel affected *everyone* . . . *everything*. . . *every day* . . . *everywhere*. Notice how the Bible describes this vibrant church in Acts 2:43-46.

- "*Everyone* was filled with awe" (v. 43). Not only the apostles and the preachers. Not just the famous folk or the well-known leaders. Everyone was full of awe for God. As we grow older, let's never lose our sense of wonder for the Lord!

- "All the believers were together and had *everything* in common" (v. 44). They even sold property and possessions so they could meet others' needs (v. 45). While this is not an all-inclusive command, it is a compelling example. Everything we own belongs to God. If he wants us to keep it, use it, spend it, save it, or give it away, we need to see everything as God's.

- "*Every day* they continued . . ." (v. 46). The first-century believers lived by faith seven days a week, not just on Sunday.

- They were devoted to Christ *everywhere*. Verse 46 says, "They continued to meet together in the temple courts [big spaces where large groups gathered]," and "They broke bread in their homes [intimate places where small groups of friends, family, and neighbors gathered] and ate together with glad and sincere hearts." They recognized that the Lord is present and relevant at school, at work, at home, at the coffee shop—in the locker room, the classroom, and the operating room.

Someone summed up senior adulthood by saying, "In your sixties, it's 'go, go, go.' In your seventies, it's 'slow, slow, slow.' In your eighties and nineties, it's 'no, no, no'!" But followers of Christ add another category. In every season of life, your faith can "grow, grow, grow." You are not too old to deepen your faith and develop a stronger relationship with God. In some ways older folk have an advantage because, if we look back at our lives through eyes of faith, we can see how the Lord has been at work over the long haul.

THREE TOOLS FOR GROWING IN SPIRITUAL MATURITY:

ADVICE

"The way of fools seems right to them, but the wise listen to advice" (Proverbs 12:15). "Listen to advice and accept discipline, and at the end you will be counted among the wise" (Proverbs 19:20). Whose advice are you following? Are you listening to the loudest voices on TV or social media, or to wise, godly advisors?

ADVENTURE

Jesus' invitation, "Come, follow me," is a call to adventure! The Lord has something bigger in mind for us than we can imagine. As we grow older, we need not be stale and inflexible. While it is natural to become more cautious with age, we are never too old to sing a new song, pray a bold prayer, or learn something new. "Old dogs" can learn new tricks! A sense of adventure helps us stay young. It has been said, "We must do things we have never done before to reach people we have never reached before." What new adventures might God have in store for you?

- Make a new friend.
- Learn a new skill.
- Find a new way to serve.
- Help a local or global mission.
- Give at a new level of generosity.
- Take a risk that stretches your faith.

ADVERSITY

We grow more during hard times than easy times. God uses hardships to deepen our faith and strengthen our character. "Suffering produces perseverance; perseverance, character; and character, hope" (Romans 5:3-4).

FIVE WAYS GOD HELPS US GROW

How does God nudge us toward spiritual maturity? I have noticed five specific methods he often uses.

1. **We grow when we stretch.**

In a sense, growth is natural and easy. When I was a boy, I don't remember growing . . . I just grew! Every year, I needed bigger shoes, pants, and shirts to wear. I didn't feel like I was growing. In fact, I was hardly even aware of it. I just grew! Some spiritual growth comes naturally as we walk with the Lord over extended periods of time. But there are times when we must "make every effort" to grow in our faith (2 Peter 1:5)—and that is where the stretching comes in.

After you have been sitting in a car for a long time, it feels good when you get out and stretch your arms and legs. Likewise, after you have been sitting in church a long time, it's good to stretch your faith.

The prophet Isaiah wrote, "Enlarge the place of your tent, stretch your tent curtains wide, do not hold back; lengthen your cords, strengthen your stakes" (Isaiah 54:2). The apostle Paul surely loved those words, because he sometimes made tents to support himself while he preached the gospel. He spent his life "expanding the tent," helping to stretch the kingdom of God to take in more people.

In Bible times, Abraham and others lived in tents. A typical nomad's tent was set up with nine poles in three rows. If you wanted to enlarge the tent, you would stretch the curtains tight and drive the stakes deep into the ground. By saying, "enlarge . . . your tent," God (through Isaiah) was telling the Jewish people to expand and make room for others. Don't just hide in the tent and stay to yourself. Open up so others can join you.

Sometimes we get too comfortable with the way things are. When that happens, the Lord says, "Enlarge your tent. Stretch your faith. Make room for others in your life. But as you grow, keep your stakes deep in the ground."

God might use uncomfortable circumstances or challenging relationships to stretch you outside your comfort zone. He might even use your own family to stretch you.

Candy was 20 years old and I was 21 on our wedding day. Marriage stretched me because I was so immature—and being married to me stretched my wife's faith quite a bit! When I became a dad, being a parent stretched me. My kids needed me to be more than just a friend or the guy who paid the bills. They needed me to act like an adult. Our own spiritual growth is one of the best gifts parents and grandparents can give our kids. They need to know that faith in God is the centerpiece of our lives, not a religious accessory.

2. We grow when we study.

We need to study the Bible to understand the will of God.

We need to study other people so we can love them well. For example, 1 Peter 3:7 instructs husbands to "be considerate as you live with your wives." (Another Bible translation says to live with wives "in an understanding way.")

We need to study our culture so we can understand what is happening in the world, like the men from the tribe of Issachar, "who understood the times and knew what Israel should do" (1 Chronicles 12:32).

We grow when we stretch. We grow when we study. And . . .

3. **We grow when we serve.**

My favorite artistic conception of Jesus is a picture Candy gave me many years ago. I keep it hanging on the wall next to my office door. It shows Jesus as a carpenter, shaping a block of wood. I like that picture because Jesus was the kind of leader who rolled up his sleeves and got his hands dirty. I also like that the artist showed the Lord carving the wood, which reminds me that he's chipping away the rough edges from my life. It is our job to be a tool in the Lord's hands. Life isn't just about us. It is about serving others.

Most of us learn best through hands-on experience. As we mature, our main question shouldn't be, "Am I being fed?" but "Who am I feeding, and how can I use my gifts to build up the body of Christ?"

You are not too old to be a servant. There comes a time when you should not only attend a small group; you should lead one. There comes a time when you should not only enjoy eating a meal; you should take responsibility to cook it and wash the dishes afterward. It was convenient when you dropped your kids off and let someone else take care of them while you attended worship services; but when will you dive in and help with ministry yourself?

When I was a boy, my parents bought my clothes, cooked my food, and paid for everything. But as soon as my brothers and I were old enough to work, Dad gave us chores to do on the farm. I fed calves and hogs every morning and evening. I gathered eggs in the chicken house. The work wasn't always fun, but it made me feel like part of the family. It helped me grow up.

In the church, we all need to be contributors, not just consumers— and this applies to every age group. In sports, players need to be on the field or court moving the ball around. People who merely sit in the stands, critiquing the action and second-guessing the coach, do nothing to help win the game. We stagnate when we focus on ourselves and put our own comforts above God's will, but we grow when we serve others. Older adults in the church should set an example of service.

Here is another way God moves us toward maturity.

4. We grow when we sacrifice.

Selfishness is a mark of immaturity. Remember when you were a little kid and your parents had to teach you to share? It is a mark of maturity to recognize that some things in life are worth sacrifice. Hebrews 13:16 says, "And do not forget to do good and to share with others, for with such sacrifices God is pleased."

I mentioned earlier how inexperienced and immature I was when I first became a father. Our first child was born prematurely, and he had to stay in the hospital for a couple of weeks. Candy was worn out from giving birth, and she was sad to come home without the baby in her arms. But I played on an industrial league softball team at the time, and instead of being there for my wife, I stayed busy playing second base. I needed to apply the Scripture that says, "Husbands, love your wives, just as Christ loved the church and gave himself up for her" (Ephesians 5:25). The ultimate sacrifice was Jesus' death on the cross—the supreme act of love, and he calls us to surrender our personal preferences for the sake of others. You and I are not too old to make sacrifices for others we love.

By the way, it is not uncommon to experience a crazy kind of joy when you sacrifice for the Lord's sake. And most of all . . .

5. We grow when we struggle.

On a mission trip to Ethiopia, I met Christians who suffer from extreme poverty and face terrible illnesses like leprosy. The sermon at the church we attended on Sunday morning was not in English, so I asked the missionary, "What is the preacher saying?" My friend explained, "He is talking about Acts 14:22, where the apostle Paul told new Christians they have to go through many hardships to enter the kingdom of God."

What does spiritual maturity require? Usually, going through many hardships.

In a sermon, Jeffrey Johnson, senior pastor at Eastern Star Church in Indianapolis, quoted Scripture that says, "Consider it pure joy, my brothers and sisters, whenever you face trials of many kinds, because you know that the testing of your faith produces perseverance. Let perseverance finish its work so that you may be mature and complete, not lacking anything" (James 1:2-4). Jeffrey explained, "As a follower of Christ, you have enrolled in the university of adversity. In this university, trials are a required course, not an elective. But fortunately, when the tests come, they are 'open-book tests'! You can open the Bible and read what God said to find the answers."[2]

The Bible reveals a spiritual growth cycle of death, burial, and resurrection. Jesus referred to this cycle when "he called the crowd to him along with his disciples and said: 'Whoever wants to be my disciple must deny themselves and take up their cross and follow me. For whoever wants to save their life will lose it, but whoever loses their life for me and for the gospel will save it'" (Mark 8:34-35).

The question, "Are we growing?" leads to a tougher question: "Are we dying?" Following the Lord means dying to selfishness, dying to sin, dying to this world and its fading glory. But resurrection and new life are ahead! So, brothers and sisters, no matter how old we are, let's join the apostle Paul and say, "Forgetting what is behind and straining toward what is ahead, I press on toward the goal to win the prize for which God has called me heavenward in Christ Jesus" (Philippians 3:13-14).

QUESTIONS FOR PERSONAL REFLECTION
AND GROUP DISCUSSION

1. It can be intimidating to "bare your soul." But guess what? Your soul is already "uncovered and laid bare" before God (Hebrews 4:13)! You can be completely vulnerable with the Lord. There is nothing to hide from him. In prayer, spend some time in honest reflection about your current spiritual condition. Which of the following words describe your relationship with God?

Apathetic	Eager	Growing
Lazy	Determined	Fruitful
Half-hearted	Enthusiastic	Hopeful
Complacent	Content	Zealous
Indifferent	Lukewarm	On fire

2. Experts say most organizations move through a life cycle that resembles a bell curve. Growth is followed by momentum, but unless the momentum is sustained, the organization tends to plateau and then decline. The same process can happen in your personal walk with God. Where would you say you are on the cycle? Are you in a season of growth and momentum, or at a plateau or in decline? What needs to happen for you to begin a new upward trend and start growing again?

3. First Peter 4:10-11 says, "Each of you should use whatever gift you have received to serve others, as faithful stewards of God's grace in its various forms. If anyone speaks, they should do so as one who speaks the very words of God. If anyone serves, they should do so with the strength God provides, so that in all things God may be praised through Jesus Christ. To him be the glory and the power for ever and ever. Amen." How are you using your spiritual gifts to build up the body of Christ?

9 | Retired or Refired?— Life Doesn't Stop When Your Career Ends

*"All ballplayers should quit when it starts
to feel as if all the baselines run uphill."*
—Babe Ruth

*"Old barbers never die;
they just can't cut it anymore."*
—Unknown

A book about aging should include a chapter about retirement, right? But I will approach this topic cautiously for two reasons: (1) The Bible has little to say about retirement, and (2) I haven't retired yet, so I can't speak about it from personal experience. I have some thoughts to share with you, though, based on my ministry experiences with others who are preparing for or moving through their retirement years.

Perspectives on retirement vary. Some of my friends retired "early" (in their fifties) while others retired "late" (in their eighties or even their nineties). I know a few hardy individuals who insist they will never retire, and others who decided to "retire and restart" by switching to an entirely different career. One friend, who was a high-profile professional athlete, retired in his thirties and now devotes his time to leading a nonprofit organization that benefits children and teens. Some retirees say they stopped working at the perfect time, while others regret quitting their jobs and wish they could rewind the clock and do things differently. Bill Gaither has continued writing songs, leading worship, and producing music into his late eighties. He told me that he doesn't think of what he does as a career, but as a responsibility that never ends.

My father was born and raised on a farm. His mother gave him birth in the house where he grew up and lived as an adult. When Dad reached age 65, he spoke about retiring, but what does retirement mean to someone whose whole life was about planting and harvesting, and who still was surrounded by the fields where he had labored his whole life? As an ordained minister, I am surrounded by a different kind of field, and I am engaged in a different kind of planting and harvesting. I plan to serve the Lord for the rest of my life whether anyone pays me to do so or not. What does retirement mean for someone like me?

As I grow older, friends and church members often ask me, *How do you know when it is time to retire?* This is an important question because in some cases, it is possible your retirement may last 20 or 30 years—a significant portion of your lifetime. The U. S. Census Bureau estimates the average length of retirement at 18 years. Yet, retirement is an inexact science; and you can't guarantee you will have complete control over the process, either. What if health issues, life circumstances, government policies, or corporate downsizing disrupt your plans? What if the Lord leads you in a different direction than you expected?

Even the word *retire* is a bit strange. Ernest Hemingway called it "the ugliest word in the language." Taken literally, *retirement* sounds like "getting tired all over again"! If you already feel tired, why would you want to "re-tire"? The poet Richard Armour wrote:

> Retired is being twice tired,
> I've thought.
> First tired of working,
> Then tired of not.

"Re-tired" makes me think of a car that needs new tires, or at least the tires need some new tread. This is a helpful analogy, because being "re-tired" doesn't mean you stop moving forward; it means getting ready for the next part of your journey. The happiest retirees are those who have "re-tired" by discovering some new tread so they can keep rolling along on their journey with the Lord.

The English word *retire* comes from the French *retirer* (from *re*, meaning "back"; plus *tirer*, meaning "draw"). Since the 1500s, the term has meant something like "withdrawing to a place of safety or seclusion." To make sure I wasn't missing something, I looked up the word in the dictionary, but that didn't make me feel any better about it. The definitions of *retiring* include:

- Retreating from action or danger—like an army that pulls back because it is being defeated in battle.

- Moving back or receding—which reminds me of my hairline.

- Going to bed—"I'm exhausted and it's time for me to retire to my room."

- Withdrawing from a position or an occupation or concluding one's working career (the classic definition of retirement).

- Pulling something out of circulation—"The company decided it is time to retire the item from their product line."

- In baseball, getting the other team out—"The pitcher retired the side without allowing a run."

Most of those definitions have a negative connotation. They make retirement sound like being defeated, giving up, quitting, or concluding something, not starting something new and good. The dictionary also reminded me of a positive example: Retirement can refer to settling an account or paying a debt in full, as in, "We finally retired our mortgage."

Maybe we should use a different analogy and think about what I call *refirement*. The happiest retirees I have met are not the ones who sit around watching TV all day. They are the ones who have been "refired." A fresh zest for life burns in their hearts. They have discovered that retirement provides the time, freedom, and passion to pursue opportunities that fire them up and motivate them to get out of the rocking chair and keep going.

One of my seminary professors spoke about "focusing and faceting." He compared growing older to the way a jeweler cuts a diamond, revealing new facets of the gem that sparkle in the light. On his sixtieth birthday, the professor told our class he was excited about the future because for many years he had "focused" on his teaching career, but now in his sixties he would have the opportunity to "facet"—to pursue new hobbies and explore new interests.

This analogy is helpful if you are considering retirement or even if you are already retired. After years of focusing on your career, retirement can offer you the chance to explore new facets of life that God may present to you.

In this chapter, I won't dodge the question, *How can you know when it is the right time to retire?* But before addressing that important issue, let's start with some . . .

Reasons NOT to Retire

DON'T RETIRE BECAUSE IT'S "EXPECTED."

When I was 59 years old, after serving for 12 years as president of a Christian university, I resigned to accept a ministry position with East 91st Street Christian Church, where I previously had served as senior minister. This move marked the beginning of a meaningful decade-plus of ministry as I continued to work full-time as the senior associate minister. Concurrent with that, I also served six years as a leadership advisor and consultant for another church. My sixties turned out to be a busy, productive, and fulfilling season of my life. However, I often encounter people who assume I am retired. Does my gray hair make me look "retired"?

You don't have to shut down your career simply because others expect you to do so when you reach a certain arbitrary age. "Retirement at 65 is ridiculous," George Burns quipped. "When I was 65, I still had pimples."

In the past, many workers didn't have a choice about when they would retire. The deadline was already decided for them because their employers had policies in place that mandated retirement. For example, for safety reasons the airline industry long enforced a policy that pilots must retire by age 60. (That age was raised to 65 in 2007.) In recent years, laws forbidding age discrimination have made it possible for many employees to continue working as long as they remain productive and add value in the workplace.

In the Bible, the only place I have found that plainly refers to retirement is in the book of Numbers, which specifies a retirement age for the Levites who served in the tabernacle. It says, "but at the age of fifty, they must retire from their regular service and work no longer" (Numbers 8:25). I have often used this verse (quoted out of context, obviously) to tease my friends when they reach their fiftieth birthdays. "It's time for you to retire," I joke, "and even the Bible says so!" When this Scripture passage is rightly interpreted in context, however, I believe the retirement age God prescribed was a reasonable and merciful rule. The intention of this law was not for the Levites to stop doing anything at all; the point was for them to cease the laborious, burdensome, physically exhausting part of their work. In a blog post entitled "The Chumps Who Had to Move the Tabernacle," one writer explains what was involved.

> The Israelites spent 40 years wandering through the wilderness on their way to the Promised Land. That's 40 years of setting up camp and taking down camp.
>
> *Forty. Years.* Every time God told them to move, it was a process. Setting up. Taking down. Setting up. Taking down. Setting up . . . And on and on and on.
>
> I'm sure that got old fast. I get tired of setting up and taking down tents after just one camping trip, and that's with a modern, lightweight tent held up by those fancy fiberglass rods that practically put themselves together. . . .
>
> But you know who had it worse than the average Israelite? The Levites. In addition to worrying about their own tents, they had to move the tabernacle—the ornately designed, beautifully crafted holy place that served as both a physical reminder of the presence of God and as the centerpiece of the Israelite camp. For forty years, the Levites were responsible for taking it apart and putting it back together. Every board, every socket, every curtain, every cord, every pillar—the Levites were the ones who had to load them up and make sure everything made it to the next campsite in the right order at the right time (Numbers 10:13-28).[1]

God mercifully gave the Levites a much-needed break after they tore down, set up, and carried the tabernacle around all those years. When they reached the age of 50, their role changed; they no longer had to do the cumbersome physical labor associated with being Levites. (Maybe they sat on lawn chairs and supervised the young whippersnappers who moved those poles around!) Retirement didn't mean their influence was over; it meant shifting to less strenuous ministry activity.

Don't retire simply because it is "expected." Perhaps you just need to adjust your expectations and modify the type of work you do. Unless the Lord, the law, or your employer have made it clear you should retire by a certain age, don't assume that you must quit your job just because you have reached a chronological milestone. Some workers should retire at 55, and some at 62 or 70 or older. Those are arbitrary numbers, not requirements etched in stone.

DON'T RETIRE SIMPLY BECAUSE CIRCUMSTANCES FORCE YOU TO QUIT YOUR CURRENT JOB.

When the pandemic hit in 2020, many weary workers (especially in fields like health care and public safety) decided they didn't want to deal with the stress of their full-time jobs anymore. But a few years later, economists say the Great Resignation was followed by the Great Regret, because many workers retired impulsively without a clear and positive plan for what comes next.

According to Megan Gerhardt, a business professor at Miami University, prior to the COVID-19 pandemic, economists were already worried about an approaching "silver tsunami," a mass exodus of Baby Boomers from the workforce. Then when the pandemic hit, "We had people who for health reasons or safety reasons felt like, 'Well, I was going to retire relatively soon, I'm just going to go ahead and do it now.' We had people who were laid off because of downsizing and other issues. And then we had the people who, when it was time to go back to work had a moment . . . of saying, 'Do I want to go back?'"[2]

If you are tired of your current job, or if you face downsizing or another situation at work that makes you want to step away, consider the alternatives to full retirement. Could you retool your role in your current job? Could you work part-time instead of full-time? Rather than retiring suddenly with little forethought, could you find another full-time job with a different company or organization? If you have the heart and skill of an entrepreneur, is this the time for you to branch out on your own and start a new business or become an independent contractor? Could you leverage your experience and make a living by consulting with others rather than working for a sole employer?

DON'T RETIRE BECAUSE YOU WANT TO
SIT AROUND AND DO NOTHING ALL DAY.

Rest is good. A change of pace is good. Taking time for sabbath is good. Freedom to set your own schedule is good. But at any age, idleness is bad for your body and soul. After retiring, you might need to take a few days, weeks, or even months to talk with God and catch up on your rest, but unless a physical or emotional disability limits your options, it's best to stay as active as possible.

My friend Russ Blowers died in 2007 after serving for 45 years as the senior minister at East 91st Street Christian Church. Russ used to chuckle about retirees who grow so idle "the only part of their body that gets any exercise is their thumb from pressing the TV remote!"

Retirement is a time to switch gears and go slower, but it's not a time for idleness. You are not too old to stay active. Your later years will be greater years if you engage in meaningful service to God and others.

DON'T RETIRE BECAUSE YOU THINK QUITTING
YOUR JOB WILL FILL THE VOID IN YOUR SOUL.

Have you ever wondered if your career—all those days and years, all those meetings, all those commutes to and from your job, all that time away from your family—really made any difference? Have you ever felt a sense of despair when you realize that eventually you must hand over the keys to your office or give up your place on the organizational chart to someone else who will come after you? Here is what King Solomon learned about the burdens of hard work.

> I hated all the things I had toiled for under the sun, because I must leave them to the one who comes after me. And who knows whether that person will be wise or foolish? Yet they will have control over all the fruit of my toil into which I have poured my effort and skill under the sun. This too is meaningless. So my heart began to despair over all my toilsome labor under the sun. For a person may labor with wisdom, knowledge and skill, and then they must leave all they own to another who has not toiled

> for it. This too is meaningless and a great misfortune. What do
> people get for all the toil and anxious striving with which they
> labor under the sun? All their days their work is grief and pain;
> even at night their minds do not rest. This too is meaningless
> (Ecclesiastes 2:18-23).

Do you ever feel that way? Even though your work has been tireless and your nights have been sleepless, do you wonder if your career has been pointless? After further reflection, Solomon recognized a positive aspect of labor: The opportunity to work is a blessing from God. The wise old king went on to say, "A person can do nothing better than to eat and drink and find satisfaction in their own toil. This too, I see, is from the hand of God, for without him, who can eat or find enjoyment?" (Ecclesiastes 2:24-25).

Work can be a blessing, and we should be thankful for the career opportunities God has given us. But work alone cannot satisfy our souls—and here is a surprise: *Not working* won't satisfy our souls, either!

While Solomon reflected on the meaninglessness and despair he felt from his hard work, he also found time to indulge himself. With nearly limitless resources at his disposal, he enjoyed the kinds of things many retirees dream about. Solomon amassed a fortune of gold and silver. He built and lived in a fine home. He planted gardens, vineyards, and orchards. But in time, Solomon discovered what many retirees have found (if they make self-indulgence their overarching goal). He said:

> I denied myself nothing my eyes desired; I refused my heart
> no pleasure. My heart took delight in all my labor, and this
> was the reward for all my toil. Yet when I surveyed all that my
> hands had done and what I had toiled to achieve, everything was
> meaningless, a chasing after the wind; nothing was gained under
> the sun (Ecclesiastes 2:10-11).

Be careful not to glamorize retirement and idealize what it will be like when you are free from your responsibilities at work. It is fine to relax, travel, and enjoy life, but it is a big mistake to think these pleasures alone will fill the void in your heart. Jesus pointedly asked, "What good is it for someone to gain the whole world, yet forfeit their soul?" (Mark 8:36).

When Is It Time to Retire?

We have examined some reasons *not* to retire. Now let's look at the flip side. When should you wrap up your career and step away?

Solomon wrote, "There is a time for everything, and a season for every activity under the heavens" (Ecclesiastes 3:1). When is it time to retire?

IT IS TIME TO RETIRE WHEN YOU "JUST KNOW."

I have spoken with many retirees who say something like this: "I woke up one morning and I just 'knew' it was time." Or, "Things changed in my workplace and I didn't feel comfortable there anymore. Rather than enduring another long season of organizational change, I decided it was time to go."

Babe Ruth voiced the emotions of many retirees when he said, "All ballplayers should quit when it starts to feel as if all the baselines run uphill."

One retiree suggests the decision to retire boils down to these three questions: (1) Do you have enough? (2) Will you have enough to do? and (3) Have you had enough? In other words, are you financially ready to halt or slow down your income stream from employment? Do you have a clear idea about what you plan to do after retirement? And have you grown so weary of your daily work that you don't want to face it anymore?[3]

IT IS TIME TO RETIRE WHEN YOUR HEALTH MAKES IT NECESSARY.

Quarterback Tom Brady won seven Super Bowl championships and kept playing professional football until he was 45, but the time finally came for him to retire. Even individuals who keep themselves in top physical condition eventually reach a point where they must recognize the limits of their ability to go on.

God mercifully told the Levites to retire at age 50 because the physical demands of the job were too great for older people to handle. It's OK to acknowledge that your body no longer can stand the strain of working long hours, lifting heavy weights, or spending 8 or 10 hours a day bent over a laptop computer. And a job's physical demands aren't the only issue to consider. What about your state of mind and your emotional health?

It's OK to say, "I don't want to attend any more planning meetings" or "I feel like I'm going to scream every time our company announces a new technology policy."

IT IS TIME TO RETIRE WHEN (OR PREFERABLY BEFORE) YOUR JOB PERFORMANCE TAKES A DOWNTURN.

Comedian George Carlin quipped, "Most people work just hard enough not to get fired and get paid just enough money not to quit."

Has your productivity started to decline? Is your heart no longer in your work? Has your supervisor given you low marks in your evaluations and reviews? Do you sense that you are slipping? Can you honestly say your daily work fits with the spirit of Colossians 3:23, which says, "Whatever you do, work at it with all your heart, as working for the Lord, not for human masters"?

This book is called *Not Too Old*, but to be clear, there will come a time when you are too old to do certain things anymore. I'll leave it to the voters to decide when a political leader is too old and frail to serve effectively in government leadership. For my part, I know that I am now too old to play tackle football with my friends like I did in my teens, and I am now too old to work 90-hour weeks like I did in my forties. With age, you can learn to work "smarter, not harder," but at some point, the smartest thing is to recognize your limitations, embrace less prominent and demanding roles, and live at a more reasonable pace.

Fay Vincent served as commissioner of Major League Baseball from 1989 to 1992. Now in his eighties, he wrote an article about aging for *The Wall Street Journal* in which he contrasted how Ted Williams finished his baseball career (by hitting a home run in his final at-bat) with the way Willie Mays continued to play long after his skills had diminished. Vincent wrote, "Leaving the stage at the right time demands self-awareness. I asked the diva soprano Beverly Sills how she knew when to retire, and she gave me this sensible answer: 'I knew that to continue would not be worthy of what my audience deserved.'"[4]

Self-awareness isn't easy, but it's important to be completely honest with yourself. If it is financially necessary to continue working, are you in the right job? If you are no longer able to make a significant contribution in the workplace, do you really want to keep working out of habit? Is the real issue that you are afraid to make a change and embrace a new season of your life? A friend of mine advises, "It's better to leave when your colleagues say, 'I miss him,' than when they say, 'Thank the Lord he's gone!'"

IT IS TIME TO RETIRE WHEN YOUNGER WORKERS ARE READY TO STEP INTO YOUR ROLE.

In preparing for my own retirement, I am torn between two polar considerations. I don't want to retire too soon if the church needs me and there is still useful work for me to do. On the other hand, I want to help younger leaders grow in their careers, not prevent them from having an opportunity to step up. If leaving too soon would be a mistake, staying too long might be an even bigger mistake.

Succession planning is easy to overlook. We get so busy handling "today" that we forget about "tomorrow." And there is a tendency to be prideful and cling to our jobs, because for many of us, work is not only a way to make money; it is where we find our identity and significance. The question, "What do you do for a living?" gets intermingled with the question, "Who are you and why are you valuable?" If we stop working, we fear losing our identity. That is why we need to find our true identity in knowing, loving, and serving the Lord. When our significance is rooted in the unchanging God, our past is forgiven, our present is secure, and our future holds promise of "an inheritance that can never perish, spoil or fade" (1 Peter 1:4).

Our careers don't define us. As disciples of Jesus Christ, no matter our age, we find our greatest significance simply in following him.

Succession planning matters in most workplaces, but it is especially important in the church. As we grow older, we need to prepare the next generation to take our place in the process of making disciples and continuing God's work.

Several leadership transitions are mentioned in the Bible. David prepared for his son Solomon to succeed him as king (1 Kings 1–2). Elijah literally passed the mantle of leadership to the younger prophet Elisha (2 Kings 2). Jesus spent three years preparing his disciples to carry on his work. Paul mentored Timothy and Titus and encouraged them to carry on the ministry.

A helpful biblical example is the story of Moses and Joshua. Two parallel passages, Numbers 27:12-23 and Deuteronomy 3:23-29, describe what happened when God confronted Moses with the need to implement a succession plan. Can you imagine how difficult it must have been to replace a leader with Moses' reputation, influence, and length of service? And even though Moses endured many frustrations while leading the Hebrews, don't you think it must have been hard for him to release the reins and encourage another leader to step in and succeed him? Here are some things we learn from the biblical text:

- *Moses cooperated with, and voluntarily participated in, the succession plan.* "Moses said to the Lord, 'May the Lord, the God who gives breath to all living things, appoint someone over this community to go out and come in before them, one who will lead them out and bring them in, so the Lord's people will not be like sheep without a shepherd'" (Numbers 27:15-17). This required great humility on Moses' part. As he grew older and faced the reality of his approaching death, he was more concerned about God's people and their future than he was about protecting his own power and influence. Have you ever prayed specifically for your successors at work? Do you sincerely want them to succeed?

- *The Lord selected a qualified person to continue the work.* God told Moses, "But commission Joshua, and encourage and strengthen him, for he will lead this people across and will cause them to inherit the land that you will see" (Deuteronomy 3:28).

- *There was a public, positive, prayerful transition from one leader to the next.* "Moses did as the Lord commanded him. He took Joshua and had him stand before Eleazar the priest and the whole assembly. Then he laid his hands on him and commissioned him, as the Lord instructed through Moses" (Numbers 27:22-23).

Bob Russell retired at age 62 after serving for 40 years as the senior minister of Southeast Christian Church in Louisville, Kentucky. In a blog post called "A Time to Retire," Bob wrote that he retired while he was "still healthy and alert" for two reasons:

First, the future of our church would need younger, more energetic leadership. . . . I had been the senior pastor through five new construction building programs for our church and numerous other stressful situations. I felt I did not have the energy to go through another significant project. I concluded that I needed to step aside for the good of the church.

Second, I retired to start another meaningful chapter in my life. I wanted to encourage younger pastors, speak at other churches and events, and continue writing while I still had the health to do it. So I needed to step away from the pressure of pastoring a megachurch. I had witnessed other older ministers stay at their church too long, and they ended up tearing down what had taken years to build up. Another megachurch minister later acknowledged, "I preached at my church for 44 years. It should have been 40."[5]

I don't recall where I heard the following observation, but I agree with the sentiment. "What is worse than an employee who becomes cynical and quits? An employee who becomes cynical and stays."

IT IS TIME TO RETIRE WHEN TRUSTED FAMILY MEMBERS AND FRIENDS THINK IT'S TIME.

Earlier in this chapter, I quoted a retiree who suggested three questions to ask: (1) Do you have enough? (2) Will you have enough to do? and (3) Have you had enough? If you are married, it is wise to add a fourth question: "What does your spouse think about the new and different future retirement will bring?"[6]

Of course, retirement is a personal decision you must make for yourself. But it is wise to seek the counsel and advice of others who know you well. Do your closest friends think you should retire? If you have adult children, what do they think you should do? Trusted friends and family can help you see yourself more objectively.

While working on a church staff throughout my sixties, I had honest, one-on-one conversations with the congregation's elders. I trust them, and I am confident they love me enough to help me make sure I'm not missing something important. And I periodically have asked my wife, Candy, "Do you think I should retire?" She knows me better than anyone else except the Lord. If she had said, "Dave, to be honest, you need to hang it up," I would have done so. But instead, she repeatedly said something like this:

"No, I don't think it's time yet. But if you wake up one morning and say, 'I'm done,' I will support you."

IT IS TIME TO RETIRE WHEN YOU ARE FINANCIALLY READY.

According to news accounts, an exterminator was called to a house in Santa Rosa, California, where he discovered a stash of acorns deposited there by acorn woodpeckers. The birds evidently had been stockpiling the nuts for years and hiding them in the chimney of the house. The acorn collection had grown to more than 20 feet deep. "The more acorns I pulled out from the wall, the more there were. It felt like it wasn't going to end," the exterminator reported. He filled and removed eight garbage bags of nuts weighing a total of 700 pounds. The story caught the attention of readers on social media. Some felt sorry for the hoarding birds that lost their stash of nuts, and one person quipped, "These woodpeckers are more prepared for retirement than I am."[7]

How many "acorns" must you save to retire comfortably? Should you stay in your house or downsize to a smaller home or condominium? Should you invest in long-term care insurance to offset the potential cost of nursing care in the future? The national average cost of a semi-private room in a nursing home has passed $100,000 a year, and the cost of a six-hour visit by a home health aide visiting five days a week averages over $30,000 a year.[8] And what about estate planning? A wise, trustworthy financial advisor can help you sort through these and other factors, such as:

- When to receive Social Security benefits and how to use them;

- What to do about health care and medical insurance coverage;

- How to handle mandatory distributions from your retirement account.

And be sure to consider the cost of taxes, for unfortunately, you can't avoid taxation simply because you are old. (Remember, "The IRS" spells "Theirs.")

My own financial advisor quotes Yogi Berra who cautioned, "It's tough to make predictions, especially about the future." But if you are wondering, "Will I run out of life before I run out of money?" my advisor recommends starting with well-grounded assumptions about your future income and spending needs. He says, "Often in retirement, expenses such as costs to commute, work clothing, and lunches out of the office fall dramatically, sometimes to zero. Likewise, it is common for nonessential spending such as travel and entertainment to increase, especially in one's initial retirement years." I spoke with another financial advisor who tells his clients to take a year or two to practice living on the amount of income they expect to earn in retirement before pulling the plug on their career. That way, they will have a realistic understanding of what their expenses will be. While visiting Turkey, I learned a Turkish proverb that says, "Stretch your legs to the limit of your blanket." In other words, adjust your spending to fit your budget.

Here are two crucial pieces of financial advice I encourage my younger readers to consider:

1. Avoid borrowing money and running up balances on high-interest credit cards. Get out of debt as soon as possible and avoid paying unnecessary interest to creditors.

2. Leverage the power of compound interest, which works to your advantage by accelerating your savings and investments over time.

My financial advisor observes, "Since time is the most essential input to growing one's savings, it is best to begin funding accounts like IRAs and employee retirement plans as soon as practically possible. As Proverbs 13:11 says, 'Whoever gathers money little by little makes it grow.'"

IT IS TIME TO RETIRE WHEN YOU HAVE A WORKABLE PLAN FOR WHAT COMES NEXT.

What are your goals for retirement? Many retirees find that after an initial time of relaxation (which feels like an ordinary vacation), they don't know what to do with their discretionary time.

Prior to retirement, we should give careful forethought to our plans. The Bible highlights both our personal responsibility and the providence of God when it says, "In their hearts humans plan their course, but the Lord establishes their steps" (Proverbs 16:9).

In their book, *Your Retirement Quest: 10 Secrets for Creating and Living a Fulfilling Retirement*, authors Alan Spector and Keith Lawrence suggest there are five stages of retirement:

1. *Anticipation.* This is a time of excitement and hope as you look forward to retirement. (It should also be a time for planning.)

2. *Honeymoon.* "You have the freedom to do what you want to do; just be you. No alarm clock, no business attire, no rush-hour drive—you are elated and enthusiastic and feel a sense of relief, independence, and discovery."

3. *Disenchantment.* The honeymoon is over and reality sets in. In this phase, you experience "letdown, loneliness, boredom, or disappointment; you may even be depressed."

4. *Rejuvenation.* You adapt to the reality of retirement and find ways to stay energized and engaged. (Careful planning can minimize disenchantment and help you identify ways to stay rejuvenated.)

5. *Fulfillment.* You are connected with others, giving back, pursuing your interests, growing as a person, and having fun (and I would add, serving God).[9]

IT IS TIME TO RETIRE WHEN THE LORD OPENS A NEW DOOR FOR MINISTRY.

We should be humble about our plans, for the Lord can alter them at any time. James wrote, "Now listen, you who say, 'Today or tomorrow we will go to this or that city, spend a year there, carry on business and make money.' Why, you do not even know what will happen tomorrow. What is your life? You are a mist that appears for a little while and then vanishes. Instead, you ought to say, 'If it is the Lord's will, we will live and do this or that'" (James 4:13-15).

My friend Rick Justice worked as a human resources program manager for a large company for 33 years, and he thought he had his retirement plans in place. Years earlier, Rick earned his PhD in educational leadership, and he had become acquainted with TCM International, an educational ministry that equips leaders to serve in Europe and other parts of the world. When TCM approached Rick about serving as its academic vice president, the timing didn't seem right, so he decided to decline. Here is the rest of the story, in Rick's own words:

During a corporate downsizing initiative in the spring of 2010, I was in a group of individuals who qualified for an early retirement package. My division was involved in mission-critical projects, and I had no plans to retire. Management was happy to hear that. At quitting time on Friday, management came by my office to confirm that I was not going to retire. I assured them that I had no plans to retire and would not be accepting the package.

Then Saturday night came. At some time in the middle of the night, I had a conversation with Someone. It did not seem like a dream or a vision. There was no audible voice, but there was a definite conversation:

"Why aren't you taking this package?" . . . "There is lots of work to do."

"I have work for you to do. Why aren't you taking this package?" . . . "My goal is to retire in two years."

"What's wrong with attaining your goal early? Why aren't you taking this package?" . . . No reply.

"Doesn't the new opportunity I'm presenting fit with the reason you completed your PhD studies? Why aren't you taking this package?" . . . No reply.

At 2:00 a.m. on Sunday, I woke my wife, Dixie, and said, "We need to talk." After telling her what had just happened, she said, "That's exactly what God has been saying to me for several days."

As if I wasn't going to listen to God *and* my wife, three individuals that Sunday independently confirmed my decision to retire without knowing there was an offer to retire and without knowing anything about what had happened Saturday night.

I went to the office on Monday and told management that I was retiring. They said, "But Friday you said you weren't going to.' I said: 'Ah yes, but *this* is what happened on Saturday. . . .'"

After retiring from his corporate position, Rick has served with TCM for more than a decade, using his experience and leadership skill to shepherd this growing ministry. To be clear, Rick isn't the kind of person who often says, "God spoke to me," and while not everyone will have the kind of conversation he had with the Lord that night, all of us can pray for God's guidance and direction. We all can pray, receive wise counsel from godly friends, and do our best to align our goals with God's Word. Proverbs 16:3 says, "Commit to the Lord whatever you do, and he will establish your plans."

Jesus said that our heavenly Father is gracious to "give good gifts to those who ask him" (Matthew 7:11), and sometimes his good gifts include new ministry opportunities during our retirement years. If God opens a door for new and fruitful service, are you willing to walk through it and "make the most of every opportunity" (Colossians 4:2-6)?

In Summary

Since I have not yet retired, let me close this chapter with some advice from someone who has done so. My friend Bob Russell offers this advice to those who want to make the most of their retirement.

- Be realistic. Everyone ages. We all reach a point of ineffectiveness.

- Get your self-worth from your identity in Christ and not from your occupation.

- Set a retirement date in advance and stick to it. You think you will know when it is time, but most do not. Be proactive. Make an unemotional decision long in advance.

- Retire to something, not just from something. It is not enough to step away from the pressure. You need something meaningful to do.

- Stay active! Identify your "sweet spot" and find ways to use your primary gifts in service to others. Author Bob Buford calls it "moving from success to significance."

- Learn to be content even though you are not as important in the eyes of the world as you once were. Who cares? You still matter to your family, your close friends, and, most importantly, to God. You are not in competition with anyone.

- Be joyful and make the most of every day. Say with the psalmist: "This is the day which the Lord hath made; we will rejoice and be glad in it" (Psalm 118:24, *King James Version*).

- Increasingly focus on eternity. Regardless of what happens to your mind and body, the best is yet to be![10]

QUESTIONS FOR PERSONAL REFLECTION AND GROUP DISCUSSION

1. How would you describe your current perspective on retirement?

   a. Excitement—I can't wait! (Or, I am already enjoying it!)

   b. Anxiety—I'm worried about it.

   c. Uncertainty—There are a lot of unknowns.

   d. Peace—I'm comfortable with the direction things are going (or already have gone) with my retirement plans.

   e. Other:

2. What is your main source of concern about retirement?

   a. Finances—making sure I have enough money to pay the bills.

   b. Purpose—making sure I still have a reason to get out of bed in the morning.

   c. Health—making sure I am strong enough to do the things I would like to do.

   d. Other:

3. Have you ever known people who retired "too soon" or "too late"? What can you learn from observing their experiences?

   Suggestion: Meet with a retiree who seems happy and productive, and ask them to share their perspective on retirement.

4. Read James 4:13-15. How do these verses impact the way you think about retirement planning?

10 | Still Part of the Body of Christ— Finding Your Place in the Church as a Senior Adult

"Samuel heard God's voice, but he needed the old man Eli to help him hear it more clearly. How can we help the next generation hear the voice of God?"
—David Kinnaman

"Be the person you needed when you were younger."
—Unknown

"Don't judge each day by the harvest you reap but by the seeds that you plant."
—Robert Louis Stevenson

My wife, Candy, and I enjoy being outdoors and hiking in the mountains, so for many years we hoped to visit Glacier National Park in Montana. The pandemic delayed our plans, but finally in 2021 we made the trip and visited the park. A friend suggested we should hike to a place called Avalanche Lake. We asked a park ranger about hiking to the lake, and he told us, "Altogether, it's about six miles—three miles up and three miles back." That didn't sound too bad, except for the part about *three miles up*. It's not hard for us to walk six miles on a flat trail, but the path uphill turned out to be a lot steeper than we expected.

Several times along the way, we thought about turning back. An interesting thing happened, though. Other hikers on their way back down the trail kept offering words of encouragement. They said things like, "You're halfway there." "You can do it." "Don't give up." "It's worth it when you get to the top." "You're just a few minutes away. It's right around the bend."

If not for the encouragement we received from the hikers ahead of us, we wouldn't have kept going. But when we finally made it to the top, we enjoyed the breathtaking view of mountains reflecting like a mirror on beautiful Avalanche Lake. It was breathtaking in a different way, too, because we were out of breath from the climb!

After savoring the view for a few minutes, it was time to head back to our car. But as Candy and I trekked back down the trail, we experienced an interesting role-reversal. Now, when we saw exhausted hikers coming up the hill, we were the ones encouraging them, just as others had done for us. We told the weary walkers, "Don't give up. You're almost there. It's worth it when you get to the top!"

Isn't that what the church should be like? I believe the Lord designed the church to be an intergenerational family where those who already have walked a little farther up the hill can encourage the others coming along behind them.

The problem is, a different vision of God's kingdom has surfaced in the American church. Many Christians are trying to climb up the mountain on their own, without connecting with others. And our vision tends to be limited to our own generation.

It grieves me when older Christians criticize the younger generation as lazy, self-centered, and lacking in spiritual maturity. (Many of us older believers struggle with those same flaws.) Likewise, it grieves me to see faithful senior adults treated like second-class citizens in the body of Christ. The Lord didn't say, "Go and make disciples of all nations—but only present the gospel to age-groups you easily identify with." When Jesus looked upon the multitudes and saw the harassed and helpless throngs, the Gospel writer didn't specify whether the individuals in the crowd were teenaged, middle-aged, or old aged. My guess is, all of those age-groups were represented, for every generation contains weary souls who are like sheep without a shepherd.

We naturally gravitate toward others with whom we have a lot in common and connect with people in our own age-groups. When I was a boy, I wanted to be outdoors playing softball or indoors playing basketball with friends my age. I couldn't understand why my parents and grandparents spent so much time talking about topics that seemed boring to me, like the weather, health problems, and the national news. It makes sense for churches to have classes, groups, and special events focused on the needs and interests of young children, students, single adults, married couples, senior adults, and others. But not only is there room in the Lord's church for all age-groups; I am convinced the church is healthier and higher functioning when it includes and intentionally engages with a variety of generations.

Haydn Shaw, an expert on different generations, categorizes the different age-groups as follows[1]:

> *TRADITIONALISTS (also known as BUILDERS): Born 1945 and before.* (That is my parents' generation. They lived through the Depression and World War II.)
>
> *BOOMERS: Born between 1946 and 1964.* (I was born in 1954, right in the middle of this generation. We Boomers grew up influenced by the Beatles and the Vietnam War.)
>
> *GEN XERS (also known as BABY BUSTERS or the LATCHKEY GENERATION): Born between 1965 and 1980.* (They saw the fall of the Berlin Wall and the birth of the personal computer.)
>
> *MILLENNIALS (also known as GENERATION Y): Born between 1981 and 2000.* (They are digital natives, for they grew up in a time marked by elevated usage of the internet, mobile devices, and social media. My adult children belong to the Gen X and Millennial generations.)
>
> *YOUNGER MILLENNIALS (also nicknamed GENERATION Z and the BRIDGERS): Born since 2000.* (My grandchildren belong to this generation.) It's widely reported that members of Gen Z struggle with heightened levels of anxiety. A Stanford University study found that a typical Gen Zer "is a self-driver who deeply cares about others, strives for a diverse community, is highly collaborative and social, values flexibility, relevance, authenticity, and non-hierarchical leadership."[2]

The Lord's church includes all five of these generations, and generational differences cause friction because our experiences are so different. How can a young person who wasn't born yet when 9/11 happened in 2001 relate to someone from the Builder generation raised during the Great Depression and World War II? How can Gen Xers and Millennials relate to older people who struggle with (and complain about) technology that younger people take for granted? How can we fulfill the vision of Psalm 78:4, which declares, "We will tell the next generation the praiseworthy deeds of the Lord"?

Eight Benefits of Intergenerational Churches

To be fair, some churches struggle to connect with different age groups because they are limited by demographics. One Sunday I served as a guest preacher for a congregation in Florida located in a region almost entirely populated by senior adults. After preaching for the growing church's three services, I was heading back to the airport in my rental car when it dawned on me that I had not seen anyone at worship that morning who appeared to be under the age of 55!

On the other hand, there are places where youth far outnumber the older population. In my thirties, I served on a church-planting team that established a new congregation in an urban area near the University of Cincinnati. The vast majority of people who attended our worship services were college students, along with a smattering of local residents. Naturally, we tailored our ministry efforts to meet the needs of young adults, including international students from other nations who were studying at the university. To effectively reach diverse communities with the gospel, churches must target their ministries toward the people who live there. That is just common sense. But eventually a church that focuses only on the under-30 crowd will face an interesting dilemma: What will happen when their current members grow older?

In the American church we must do more to bring different age-groups together. Churches that decide to reach across the generational divide and bring people of different ages together will face many challenges, but they also will experience great blessings. Before listing eight benefits of such churches, I want to make a small but significant distinction between the words *multigenerational* and *intergenerational.* A congregation could have multiple generations in its membership, yet those different age-groups seldom interact. If the older members isolate themselves in their own classrooms while the students stay in another part of the church building, the church might be *multigenerational* but it hardly qualifies as *intergenerational*. In my view, a truly *intergenerational* church is one that makes intentional, prolonged efforts to engage different age-groups in mission and ministry, worship and prayer, service and outreach. Ideally, in a community where a variety of age-groups are represented in the population, it is possible and desirable for a church to be both *multigenerational* and *intergenerational*.

Think about the span of care in your church. In the congregation where I serve, East 91st Street Christian Church in Indianapolis, our span of care literally extends for a full century—from age 0 to age 100—from tiny babies in the nursery to aging saints approaching the century mark. What other organization on earth has such a wide reach as the kingdom of God? If you go to a football game, you will see young and old fans. But where else but in the church can you see different generations sharing a common mission and serving together week after week, year after year?

Things are more complicated when different generations worship and serve together, but the blessings are worth the effort. We naturally connect with people our own age, so we need to take deliberate steps to widen the circle. Here are eight benefits of including, valuing, and engaging all generations in the Lord's church.

1. ***An intergenerational community reflects the mindset of the Israelites in the Old Testament.*** It's hard to think of the patriarchs Abraham, Isaac, and Jacob apart from each other. We often say their names together: "Abraham, Isaac, and Jacob." These imperfect individuals successfully transferred their faith in God from generation to generation. In fact, that may have been their most significant accomplishment! Hebrews 11:20 eloquently says, "By faith Isaac blessed Jacob and Esau in regard to their future." Don't you want to be like Isaac and bless the next generation "in regard to their future"?

Passing along God's truth was an intergenerational task for the Israelites. The psalmist wrote, "We will tell the next generation the praiseworthy deeds of the Lord, his power, and the wonders he has done . . . so the next generation would know them, even the children yet to be born, and they in turn would tell their children. Then they would put their trust in God . . ." (Psalm 78:4, 6-7). This intergenerational passing of the torch didn't happen in a vacuum. It happened because parents and grandparents talked with their kids amid the normal interactions of daily life—when they sat at home, walked along the road, tucked their kids into bed at night, and got up in the morning to face a new day (see Deuteronomy 6:4-9). It happened on special occasions like the Feasts of Passover and Tabernacles when families traveled to Jerusalem together for memorable times of worship and celebration. It happened when young people overheard the elders' conversations at the city gates, and when youngsters like 12-year-old Jesus sat among the teachers, listening and asking questions in the temple (Luke 2:46-47).

2. *An intergenerational congregation follows the example of the New Testament church.* On the Day of Pentecost, the apostle Peter told the gathered crowd to repent and be baptized for the forgiveness of sins and they would receive the gift of the Holy Spirit—and this promise, he told them, "is for you and your children and for all who are far off—for all whom the Lord our God will call" (Acts 2:38-39). The gospel is not only for us, but also for our children and for those who follow after them.

In biblical times, several generations often lived together in the same home. Grandpa and Grandma lived right there in the house with the kids, or they lived nearby. The early Christians often met together in homes where the old and young ate, served, learned, and worshipped together. The households of Cornelius, the Philippian jailor, and others believed in Christ and were baptized as a family, which presumably means parents, their believing children, and perhaps servants or others connected to their families were included in these household conversions. (See Acts 10:24, 48; 16:31-34; and 1 Corinthians 1:16.)

An intergenerational prayer gathering took place after the apostle Paul met with the elders of the church in Ephesus. The inspired writer Luke, who accompanied Paul, wrote that as they prepared to say goodbye to Paul, "all of them, including wives and children, accompanied us out of the city, and there on the beach we knelt to pray" (Acts 21:5). The elders and their kids—all those moms and dads—everyone had sand on their knees after praying together on the beach!

Paul envisioned the church as an intergenerational body. Remember how he told Timothy not to let anyone look down on him for being young? I used to read the verse and think, "Yeah, you older folk shouldn't look down on me." But now I am in the season of life when I need to be warned not to look down on those younger than I am! Paul not only instructed Timothy to "set an example for the believers in speech, in conduct, in love, in faith and in purity," he also cautioned him not to treat older folk harshly, but to view them with respect as spiritual moms and dads (see 1 Timothy 4:12; 5:1-2).

3. *An intergenerational church creates multiple opportunities to practice the Golden Rule.* Jesus taught, "Do to others what you would have them do to you" (Matthew 7:12). When different age-groups worship and serve together, they are more likely to ask questions like, "How will I want to be treated when I am old?" and "How did I want to be treated when I was young?"

4. *An intergenerational church illustrates how Jesus Christ is the same "yesterday, today, and tomorrow" (Hebrews 13:8).* Should the church think about the past or focus on the future? That question presents a false choice, for the answer ought to be "both." If we forget about the past, we will repeat terrible mistakes and fail to learn from previous generations. But if we focus only on the past, we will not move forward in faith and embrace positive change. Our eternal God is the Lord of the past, the present, and the future. He is the God of Abraham, Isaac, and Jacob—and I want him to be the God of my great-grandchildren, too. Healthy churches remember what the Lord has done in the days gone by, while faithfully pursuing what still lies ahead.

5. *An intergenerational approach to ministry opens doors for outreach and evangelism.* In most communities today, you can find unsaved, unreached, unchurched people who need Christ among all generations. If you haven't already done so, I encourage you to take a close look at the demographics of your local area, perhaps within a one-mile, five-mile, and 10-mile radius of your church's meeting place. (Demographic data for most American communities are available online, from market research firms, and in public

libraries.) We must be careful not to overlook reachable groups of people within our circles of influence.

6. *An intergenerational church demonstrates God's love for all people.* We live in an increasingly polarized world where individuals made in God's image are separated by politics, ideology, and race. By contrast, the Bible casts a different vision when it says, "So in Christ Jesus you are all children of God through faith, for all of you who were baptized into Christ have clothed yourselves with Christ. There is neither Jew nor Gentile, neither slave nor free, nor is there male and female, for you are all one in Christ Jesus" (Galatians 3:26-28). It says something powerful to a watching world when young children from a Sunday school class visit shut-in senior adults, or when older Christians become prayer partners with high school students in the youth group.

7. *An intergenerational church provides opportunities for all ages to engage in ministry and mission together.* The church is supposed to be a lifeboat, not a cruise ship. We are on a rescue mission, not a pleasure cruise. On a cruise ship, you coast along, feast on the food, and enjoy the entertainment. Everything that happens on a cruise ship is designed to create an enjoyable experience for the passengers. But a lifeboat isn't for entertainment. On a lifeboat, your goal is to rescue as many people as you can. On a lifeboat, everything you do is geared toward saving others.

In intergenerational churches, people of different ages share in activities like these:

- Mission trips where volunteers from different generations travel and serve together.

- Workdays where teenagers sweat and serve alongside senior adults, painting walls, spreading mulch, and trimming hedges to beautify the church grounds.

- Worship services where people with gray hair sing and praise God along with younger believers.

- Baptisms where parents baptize their children (or vice versa) and grandparents baptize their grandchildren (or vice versa).

- Fund-raising campaigns for benevolence, building, or mission projects that invite (and expect) different generations to participate by giving according to their means. When our church raised funds to pay off the mortgage on our property, we intentionally included a teen leader on the planning team, one of our young adults served as a co-chair of the team, and we placed a coin collection bin in the children's ministry area so the kids could contribute, too. Future generations will benefit from having a paid-off facility, so why not invite them to share in raising the funds so they can learn the joy of giving? And speaking of money . . .

8. ***An intergenerational approach to ministry opens avenues for financial support of the Lord's work.*** Sadly, I have known situations where church leaders paid little or no attention to their older members— until it was time to ask for money to fund the church's programs. It is shortsighted to overlook the giving capacity of the older generation. According to one estimate, in many churches, 70 percent of the money comes from donors over age 70.[3] Of course, this doesn't mean the folks with money should be allowed to solely determine the church's direction. (Have you heard the twisted version of the Golden Rule that says, "Those who have the gold make the rules"?) No, churches shouldn't bend to the whims of potential donors. But does it make sense to ignore the spiritual needs and concerns of older Christians while expecting them to support leaders who consistently neglect or offend them? Wise leaders build trust across generational lines, so when it is time for the congregation to give, generosity is a natural and cheerful response.

Psalm 100:3 says, "We are his people, the sheep of his pasture." Some of God's sheep are young lambs, and some of us are old with thick, heavy wool, but we all need the Lord as our shepherd. This is not a time to "put senior adults out to pasture" as if they are unimportant and have nothing to offer. This is a time to deploy senior adults in God's service.

WHAT DOES IT MEAN TO BE PART OF THE CHURCH?

The word translated "church" in the New Testament is the Greek term *ekklesia* (*ek*, meaning "out"; plus *klesia*, meaning "called"). The church isn't a physical building. It's the assembled, chosen people of God who are called out from the world to go out to the world.

The church is far more than a mere human institution. It is the Lord's idea and it belongs to him, for Jesus promised, "I will build my church" (Matthew 16:18). The Bible compares Christ's love for the church to the way a groom loves his bride (Ephesians 5:25-30). The church is Christ's body (Ephesians 1:22-23; 1 Corinthians 12:27) and the household or family of God (1 Timothy 3:15; compare Mark 3:33-35).

If you have placed your faith in Christ and have been baptized into him—that is, if you are a disciple (devoted follower) of Christ—you belong to his church. You are a "living stone" in a spiritual house where the Lord lives (1 Corinthians 3:16; 1 Peter 2:4-8). Some stones in God's dwelling-place are shiny new Christ followers while some of us long-term disciples look a bit weathered and worn. But by God's grace we all belong to a church that is gloriously multigenerational by design. "To him be glory in the church and in Christ Jesus throughout all generations, for ever and ever! Amen" (Ephesians 3:21, emphasis added).

A healthy church helps you discover your authentic identity in Christ. You are "a chosen people, a royal priesthood, a holy nation, God's special possession, that you may declare the praises of him who called you out of darkness into his wonderful light. Once you were not a people, but now you are the people of God; once you had not received mercy, but now you have received mercy" (1 Peter 2:9-10).

What does a healthy church look like? Acts 2:42 gives us one example: "They devoted themselves to the apostles' teaching and to fellowship, to the breaking of bread and to prayer." And Acts 9:31 paints a beautiful portrait when it says, "Then the church . . . enjoyed a time of peace and was strengthened. Living in the fear of the Lord and encouraged by the Holy Spirit, it increased in numbers."

What Should the Church Do for Older Adults?

Older people need the same things everyone else does.

Love them. If you are young, ask yourself, "How will I want to be treated when I am in my sixties, seventies, or eighties?"

Disciple them. Jesus' command to "make disciples of all nations" includes older adults. The word *disciple* appears 269 times in the New Testament. It is both a noun (Greek *mathetes*) and a verb (*matheteuo*). The noun form appears in Matthew 28:16, where the disciples met Jesus and received the Great Commission. The verb form appears three verses later when Jesus says to "go and make disciples of all nations, baptizing . . . and teaching them" (Matthew 28:19-20). It is accurate to say, "The New Testament is a book about disciples, by disciples, and for disciples of Jesus Christ."[4]

Making disciples means persuading our families and friends to follow Christ, learn from him, serve him, and be apprenticed to him for life. It means growing together, "admonishing and teaching everyone with all wisdom, so that we may present everyone fully mature in Christ" (Colossians 1:28). We don't outgrow our need for discipleship just because we are older.

Dietrich Bonhoeffer's 1937 book, *The Cost of Discipleship,* challenged the concept of "cheap grace" and emphasized Jesus' call to complete and costly surrender. But author Dallas Willard pointed out that "the cost of nondiscipleship is far greater . . . than the price paid to walk with Jesus." Willard observed, "Nondiscipleship costs abiding peace, a life penetrated throughout by love, faith that sees everything in the light of God's overriding governance for good, hopefulness that stands firm in the most discouraging of circumstances, power to do what is right and withstand the forces of evil. In short, it costs exactly that abundance of life Jesus said he came to bring (John 10:10)."[5]

If church membership means little more than showing up for an hour on Sunday, listening passively to the sermon, and dropping a few dollars into the offering, it is no wonder many churches are withering on the vine. Older adults need to be involved in one-on-one and small-group discipleship. Our later years will be greater years if we pour ourselves into relationships that nurture faith, reinforce biblical values, and model obedient service to the Lord.

Engage them in service. By the time George Plimpton died at age 76, he had experienced an amazing variety of adventures. He believed a writer must get personally involved with his subject—not merely observe it—to know it well. Plimpton called himself a "participatory journalist." He boxed against Sugar Ray Robinson and got his nose bloodied by champion boxer Archie Moore. (It hurt so much that Plimpton cried.) He trained with the Detroit Lions football team in 1963 and wrote *Paper Lion,* a book based on that experience. Arnold Palmer and Jack Nicklaus easily defeated him in golf, and Pancho Gonzalez beat him in tennis. He pitched less than one inning of an exhibition baseball game between the National and American League All-Stars before leaving the mound exhausted. He performed on a circus trapeze and played several cameo roles in movies. Plimpton wasn't a great athlete or actor, but you have to admire him for getting involved in the stories he wrote about.

We could use more "participatory Christians" in the church. The Bible says, "Each of you should use whatever gift you have received to serve others, as faithful stewards of God's grace in its various forms" (1 Peter 4:10). The ministry of all believers is more than a theoretical principle; it is a dynamic strategy for expanding God's kingdom. Older believers need to be participatory Christians who don't merely listen and observe, but who get down on the playing field where the action is.

Listen to them. Don't cater to senior adults' whims, but pay attention to their wisdom.

In some churches older people have earned a reputation as the group that mainly whines and complains. Sadly, in some cases this reputation is well-deserved. Some older believers are never satisfied. They nitpick at picnics, fill the ministry staff's email boxes with petty criticism, and create the impression that instead of trying to worship in spirit and truth, they are more interested in complaining because the music is too loud. I don't want to be that kind of older Christian, and I don't think you do, either. But sometimes what young leaders interpret as grumbling or a negative attitude is actually a cry of pain from older Christians who genuinely love the Lord, love their church, love their ministry leaders, and welcome positive change—but they wish someone would truly care about them and listen to them with gentleness and respect.

Wise leaders keep the lines of communication open and seek the counsel of mature believers who have the best interests of the church at heart.

What Should Older Adults Do for the Church?

Listen to and learn from the younger generation. Yes, older people have wisdom to share; but it works the other way as well. Timothy was a young preacher, but the older members of the church needed to respect him, not denigrate him for being young. They needed to learn from his Christlike example and listen carefully as he taught them the Scriptures (1 Timothy 4:11-16). People who know and obey God's Word have valuable insights to share, no matter how young or old they happen to be. Psalm 119:100 says, "I have more understanding than the elders, for I obey your precepts."

As one of the oldest full-time staff members at East 91st Street Christian Church, I work on a regular basis with other leaders and volunteers who are years (or even decades) younger than I am. I hope they learn some things from me, but I certainly learn a lot from them!

Our creative arts pastor, Josh Mathews, is in his twenties. He and I meet frequently to discuss, plan, and lead the church's worship services. Josh and I have become good friends, and I learn a lot from him. It makes us chuckle when the two of us meet and he has all his notes on a cellphone or a laptop, while I hold an old clipboard and a pen in my hands.

At one of our meetings, we discussed how much light should be in the room when the congregation meets for worship. I explained that many older believers prefer brighter lights so we can see what is happening. "Light is cheerful," I said as I pressed my case, "and it helps you to see your Bible and see the other people in the room." Nailing down my argument, I said, "And theologically, we know Jesus is the light of the world."

Josh listened patiently, but then he offered a different perspective. From his point of view, a brightly-lighted room may create unnecessary distractions. He prefers to dim the lights during times that are more reflective or introspective and bring up the lights at times when we want to emphasize the corporate aspect of a worship gathering. Josh and I still don't fully agree on this point, but our conversations have deepened our friendship, led to better mutual understanding, and helped us do a better job leading as a team. Instead of making assumptions and letting our frustrations build up, we have come to appreciate each other's points of view.

Another time, Josh and I were discussing when the traditional candle-lighting and singing of "Silent Night" should happen during our Christmas Eve services. I offered my point of view: "Most of our older members prefer to close the service with 'Silent Night,' because holding our candles and singing that quiet song ends the service on a beautiful solemn note."

Josh looked puzzled. "It's Christmas Eve!" he exclaimed. "Why would we want to send people away sad? Wouldn't it be better to close the service with a cheerful, upbeat song like 'Joy to the World'?"

We had different understandings of the word *solemn*. That word makes me think of holy reverence and awe-inspiring moments when we seriously ponder the things of God. To Josh, however, *solemn* suggests something sad, depressing, stern, humorless, and gloomy. We decided to resolve our disagreement by looking up the word in the dictionary, but when we did so, we found both definitions are legitimate! In other words, there was some truth in both of our arguments.

Generational expert Haydn Shaw says, "To handle this new world, we need generational intelligence. The reason we struggle with other generations is not that they are 'the problem.' The reason we struggle with other generations is that we don't understand them. We don't know why they think differently, so we stereotype, criticize, or make jokes. But when we start to understand another generation—rather than attempting to maneuver others into seeing things our way—we open ourselves to new possibilities of relating, helping, reaching, encouraging, and loving them."[6]

HAVE YOU CALLED A TRUCE IN THE WORSHIP WARS?

Musical styles and preferences have torn apart churches far too long. Healthy intergenerational churches see worship as a lifestyle, not merely a Sunday morning event—and they find ways to bridge the gap so believers from different age groups can worship the same Lord. Here are some suggestions.

- Keep your primary worship audience in mind. It is misguided to think of the preacher and worship leader as the performers and the congregation as the audience. In true worship, the audience is the Lord and individual worshippers are the performers, praising God for his supreme "worth."

- Keep the whole spectrum of worship participants in mind. When congregations gather, there are new believers who need to be taught, equipped, encouraged, and uplifted; maturing believers who need to be challenged and deployed into service; and seekers and unbelievers who need to hear the gospel and learn what it means to love and follow Christ.

- Prioritize the church's mission over personal preferences, valuing unity over self-interest. Following Christ means making personal sacrifices for the sake of the body rather than having our own way.

- Expect, welcome, and plan for variety. Worship includes music, but it involves far more than that. Testimonies, videos, interviews, participatory prayer times, mission moments, uplifting offering times, thoughtfully prepared and well-presented Communion introductions, practical next steps for applying Scripture, and other creative elements bring freshness to services of any style. It is possible to "sing to the Lord a new song" (Psalm 96:1) while also valuing and incorporating time-honored "psalms, hymns, and songs from the Spirit" (Colossians 3:16) that link us to past generations of believers.

- Don't try to clone your congregation by imitating what trendy churches are doing. What works somewhere else may not fit your church well. Have the courage to prayerfully find your own unique sweet spot when it comes to worship style. Don't just copy other churches. Ask the Lord to help the members of your congregation be your best selves as you praise and worship him together.

Speak well of others. Don't be the kind of senior adult who is always griping, grumbling, and spreading negative talk. First Thessalonians 5:11 exhorts us to "encourage one another and build each other up." Instead of tearing down other generations, we need to speak uplifting words. Empathize more than we criticize. Listen more than we lecture.

The apostle Paul described his young friend Titus to others with glowing terms like *enthusiasm, initiative, partner,* and *co-worker.* He called young friends "representatives of the churches and an honor to Christ" (2 Corinthians 8:16-24). He considered Timothy and Titus his "dear [true] sons" in the faith (2 Timothy 1:2; 2:1; Titus 1:4). We older adults need to speak positively about younger Christians whenever we can and cultivate the habit of encouragement. Let's be "balcony people" who uplift and cheer on the next generation, not "basement people" who drag them down.

Mentor someone. Leadership coach John Maxwell says, "Many people go far in life because someone else thought they would." Many young adults would appreciate having older Christians who take a personal interest in them and make themselves available for consultation, coaching, and encouragement. The website mentoringgroup.com contains articles and practical suggestions about mentoring. Pastor and author Wayne Cordeiro says, "We teach what we know, but we reproduce what we are." Character development and practical leadership skills transfer best in high-trust relationships marked by candid communication and regular interaction. Cordeiro reminds us, "You don't dim the light of your own candle by lighting the candle of another."

Generational expert Haydn Shaw states:

> One of the beautiful things about the Millennials is that they really want to know what older generations think, and how they've sorted things through. So this is a match made in heaven. You've got older people who are living longer and want to know how to make an impact in their retirement. You've got younger people who are wanting somebody in addition to their parents that they can go to, and think out loud with, and sort through all the new choices that previous generations didn't have and didn't have to make.[7]

Engage in "culinary diplomacy." This phrase has been used to describe how government officials from different nations and cultures exchange ideas and learn to get along. Culinary diplomacy happens when a president or ambassador hosts a state dinner for another head of state or diplomats from another country. Government officials understand it is easier for people to open up and talk when they share a common meal. I learned the same lesson as a parent. The times my children were likely to open up and talk were late at night when they (and I!) were very tired, and over meals when we relaxed and ate together. If you are an older adult who wants to connect with younger people, try some culinary diplomacy! Invite your church's student ministry leaders out to lunch and ask how you can help them and pray for them. Host a pizza party for the church's middle schoolers at your home or at the church building. Invite some young adults over for dessert and coffee and spend the evening in conversation. Intergenerational ministry doesn't happen without taking intentional steps to connect. Eating together is a great place to start.

Pass the baton. As senior adults, we now find we are older than the heroes and authority figures we once so admired and looked up to when we were youngsters. Schoolteachers and police officers used to seem so old. When I was a boy, professional baseball players seemed larger than life; but now, I have grandchildren the age of Major League ballplayers. It seems a bit strange to trust my health to doctors half my age—but I do. And what about the ministers who lead our churches? A woman in her fifties told me, "My church has gone through a leadership transition. The preacher who led our church for decades used to be like everyone's dad or grandpa. Now our new young preacher is like our son." Transitions are inevitable. One challenge of senior adulthood is how to prepare, accept, encourage, and follow the next generation of leaders.

Like runners in a relay race, older Christians must pass the baton of faith, service, and leadership to our younger teammates so they can run the next leg of the race. A favorite Scripture of mine is 2 Timothy 2:2, where the apostle Paul says, "And the things you have heard me say in the presence of many witnesses entrust to reliable people who will also be qualified to teach others." G. K. Chesterton said, "The true soldier fights not because he hates what is in front of him, but because he loves what is behind him." Love motivates us to equip the next generation. Who will carry on the Lord's work after you and I have finished the race? Who are we preparing to succeed us?

In their book *Growing Young,* authors Kara Powell, Jake Mulder, and Brad Griffin talk about what they call "keychain leadership." They point out, "Whoever holds the keys has the power to let people in or to keep people out. Keys provide access to physical rooms, as well as to strategic meetings, significant decisions, and central roles or places of authority. The more power you have, the more keys you tend to possess." Keychain leaders are those who are "acutely aware of the keys on their keychain, and intentional about entrusting and empowering all generations, including teenagers and emerging adults, with their own set of keys."[8]

Be firm about what matters most, but be flexible where you can. Jesus was full of both grace and truth (John 1:14). Christians need to stand solidly on the truth of Scripture while showing lots of grace to others and being flexible about our personal preferences. This balance can be difficult to find at any age, but older believers need to be especially careful not to abandon the core doctrines of our faith. On the other hand, neither should we become rigid, legalistic, and inflexible about our opinions. It has been said, "Methods are many, doctrines are few. Methods always change, doctrines never do."

I have spoken at a church in Katy, Texas, called "Current—A Christian Church." The name "Current" applies to the church for several reasons. Something is *current* if it's happening now, and my friends in Texas want people to know the church is relevant and God's Word still applies today. *Current* also refers to the way wind, water, and electricity are always moving. Our relationship with the Lord should never stagnate, but always keep us moving toward growth and vitality. And our faith should flow toward others as a witness of the transforming power of Jesus. As a visual example, the front of the Current church's property contains a beautiful plaza with the cross as its centerpiece. A water feature bubbles up from the rock formation at the base of the cross. The water winds around the plaza, flowing out toward the community. Whether we are young or old, we all are part of the "current" generation. We can stay anchored to the Rock, with Jesus' sacrifice on the cross at the center of our faith. Our faith can be alive and vibrant, flowing outwardly to those who need the Lord.

Candy and I once visited Mount Sinai. We hiked up the mountainside on a Sunday afternoon and arrived at the top while there was still just enough daylight to read the Ten Commandments before the sun set. Our tour group included people in their twenties and thirties, and some in their seventies and eighties, but we all climbed the mountain together.

Whether we are young or old, Jesus invites us, "Come, follow me." Let's climb the mountain together.

QUESTIONS FOR PERSONAL REFLECTION AND GROUP DISCUSSION

1. Does your circle of friends include people from different age groups? If not, what could you do to cultivate relationships with individuals who are younger and older than you are? Suggestions:

   • Eat a meal or have coffee together.

   • Ask each other questions like, *What stresses you out? What gives you joy? What worries you about the future? What are you looking forward to in the years ahead?* Look for things you have in common, as well as areas where you have different points of view.

   • Talk about what you believe. Discuss your faith in the Lord and what it means to follow Christ in today's cultural environment.

   • Share favorite Scripture verses with each other and explain why you appreciate these texts.

2. Ponder the apostle Paul's instructions recorded in Titus 2:2-6. What does this text tell you about what older and younger people can learn from each other? If you were writing a letter to young church leaders today, what would you tell them about how different generations should interact?

3. How well do you think the church you attend (or other churches you know) value and include senior adults? What step(s) could you take to help senior adults engage in a more positive way as members of the body of Christ?

11 | You Can't Take it with You— So What Should You Do with It?— Money Management for Older Adults

*"Fortune cookies do not have money in them,
making them the most disappointingly named cookies ever."*
—Unknown

*"Money may be the husk of many things, but not the kernel.
It brings you food but not appetite; medicine but not health;
acquaintances but not friends; servants but not faithfulness;
days of joy but not peace or happiness."*
—Henrik Ibsen

"We make a living by what we get, but we make a life by what we give."
—Unknown

On average, here is what things cost in the year I was born (1954):
        House: $8,650
        Ford car: Between $1,548 and $2,415
        Milk: 92 cents per gallon
        Gasoline: 21 cents per gallon
        Bread: 17 cents per loaf
        Postage stamp: 3 cents
        T-bone steak: 95 cents per pound[1]

Ah, how things have changed. Today, buyers pay as much for a new car as I paid for my first house.

But prices aren't the only things that change. Money changes people, too It can be a tool for good, but if we're not careful, it also can become a substitute for God.

As we grow older, the unbridled pursuit of money can lead to greed, frustration, and disillusionment. You can drive a nice car and live in a full house and still have an empty heart. In their book, *God and Money: How We Discovered True Riches at Harvard Business School,* authors John Cortines and Gregory Baumer write, "Wealth is like dynamite, with great potential for both good and harm."

King Solomon lived in a palace, but he discovered earthly possessions are fleeting and do not satisfy a person's soul. He advised, "Do not wear yourself out to get rich; do not trust your own cleverness. Cast but a glance at riches, and they are gone, for they will surely sprout wings and fly off to the sky like an eagle" (Proverbs 23:4-5). Jesus warned, "You cannot serve both God and money" (Matthew 6:24). According to Benjamin Franklin, "Money has never made man happy, nor will it, for there is nothing in its nature to produce happiness. The more of it one has, the more one wants."

But we can't avoid thinking about money, and as we age, worries tend to cross our minds. Do you ever find yourself pondering questions like these?

- How can I have financial security when the global economy seems so unstable? What about the soaring national debt and never-ending inflation?

- Medical care and nursing care are expensive. How can I afford them while living on a fixed income?

- How long should I keep working full-time or part-time? Have I saved enough money to pay my bills after I retire?

- In the future, how can I avoid being a financial burden to my children?

I am not an economist, but Candy and I have learned a lot of practical lessons about money during our half century of marriage. Looking back, we recognize several things we should have done differently. For example,

I wish we had found a financial advisor early in our marriage—a high-integrity individual filled with godly wisdom who has the heart of a teacher. We didn't think much about money in our early years of marriage because we didn't have much money to think about! I earned a modest salary from my work as a minister and Candy supplemented our income by babysitting and cleaning houses (while caring for our three children and serving alongside me in ministry). We did the best we could, but we had no financial strategy to guide us. By God's grace we kept our bills paid, bought a small life insurance policy, and eventually started making modest investments in a retirement account. It wasn't until much later in our marriage that we found a professional financial planner who has become a trusted friend, helping to guide us through the financial wilderness.

Unless you are uniquely gifted in handling money, I suggest you find a skilled, capable, trustworthy advisor who can help you make the most of your finances.

Money alone isn't the key to a happy life, but wise financial management can help to turn your later years into greater years.

In this chapter, I want to highlight four foundational money management principles that are relevant at any age, but they are especially important during the final third of your life. You are not too old to learn something new about finances. You can't take it with you, so what should you do with it?

The first step is to thank God for what you have.

Gratitude

I realize this might seem like a strange place to start. Money management is about hard numbers, right? Spread sheets. Profit and loss ratios. Cost of living increases. Tax rates, interest rates, and inflation rates. Stocks and bonds, and real estate investments.

By contrast, *gratitude* sounds like a soft word. It brings to mind Thanksgiving dinners with turkey, mashed potatoes, and pumpkin pie—not real-world stuff like bank accounts and retirement portfolios. The truth is, though, a grateful heart is "real-world stuff." In fact, as you grow older, a grateful heart will prove to be more important than your bank balance.

Why does the Bible say to "give thanks in all circumstances" (1 Thessalonians 5:18)? Why does it say to present your requests to God "with thanksgiving" (Philippians 4:6)? Why does it say, "And whatever you do, whether in word or deed, do it all in the name of the Lord Jesus, giving thanks to God the Father through him" (Colossians 3:17)? Gratitude is more than a nice little add-on in the Christian life. What if it's not a soft word after all? What if gratitude is actually a tough, gritty, real-world survival tool? Life isn't a playground; it's a battleground where we fight "against the powers of this dark world and against the spiritual forces of evil in the heavenly realms" (Ephesians 6:12). What if gratitude is actually one of our most powerful weapons to use in spiritual warfare?

Peter urged, "Be alert and of sober mind. Your enemy the devil prowls around like a roaring lion looking for someone to devour. Resist him, standing firm in the faith" (1 Peter 5:8-9). Gratitude is part of having an "alert" and "sober mind." A grateful heart will equip you to fight against complacency, for you won't take for granted what God has given you. It will shield you against jealousy and envy, for if you are grateful for your blessings, you will be less likely to covet what others have. It will help you fight off discouragement and focus on your joys rather than your worries. It will protect you against hopelessness and despair and help you recognize God's hand at work in your life.

Yet, gratitude is rare today. After eating a meal in a restaurant, I asked to speak to the manager, and the woman who had served our table looked nervous. Evidently, she thought I was going to register a complaint. But I reassured her and said, "I want to thank the manager for an excellent meal and compliment you for doing a great job." Sadly, in our culture we are conditioned to expect complaints, criticism, and negativity rather than appreciation.

Gratitude makes life more enjoyable. The actor Denzel Washington said, "Give thanks for your blessings every day. A bad attitude is like a flat tire. Until you change it, you're not going anywhere."

A friend of mine grew up as an orphan in a communist country. When she attended the Christian university where I worked, some students asked, "Do we *have to* go to chapel?" But this young woman enthusiastically exclaimed, "I'm so glad I *get to* go to chapel!"

Do you have a "get to" attitude? "Get to" is better than "have to." "Get to" nurtures gratitude; "have to" generates grumpiness. Reluctant workers crawl out of bed on Monday morning muttering, "I wish I didn't have to go to work." But considering the alternatives of being sick, injured, or unemployed, isn't it better to say, "Thank you, Lord, that I get to go to work today"?

Parenting young children is a difficult task, but dads and moms make it harder when they wallow in self-pity and tell themselves, "I have to cook dinner, pay the bills, drive the kids to school, and do the laundry." Joy increases if they remember to say, "Thank you, Lord, that I get to invest in the lives of my kids."

Do we *have to* pray? Actually, we *get to* pray. Does the Lord require his followers to be baptized? Yes, but it's not a burden; it is a joy to express our faith in baptism. Do we *have to* worship God? Actually, we *get to*! Do we *have to* give our tithes and offerings? We *get to*! Life is so much better if we serve the Lord with gladness.

In the aftermath of the Union Army victory at Gettysburg, President Abraham Lincoln announced that the nation would celebrate an official Thanksgiving holiday on November 26, 1863. Lincoln delivered his famous Gettysburg Address one week earlier, on Thursday, November 19, 1863. Ironically, the leader who helped to formalize America's Thanksgiving tradition fought clinical depression all his life. If Lincoln were running for office today, his moodiness would be considered a political liability. Yet his willingness to confront America's painful divisions equipped him to lead the nation through its darkest hours. Thanksgiving isn't just for the happy and the lighthearted; it is also for the depressed and the discouraged. Like Abraham Lincoln, even during our darkest hours we can find reasons for gratitude.

JESUS AND THANKSGIVING

Jesus taught by example what it means to "give thanks in all circumstances" (1 Thessalonians 5:18).

- He gave thanks during high-pressure ministry moments. Prior to feeding the 5,000, feeding the 4,000, and raising Lazarus from the dead, Jesus didn't beg for miraculous power; he calmly gave thanks in advance for the miracles before they occurred (Matthew 14:19; Mark 8:6; John 11:41-44).

- He gave thanks when facing imminent death. At the Last Supper, on the night before he died on the cross, he gave thanks for the bread and the cup as he celebrated the Passover Feast with his disciples (Matthew 26:26-27).

- He gave thanks again after rising back to life, as he broke bread with his followers (Luke 24:30).

An old song says, "count your many blessings," but we also should thank the Lord for our "mini blessings"—God's small gifts that are easy to overlook. Cold, clear water to drink. A good book to read—and eyes that see the words and minds that comprehend them. Nature's scenery to enjoy. Friends who encourage us and support us in prayer. The rich flavors and aromas of coffee and casseroles and cake, and the sweet sounds of laughter and friendly conversation.

Do you thank God for the fresh air that fills your lungs when you walk outdoors on a chilly morning? Do you thank him for the times when you made a mess of things, but he redeemed the situations anyway and used your mistakes to help you grow?

David prayed, "Many, Lord my God, are the wonders you have done, the things you planned for us. None can compare with you; were I to speak and tell of your deeds, they would be too many to declare" (Psalm 40:5). We can't literally count all our blessings, for there are too many of them to list. But with childlike awe, why not lift an eyelid and give it a try? Money management starts by thanking God for what we have.

PRACTICAL WAYS TO SHOW GRATITUDE

My friend Louie LaPlant shared these suggestions during a devotion he led for the elders at East 91st Street Christian Church.

- Keep a gratitude journal and write down what you are thankful for.
- Limit the amount of negative input you allow into your mind.
- Share your gratitude with others and thank them for acts of kindness large or small.
- Break the habit of grumbling and complaining.
- Start and end each day with a prayer of thanksgiving.
- Keep an eternal perspective and thank the Lord for handling the big picture with so much wisdom and grace.

Stewardship

Another key financial principle found in Scripture is the concept of stewardship. The biblical perspective on money starts with the fact that God owns it all. "The earth is the Lord's, and everything in it" (Psalm

24:1). According to Psalm 50:10-11, he owns "every animal in the forest," "the cattle on a thousand hills," and "the insects in the fields." (Yes, even those annoying mosquitoes belong to the Lord.)

Isn't it amazing that Almighty God would choose unmighty human beings as his business partners? That is exactly what he has done. The Great Commission (Matthew 28:18-20) reminds us that we are on a great "co-mission" with God! In awe, David asked the Lord, "What is mankind that you are mindful of them, human beings that you care for them?" He continued, "You made them rulers over the works of your hands; you put everything under their feet" (Psalm 8:4, 6). Paul wrote, "Now it is required that those who have been given a trust must prove faithful" (1 Corinthians 4:2). God has trusted us with time, talents, and treasure. Stewardship isn't just about money; it's about all of life. The whole universe belongs to God.

We are designed to be stewards (caretakers) of all he provides. We are not the owners; God is the owner and we are his property managers. This fact has practical implications for us as we grow older.

Anyone can open a can, but if you want to cook your own homemade soup, you need to be careful what you put into the pot first. As a novice soup-maker, I made a common mistake: I dumped all the ingredients into the kettle at the same time. After an hour of simmering, some items remained undercooked, while others were limp and overdone. Eventually I learned to start with the firmer items (potatoes, dry beans) and add the softer items (onions, celery, and seasoning) later in the process.

Soup isn't the only thing that turns out better if you start the process right. Wisdom means deciding what takes priority and doing that first. Before construction workers nail the first board, they study the blueprints. Before musicians play a song, they tune their instruments. Before an athletic contest begins, coaches draw up a game plan. Before farmers harvest their crops, they till the soil and plant their seed. When you put on a shirt and get the first button wrong, the rest of the buttons don't fasten correctly. Position the first button correctly, and the rest of them fall into place.

What comes first in your life? Jesus said to "seek first his kingdom and his righteousness," not your own self-interest or your own righteousness, and he added that when your priorities are right, "all these things" (including your physical, earthly needs) "will be given to you as well" (Matthew 6:33). God's kingdom and his righteousness deserve top priority.

Luke 12 contains several other teachings of Jesus pertaining to stewardship.

- *Watch out for materialism—it's deadly.* "Be on your guard against all kinds of greed; life does not consist in an abundance of possessions" (v. 15).

- *Live by faith, not fear.* "Do not worry about your life, what you will eat; or about your body, what you will wear" (v. 22). "Do not be afraid, little flock, for your Father has been pleased to give you the kingdom" (v. 32).

- *Take your cues about money and possessions from God, not from the culture around you.* "For the pagan world runs after all such things, and your Father knows that you need them. But seek his kingdom, and these things will be given to you as well" (vv. 30-31).

- *Make giving a priority.* "Sell your possessions and give to the poor" (v. 33a).

- *Keep in mind God's priorities and the world's uncertainties.* "Provide purses for yourselves that will not wear out, a treasure in heaven that will never fail, where no thief comes near and no moth destroys" (v. 33b). The English preacher Charles Spurgeon wrote, "If we would remember that all the trees of earth are marked for the woodman's axe, we should not be so ready to build our nests in them."

Bob Russell tells the humorous story of a wealthy man who begged God to allow him to take his money with him when he died. He was so persistent that the Lord finally gave in and allowed him to bring along one sack of money, so the man liquidated all his assets and filled the sack with gold bars. When the fellow died, at heaven's gate Saint Peter examined his sack of gold, and then telephoned the Lord. "There's a guy here who insists you gave him permission to bring one sack with him," Peter reported, "but for the life of me, I can't figure out why he would want to bring pavement!"[2]

Heaven is so beautiful that the streets are paved with gold. Why should we put so much value on earthly wealth that pales in comparison?

Another money management principle to keep in mind as we grow older is contentment.

FINANCIAL WISDOM FROM THE BOOK OF PROVERBS

Times change, but wise financial principles apply in every generation. The ancient book of Proverbs contains tried-and-true money management methods that will help anyone who wants to make ends meet.

Save regularly. "Dishonest money dwindles away, but whoever gathers money little by little makes it grow" (Proverbs 13:11).

Work diligently. "All hard work brings a profit, but mere talk leads only to poverty" (14:23).

Spend prudently. The "wife of noble character" shows wisdom when she "considers a field and buys it; out of her earnings she plants a vineyard" (31:16).

Avoid unnecessary debt and unwise lending. "The rich rule over the poor, and the borrower is slave to the lender" (22:7; see also 11:15; 22:26-27).

Never acquire funds dishonestly. "A wicked person earns deceptive wages" (Proverbs 11:18; see also 28:6).

Make smart decisions. "The prudent give thought to their steps" (14:15).

Keep track of your property and take proper care of it. "Be sure you know the condition of your flocks, give careful attention to your herds" (27:23).

Give generously to honor God. "Honor the Lord with your wealth, with the firstfruits of all your crops" (3:9).

Give generously to help others. "The generous will themselves be blessed, for they share their food with the poor" (22:9).

Provide for the needs of your children and grandchildren. "A good person leaves an inheritance for their children's children, but a sinner's wealth is stored up for the righteous" (13:22).

Don't expect money to buy happiness. "Those who trust in their riches will fall, but the righteous will thrive like a green leaf" (11:28).

Trust God more than you trust your own ability to make and manage money. "Do not wear yourself out to get rich; do not trust your own cleverness" (23:4).

Contentment

Today we are bombarded by advertising strategically designed to fan the flames of discontent. The marketing industry studies our buying habits and generates profiles based on our online searches. Advertisers try to get us to purchase nicer cars, newer technology, and more fashionable clothes.

The Bible says, "Do everything without grumbling or arguing" (Philippians 2:14), but in today's world grumbling has become a way of life. Contentment goes against the grain, but it is a vital quality for anyone who wants to age well. Cranky old codgers become that way because they haven't learned how to find joy in simple things, and they have sought worldly possessions more than "the peace of God, which transcends all understanding" (Philippians 4:7).

George Vanderbilt spent a fortune and a good portion of his life building the Biltmore Estate near Asheville, North Carolina. Finished in 1895, his massive house and gardens are marvels of design. Tourists pay to see oversized rooms full of imported furnishings, walls covered in Spanish leather and gold leaf, a four-story high chandelier, a swimming pool, and a bowling alley in the basement. However, Vanderbilt died an untimely death in his early fifties and didn't get to enjoy the mansion in his twilight years.

In the 1700s, the Austrian royal family built Schonbrunn Palace in Vienna, a showplace still toured by visitors from around the world. When he was 6 years old, the musical prodigy Mozart performed in the parlor—one of the palace's 1,441 rooms! By contrast, the little palace I call home has no bowling alley in my basement. I won't live in a mansion till I get to heaven, but I don't feel shortchanged. Since I am a child of the King, my name is already on the deed for a heavenly estate. Meanwhile, God has given me more blessings than I can count.

My home has central air conditioning—a blessing even the palace in Vienna couldn't claim. No servants prepare my dinner, but the Austrian royal family would have envied the microwave oven that heats my meals, the refrigerator that preserves my food, and my computer that links me with people all over the world.

Discontent can arise from different sources. For me, the greater temptation has not been my desire to own things, but my drive to achieve things. My workaholic tendencies and my unhealthy drive for accomplishment pushed me toward chronic discontentment. I was trying to do lots of "good" things, but I wasn't enjoying the "best" things—peace with God and joy in the moment. Looking back, I realize the wisdom of this line from William Shakespeare: "Striving to better, oft we mar what's well."

Here are some things I have learned about contentment. As we grow older, we should ask God to help us . . .

- *Notice and appreciate simple joys.* Some of life's greatest blessings are the everyday ones we can see all around if we open our eyes: a hot shower, a soft bed, a delicious meal, a caring friend.

- *Eliminate "evil desires and greed, which is idolatry" (Colossians 3:5).* Greed is idolatry because it puts earthly things in the place only God should occupy.

- *Learn not to put too much faith in personal wealth.* John D. Rockefeller said, "The poorest man I know is the man who has nothing but money."

- *Tamp down the constant desire to have more, do more, achieve more, and experience more.* Thomas Fuller said, "Contentment consists not in adding more fuel, but in taking away some fire."

- *Refuse to accept the world's perspective that money is the key to happiness.* Ecclesiastes 5:10 warns, "Whoever loves money never has enough; whoever loves wealth is never satisfied with their income. This too is meaningless."

Here are some of my favorite Bible verses about contentment:

- "Better a little with the fear of the Lord than great wealth with turmoil. Better a small serving of vegetables with love than a fattened calf with hatred" (Proverbs 15:16-17).

- "Better a dry crust with peace and quiet than a house full of feasting, with strife" (Proverbs 17:1).

- "I have learned to be content whatever the circumstances. I know what it is to be in need, and I know what it is to have plenty. I have learned the secret of being content in any and every situation, whether well fed or hungry, whether living in plenty or in want. I can do all this through him who gives me strength" (Philippians 4:11-13).

- "But godliness with contentment is great gain. For we brought nothing into the world, and we can take nothing out of it. But if we have food and clothing, we will be content with that" (1 Timothy 6:6-8).

- "Keep your lives free from the love of money and be content with what you have, because God has said, 'Never will I leave you; never will I forsake you'" (Hebrews 13:5).

We have looked at the money management principles of gratitude, stewardship, and contentment. Now we come to another key principle, the one known as . . .

Generosity

In her novel, *Little Men*, one of Louisa May Alcott's characters says, "I've been so bothered with my property that I'm tired of it, and don't mean to save up any more, but give it away as I go along, and then nobody will envy me, or want to steal it, and I shan't be suspecting folks and worrying about my old cash." There comes a point in life when we don't need to save up any more, "but give it away as we go along."

Our English word *generous* comes from the same root as the words *genetics* and *genealogy*. God genetically designed us to be generous! God is the supreme giver, and we are created in his image. Every breath of air, every beat of our hearts, every morsel of food we enjoy—all are gifts of God.

Although we are designed to be generous, we tend to be selfish. My wife and I will be snuggled under warm blankets on a cold winter night, and suddenly we realize we didn't put the garbage out—and the garbage truck comes early the next morning. Someone needs to go out in the cold and put the garbage out. Why does something inside of me say, "*She* should be the one to do it"?

How can we learn to shun selfishness and embrace generosity? The answer is found in God's unmerited mercy and grace. "We love because he first loved us" (1 John 4:19). We give because he first gave to us. Giving is an act of worship. It's not just about money. It's about delighting the heart of God. After all the Lord has done for us, we want to give him joy. When the Israelites offered animals on the altar, those animal sacrifices foreshadowed the ultimate sacrifice when Jesus died on the cross for us. As someone has pointed out, "The smoke of the Old Testament sacrifices blows in the direction of Calvary."

When the Hebrews built the tabernacle, the people donated so much that Moses finally told them to stop giving (Exodus 36:6-7). When it was time to collect money to pay for the temple in Jerusalem, the people responded so generously that King David told the Lord, "But who am I, and who are my people, that we should be able to give as generously as this? Everything comes from you, and we have given you only what comes from your hand" (1 Chronicles 29:14). Giving is at the heart of the gospel. "For God so loved the world that he gave his one and only Son" (John 3:16).

In biblical terms, generosity means:

- Holding things loosely, not hoarding them (and hoarding—trying to hold onto our earthly possessions—is a particularly strong temptation as we grow older).

- Prioritizing heaven's treasures over earthly ones (and as we age, our true priorities tend to become clearer and can no longer be hidden).

- Sacrificing for others, not demanding what's ours.

But let's consider what generosity does *not* mean.

Generosity doesn't mean giving to impress others. Jesus said not to imitate the hypocrites who were virtue-signaling and trying to make themselves look good by making a public display of their donations (Matthew 6:2-4).

Generosity doesn't mean giving with a grudging attitude. Gifts should come from a willing, cheerful heart, not from a sense of obligation. "Each of you should give what you have decided in your heart to give, not reluctantly or under compulsion, for God loves a cheerful giver" (2 Corinthians 9:7).

Generosity doesn't mean giving so you will get in return. To be clear, giving does bring blessings. Jesus said, "It is more blessed to give than to receive" (Acts 20:35) and, "Give, and it will be given to you" (Luke 6:38). You truly can't outgive the Lord. "A generous person will prosper; whoever refreshes others will be refreshed" (Proverbs 11:25). But God is not a vending machine, where you put something in and expect something back in return. Our motives matter.

In Agatha Christie's novel, *The Mysterious Affair at Styles*, she described a woman named Emily who "was a selfish old woman in her way. She was very generous, but she always wanted a return. She never let people forget what she had done for them—and, that way she missed love." Is it possible to be generous, yet miss love? Yes! Even if you give all your possessions to help the poor, the gift means little if you don't offer it out of love (1 Corinthians 13:3). But if you give with pure motives, the Lord will bless you with what matters most—and what matters most doesn't necessarily have a dollar value assigned to it.

Generosity doesn't mean you never say "no" to a request. When James and John (and their mom!) asked Jesus for a favor, the Lord answered, "You don't know what you are asking" (Matthew 20:22). When a man who couldn't walk begged for money, Peter responded, "Silver and gold I do not have, but what I do have I give you" (Acts 3:6), for the man needed healing and hope more than he needed silver and gold. If a two-year-old asks for the car keys, you will say "no." Even God says "no" sometimes, especially if our main goal is simply to spend what we get on our pleasures (James 4:3). It's OK for you to have boundaries, too.

Generosity doesn't mean giving only when it's fun and exciting. Paul complimented some first-century Christians because, "In the midst of a very severe trial, their overflowing joy and their extreme poverty welled up in rich generosity. . . . they gave as much as they were able, and even beyond their ability. Entirely on their own, they urgently pleaded with us for the privilege of sharing in this service to the Lord's people" (2 Corinthians 8:2-4).

Giving should be a consistent way of life, not just something we do impulsively when the mood strikes. Some of the most generous and hospitable people I have ever met have limited incomes.

When Candy and I were newlyweds, we didn't have much money. I was a full-time student working part-time for a nonprofit ministry, and she was a server in a restaurant. We rolled up the quarters she earned from tips and used the coins to buy groceries. In spite of our limited resources, Candy insisted that we should tithe and give at least the first 10 percent of our earnings back to God. I'm embarrassed to admit it, but I hesitated. I didn't think we could afford it. But she was right. We needed to make giving a habit, even when it was difficult.

DON'T PUT YOUR HOPE IN MONEY!

"Command those who are rich in this present world not to be arrogant nor to put their hope in wealth, which is so uncertain, but to put their hope in God, who richly provides us with everything for our enjoyment. Command them to do good, to be rich in good deeds, and to be generous and willing to share" (1 Timothy 6:17-18).

The Bible encourages us to "excel in this grace of giving" (2 Corinthians 8:7). We shouldn't be sloppy or halfhearted about generosity. Here are seven points to keep in mind if you want to excel in giving as you grow older.

1. *Cultivate your love for God, and generosity will follow.* Give yourself "first of all to the Lord" (2 Corinthians 8:5) and generosity will be a joy, not a burden. Put him first and "honor the Lord with your wealth" (Proverbs 3:9-10).

2. *Make giving a healthy rhythm in your life.* Keep setting aside "a sum of money in keeping with your income" (1 Corinthians 16:2). Be consistent and intentional about it. Many believers find that tithing (described in Malachi 3:10) gives them a starting point for consistent giving. You simply decide that the first 10 percent of your income belongs to God, and then grow from there. In your later years, you may not be able to give at the same level you did when you earned a larger income; but you can still give with a cheerful heart. The depth of your commitment and the intent of your heart matter more than the amount you give. Jesus complimented a poor widow who gave sacrificially from her limited means (Mark 12:43-44).

3. *Include generosity in your long-range estate planning.* "Commit to the Lord whatever you do, and he will establish your plans" (Proverbs 16:3).

4. *Consider how you can bless your children and grandchildren financially—but do this wisely and prayerfully.* Give your kids too much, and you prevent them from learning responsibility. But the Bible does say, "A good person leaves an inheritance for their children's children" (Proverbs 13:22). To illustrate a point about his own apostleship, Paul stated

matter-of-factly, "After all, children should not have to save up for their parents, but parents for their children" (2 Corinthians 12:14).

5. *Consider the possibility that God might give you a special capacity to provide financial help to others.* In the body of Christ, the Lord gives his followers unique abilities for building up others. The list of spiritual gifts includes the gift of giving (Romans 12:8). Of course, every Christian should be a giver, just as every Christian should be hospitable—but some have a special aptitude for hospitality. Likewise, every Christian should be a giver—but some have extra resources to share and find extra joy in doing so. And by the way, if you have the gift of giving, it is likely you also have the gift of earning, so you have the means to give! The point is, God grants some believers an exceptional ability to bless others financially. If you have the gift of giving, I urge you to recognize, develop, and use it for God's glory.

6. *Remember that generosity isn't only about money; it also means sharing your time and your possessions.*

I have written this little reminder on the weekly "things-to-do" list I keep on my desk: "Interruptions are God's appointments." Yes, Jesus had boundaries. He often retreated from the crowds and found solitary places where he could pray. But when Jesus was "on," he shared his time generously. He was interrupted by little kids and their parents . . . by a centurion whose servant was sick . . . and by a woman who touched the hem of his garment so she could be healed. Jesus couldn't even *die* without being interrupted! The thief on the cross next to him asked him for a favor: "Remember me when you come into your kingdom" (Luke 23:42). Being like Christ means we must be willing to share time with others.

And when it comes to sharing your possessions, remember this example from the early church: "All the believers were one in heart and mind. . . . [and] they shared everything they had" (Acts 4:32). Do you have more items than you need in your closet or your garage? It's amazing how much we tend to accumulate as we grow older. While giving my garage a thorough cleaning, I found items I had forgotten I owned, including a set of golf clubs and some new never-used golf shoes (still in the box) someone gave me years ago. I had kept these items in my garage for years, even though I don't play golf! It was a joy and a relief to give them to someone who would use and enjoy them.

After years as a Bible teacher, I have accumulated more than 1,000 books. They fill the shelves of my office at work and my study at home. It's hard to get rid of them, because my books are like familiar friends to me. But now in my senior adult years, it is time to let go.

What could you give away that would be a blessing to someone else? If your family members and friends don't need your extra books, clothes, furniture, tools, vehicles, dishes, and sports equipment, there are ministries and nonprofit organizations in your local area that will gladly receive your donations. As someone has said, "Sharing what you have is greater than having what you have."

7. *Have fun with giving!* Some senior adults get a kick out of giving anonymous gifts that surprise and encourage the recipients, whether they are friends in need or missions and nonprofit ministries that could use some extra help. One grandmother told me about a creative approach she uses with Christmas presents for her grandchildren. She gives them cash to spend on themselves, but she also gives each grandchild an extra cash gift they can use to bless someone else.

When Mary broke "an alabaster jar of very expensive perfume, made of pure nard" and poured it onto Jesus' head, some observers called it wasteful. But Jesus commended her and said, "She has done a beautiful thing to me" (Mark 14:1-6; see also John 12:1-8).

"To me." She did it to Jesus and for Jesus. That's what makes generosity beautiful.

Whenever you go all out for the Lord, some observers won't understand. When I was a senior in high school, a guidance counselor warned me that if I went to Bible college, I would waste my life. I'm glad I ignored his advice. Do you know what is truly a waste? Hanging onto something you should give to honor Jesus!

The Lord said of his friend Mary, "She did what she could" (Mark 14:8). May the same be said of us all.

QUESTIONS FOR PERSONAL REFLECTION AND GROUP DISCUSSION

1. When you think about finances in your senior adult years, what is your biggest cause for concern?

    a. Having enough savings to do what I want to do (traveling, giving, spending time with grandchildren, etc.)

    b. Running out of money and becoming a financial burden to others.

    c. The escalating cost of living—keeping up with inflation.

    d. Paying for my health care.

    e. The possibility of having to move out of my house.

    f. Other:

2. How has your approach to earning, saving, spending, and giving changed with age—and how do you expect your approach might change again in the future?

3. Which of the four key concepts described in this chapter (gratitude, stewardship, contentment, and generosity) do you find most challenging? Why?

4. What step(s) can/should/will you take to improve the way you view or handle money?

12 | Old Friends, New Friends— Cultivating Lasting Relationships as You Age

"A friend is a gift you give yourself."
—Robert Louis Stevenson

"Make new friends, but keep the old.
Those are silver, these are gold."
—Joseph Parry

Leonard Sweet writes about a Northerner who traveled through West Virginia and stopped at a restaurant for breakfast. The server asked if he wanted grits, and the traveler said, "OK, I'll try one."

The server replied, "Honey, you can't get just one grit. Grits're like a community. They come in groups."[1]

We're all like grits. At every age, we need friends.

DON'T TRY TO LIVE AT POINT NEMO

Have you heard of Point Nemo? It is not well-known. And it has nothing to do with a cartoon fish in a Disney movie.

Point Nemo is the place in the ocean farthest from land. Technically it is known as the "oceanic pole of inaccessibility." Talk about being "out in the middle of nowhere"! Located in the South Pacific, Point Nemo is the most remote location on earth—more than 1,000 miles from land in any direction. From that spot a person would have to travel over 1,000 miles to get to the Pitcairn Islands in the north, Antarctica in the south, or Chile to the east. *Nemo* is Latin for "no one," and it was the name of the submarine captain in Jules Verne's classic book, *20,000 Leagues Under the Sea.* Point Nemo is such a remote location that the astronauts on the International Space Station are frequently the closest human beings to the spot—and most of the time they are about 258 miles from the earth's surface.[2]

Sadly, some of us decide to live in a spiritual and relational version of Point Nemo. We try to isolate ourselves from others and remain distant and alone. Now, there are times when we need to stay away from others. If we are sick with a contagious disease, we should keep our distance. If we need quiet time alone, we should follow Jesus' example and withdraw to lonely places where we can pray (see Luke 5:16). Many of us would benefit by practicing the spiritual disciplines of silence and solitude. But while some isolation is necessary, healthy, and spiritually profitable, many of us engage in a form of isolation that is unnecessary, unhealthy, and self-inflicted.

A famous line of poetry says, "No man is an island." God designed us to be like grits—connected with others in community.

WE NEED FRIENDS IN EVERY STAGE OF LIFE– BUT ESPECIALLY AS WE GROW OLDER

John Donne was the English poet who wrote, "No man is an island." Donne suffered a variety of griefs. He secretly married a young woman named Anne More, but her father and his boss—both high-ranking officials in London—vehemently opposed their marriage. Donne lost his job and spent time in jail, prompting him to write a note to his wife and sign it, "John Donne, Anne Donne, Un-done." Anne bore 12 children in 16 years, and she died after giving birth to their twelfth child, a stillborn girl. Four of his other children died before reaching the age of 10, and another daughter named Lucy died when she was 18. After experiencing so much tragedy and heartache, it is no wonder Donne concluded no one should be an island.

We all need friends—especially in times of suffering. The Bible says, "A friend loves at all times, and a brother is born for a time of adversity" (Proverbs 17:17). Columnist and news commentator Walter Winchell once said, "A real friend is the one who walks in when the rest of the world walks out." Helen Keller was blind, but she believed, "Walking with a friend in the dark is better than walking alone in the light."

ARE YOU FILLED WITH PHILOS?

The ancient Greeks had different words for *love*. One of those words was *philos*, which we translate as "friend" or someone who is "devoted" or "kindly disposed." Philosophers are devoted to the pursuit of wisdom and philanthropists are kindly disposed toward the needs of others. Forms of the word *philos* are used frequently in the Greek New Testament. Here are some verses where the word appears:

- Matthew 11:19 . . . Jesus was called "a *friend* of tax collectors and sinners."

- Luke 7:5 . . . Jewish elders in Capernaum praised a centurion as a friend of the Jews who "*loves* our nation and has built our synagogue."

- Luke 21:16 . . . Jesus warned his disciples, "You will be betrayed even by parents, brothers and sisters, relatives and *friends*."

- Luke 23:12 . . . On the day of Jesus' trial and crucifixion, "Herod and Pilate became *friends*—before this they had been enemies."

- Acts 10:24 . . . A centurion named Cornelius "called together his relatives and close *friends*" to hear what Peter had to say.

- James 4:4 . . . "Don't you know that *friendship* with the world means enmity against God?"

- 3 John 15 . . . "The *friends* here send their greetings. Greet the *friends* there by name."

Kids understand the need for friendship. When I was a boy growing up on our Ohio farm, my friend Garry Barr lived about a quarter mile down the road. (He had a sister, by the way, named Candy Barr.) In the summer we played softball together and built a fort in the field next to our school building. In the winter we played ice hockey on the frozen creek behind his house and basketball in the barn behind my house. The first time I ever knowingly ate a mushroom was at Garry's house. His parents gathered them in the woods and his mom sauteed them in a frying pan. I don't know why I still remember that detail, but I do. Most likely, you have some unique memories of your own about childhood friends.

The psalmist David recognized the value of friendship. He wrote, "How good and pleasant it is when God's people live together in unity!" (Psalm 133:1). He and his fellow soldier Jonathan became close friends even though Jonathan's father, King Saul, hated David (1 Samuel 18:1-4). When Jonathan died, David mourned and said, "I grieve for you, Jonathan my brother; you were very dear to me" (2 Samuel 1:26).

King Solomon understood the importance of friends. He wrote:

> Two are better than one, because they have a good return for
> their labor: If either of them falls down, one can help the other
> up. But pity anyone who falls and has no one to help them up.
> Also, if two lie down together, they will keep warm. But how can
> one keep warm alone? Though one may be overpowered, two
> can defend themselves. A cord of three strands is not quickly
> broken (Ecclesiastes 4:9-12).

Jesus valued friendship. He declared, "Greater love has no one than
this: to lay down one's life for one's friends" (John 15:13). And he went on
to say, "I no longer call you servants, because a servant does not know his
master's business. Instead, I have called you friends, for everything that I
learned from my Father I have made known to you" (v. 15). Jesus cultivated
healthy friendships with his disciples, especially those in his inner circle of
Peter, James, and John. Remarkably, by believing in the Lord's promises we
can be like Abraham who "was called God's friend" (James 2:23).

Jesus' apostles modeled friendship. Why did the Lord send them
out two by two, rather than one by one (Luke 10:1)? Two people serving
together can assist and encourage each other. They are more resistant to
loneliness. They bring different personalities and spiritual gifts into their
conversations with others, doubling their ministry capacity.

The apostle Paul knew what it was like to be alone, but he also had a
long list of friends and companions who served with him. He even had
a special word for them: *synerges,* often translated "co-worker" or "fellow
laborer." They were Paul's "synergizers"!

In Romans 16, Paul sent greetings to one person after another,
which makes it a bit tedious to read. But a chapter like this one reveals
how important friends can be. "Greet Priscilla and Aquila, my coworkers
in Christ Jesus," Paul wrote. This married couple made tents with Paul
(Acts 18:2-3) and in some way not specifically explained in Scripture,
Paul remembered, "They risked their lives for me" (Romans 16:3). Paul
continued, "Greet my dear friend Epenetus, who was the first convert to
Christ in the province of Asia" (v. 5). Paul fondly remembered how, early
in his missionary endeavors, Epenetus was the first to respond by faith
in a region that later saw thousands accept Christ. The list continued:
"Greet Urbanus, our co-worker in Christ, and my dear friend Stachys.

Greet Apelles, whose fidelity to Christ has stood the test" (vv. 9-10). Paul mentioned "Tryphena and Tryphosa" (two sisters, evidently—maybe twins?), "women who worked hard in the Lord" (v. 12), and the mother of Rufus, "who has been a mother to me, too" (v. 13). Personal relationships like these meant a lot to Paul. He loved his friends, spoke fondly of them, and remembered what they had gone through together with him.

Even some animals apparently grasp the importance of having friends. Dogs have long been known as "man's best friend." Scientists have found that unrelated chimpanzees, dolphins, hyenas, elephants, baboons, horses, and other animals can develop strong, durable connections that last for years. A *Time* magazine article explains, "Animal friendship is about enduring bonds defined by sharing, sacrificing and, when circumstances warrant it, grieving. Not all animal friends exhibit all those behaviors, but they exhibit enough of them—with enough consistency—that something deep is clearly going on." The author concludes, "One thing is clear: humans have always known that it's hard to get through life without friends, and it appears that animals are wise to that secret too."[3]

Friends are important in every stage of life, but they have added significance as we grow older. Senior adults who drift toward Point Nemo—staying as far as possible from other people—diminish their quality of life. From a scientific perspective, physicians Harry Lodge and Allan Hamilton describe how a vibrant social network benefits aging minds:

> First, maintaining complex social relationships keeps our minds fine-tuned to be good listeners; we need to catch nuances of intonation and the secrets of body language and practice empathetic listening, which requires full cognitive engagement. Second, people who have strong social networks have fewer cardiovascular events and experience less stress, both of which impede brain processing. Finally, the brain's internal milieu works best when there is a rich and satisfying emotional life. It amplifies the secretion of neurotransmitters (such as oxytocin, endorphins, and dopamine) that lead to enhanced sharpness of focus but also streamline regional interactions within the brain.[4]

The directors of the Harvard Study of Adult Development disclosed their findings in a *Wall Street Journal* article called "The Lifelong Power of Close

Relationships." For more than 85 years, this study has tracked an original group of 724 men and more than 1,300 of their male and female descendants over three generations. For decades, people in this unique study group have been asked thousands of questions and hundreds of measurements have been taken in an effort to learn what keeps people healthy and happy. Here are the authors' conclusions:

> Through all the years of studying these lives, one crucial factor stands out for the consistency and power of its ties to physical health, mental health and longevity. Contrary to what many people might think, it's not career achievement, or exercise, or a healthy diet. Don't get us wrong; these things matter. But one thing continuously demonstrates its broad and enduring importance: good relationships.
>
> In fact, close personal connections are significant enough that if we had to take all 85 years of the Harvard Study and boil it down to a single principle for living, one life investment that is supported by similar findings across a variety of other studies, it would be this: Good relationships keep us healthier and happier. Period. If you want to make one decision to ensure your own health and happiness, it should be to cultivate warm relationships of all kinds.[5]

Friendships are even more important with the passing of time. As we grow older, we grieve the death of longtime friends, which should make us thankful for those who remain. Here are some further conclusions from the extensive Harvard Study of Adult Development:

> Over and over again, when the participants in the Harvard Study reached their 70s and 80s, they would make a point of saying that what they valued most were their relationships with friends and family. If we accept the wisdom—and, more recently, the scientific evidence—that our relationships are among our most valuable tools for sustaining health and happiness, then choosing to invest time and energy in them today becomes vitally important. It is an investment that will affect everything about how we live in the future.[6]

Clearly, if you want your later years to be greater years, you need to build strong relationships with others. You are not too old to enjoy your friends—and to make some new ones, too!

Different Kinds of Friends

If you want to build strong friendships in your later years, what kinds of friends should you pursue? Here is a better question: What kind of friend are you willing to *be*? The best way to find a friend is to be one.

True friends are:

- *Honest.* They don't just tell you want you *want* to hear. They tell you what you *need* to hear, and they tell you the truth in a way that enables you to hear it.

- *Available.* Whether in person or by phone, text, letter, or e-mail, they stay in touch.

- *Wise.* True friends provide godly counsel and lead you toward God and his Word, not farther away.

- *Loyal.* They don't stab you in the back with gossip or trade you in for a newer model as soon as they discover your unlikeable traits.

- *Trustworthy.* True friends will not betray your confidences or stab you in the back with gossip. George Washington advised, "Be courteous to all, but intimate with few, and let those few be well tried before you give them your confidence."

- *Uplifting.* True friends "carry each other's burdens" (Galatians 6:2), but their conversations are more than just gripe sessions for airing mutual grievances. Supportive friends laugh together easily and lift each other's spirits. They enjoy the refreshing kind of relationship that moved the apostle Paul to tell his friend Philemon, "Your love has given me great joy and encouragement, because you, brother, have refreshed the hearts of the Lord's people" (Philemon 7). Someone said, "If laughter is the best medicine, good friends are the best physicians."

Here are three kinds of friendships to pursue as you age. I call them *old* friends, *bold* friends, and *gold* friends.

OLD FRIENDS

Some acquaintances are easy to be around because you have known them for a long time. "Old friends" don't have to be chronologically old in years; but they are people with whom you have comfortable chemistry and lots of shared experiences.

Are you thankful for the faithful friends you see at church every Sunday? The widow down the street who keeps her lawn neatly trimmed and says "hello" whenever you walk past her house? The postal worker who waves each morning when she delivers your mail? The former classmate you have known since high school or college who still keeps in touch? The funny friend who occasionally sends you a text or Facebook message that makes you laugh?

If you have some *old* friends in your life, appreciate them. Stay in touch. Don't take them for granted.

But don't restrict yourself to those *old* friends. You also need some . . .

BOLD FRIENDS

These are relationships that stretch you and make you uncomfortable (at first). It is relatively easy to connect with *old* friends because it is comfortable to be with them. But *bold* friendships are the new ones . . . the unexpected ones . . . the surprising ones . . . the ones that don't come easily but require intentional pursuit, deliberate cultivation, and persistent effort. Here are some *bold* friendships to consider pursuing:

MAKE FRIENDS WITH SOMEONE FROM A DIFFERENT RELIGIOUS, CULTURAL, OR ETHNIC BACKGROUND THAN YOUR OWN.

Over the years, as Candy and I have served in ministries in New York, Ohio, and Indiana, we have been blessed by making friends from a wide variety of ethnic and cultural backgrounds, including international students from various nations. When I served as president of a Christian university, we hosted barbeques and Christmas dinners at our house attended by two dozen different nationalities.

When we moved to Indianapolis to serve on the staff of East 91st Street Christian Church, our neighbors for a time included a Muslim family who lived across the street from our house. Friendly and hospitable, they welcomed us into their home where we ate delicious Turkish food, drank tea, and talked about our different customs and beliefs. Although they did not share our faith in Christ, we had the chance to plant seeds of the gospel and dispel some of their misconceptions and fears about Christianity.

It will enrich your life if you diversify your circle of friends and build relationships with people from ethnic backgrounds different from your own.

MAKE FRIENDS WITH SOMEONE WHO IS SEEKING GOD.

You might be surprised how many of your neighbors are open to engage in honest, heart-to-heart conversations about faith. God "rewards those who earnestly seek him" (Hebrews 11:6), and there are many earnest seekers around. They aren't looking for entertainment; they are looking for God. They are curious about the Bible, concerned about their families, anxious about this troubled world, and interested in the power of prayer.

I have found that if I pray for opportunities, the Lord opens doors for me to share my faith in natural ways, much like he did when Philip encountered an Ethiopian government official who was curious about God but needed someone to explain God's Word to him (Acts 8:30-31). The old adage is true: People don't care how much you know unless they first know how much you care. Friendships with seekers keep our faith sharp and create natural bridges for communicating the gospel.

After suffering a stroke, a man in his eighties was living in a rehab center. A friend asked me to visit him there. During my first few visits, the fellow was cranky and suspicious of me, and he acted like he didn't want to talk about the Lord.

He asked, "What do you want from me?"

"I don't want anything from you," I responded. "I want something *for* you—something only the Lord can give."

Unimpressed, he peppered his language with profanity and showed no interest in spiritual matters. To be honest, talking with him wasn't a pleasant experience, and I wondered if my visits were making any difference at all. But I kept going—and during each visit, I talked about the Lord's love.

I took an extended trip overseas and was away for a couple of weeks. Upon my return, I went back to see my cranky friend, but this time there was something different about him. His attitude was pleasant, and he seemed glad to see me. When I asked how he was doing, he answered, "I'm finding that the Lord is the main thing that matters."

Surprised, I blurted out, "Did someone tell you about Jesus?"

"*You* did!" he exclaimed. Evidently, he had been listening to my words about the gospel during my visits, even though I didn't think he was paying any attention.

The Bible says, "Make the most of every opportunity. Let your conversation be always full of grace, seasoned with salt, so that you may know how to answer everyone" (Colossians 4:5-6). If you season your conversation "with salt," it will make people thirsty for the Lord. Even if sharing your faith feels a bit clumsy and awkward, God can use your earnest testimony to open hearts to the gospel.

Here is another kind of "bold" friendship to consider . . .

MAKE FRIENDS WITH SOMEONE YOU DON'T LIKE.

Admittedly, this is a hard one! But we must attempt it, because Jesus said, "Love your enemies and pray for those who persecute you," and he asked, "If you love those who love you, what reward will you get?" (Matthew 5:44, 46). Followers of Christ are to build positive relationships that go beyond the norm—even showing kindness to those who mistreat us. The apostle Paul wrote, "If your enemy is hungry, feed him; if he is thirsty, give him something to drink." He urged, "Do not be overcome by evil, but overcome evil with good" (Romans 12:20-21). Abraham Lincoln asked, "Do I not destroy my enemies when I make them my friends?"

God might give you the chance to build unexpected friendships with people you currently don't like at all. Do you think first-century Christians expected to have a close friendly relationship with Saul of Tarsus when he was persecuting them and throwing them in jail? Yet, after his conversion, that same man wrote a warm, cheerful letter to his fellow believers and said, "I have you in my heart" and "I long for all of you with the affection of Christ Jesus" (Philippians 1:7-8).

MAKE FRIENDS WITH SOMEONE FROM A GENERATION OTHER THAN YOUR OWN.

As we grow older, it is tempting to grow complacent and associate with friends we already know. *Old* friends are great, but we miss out on

WORDS FROM THE WISE ABOUT FRIENDSHIP

"A perverse person stirs up conflict, and a gossip separates close friends" (Proverbs 16:28).

"A friend loves at all times, and a brother is born for a time of adversity" (Proverbs 17:17).

"One who has unreliable friends soon comes to ruin, but there is a friend who sticks closer than a brother" (Proverbs 18:24).

"Wounds from a friend can be trusted, but an enemy multiplies kisses" (Proverbs 27:6).

many blessings when we restrict our social connections to members of our own age groups. Sure, we already have a lot in common with them, so it's comfortable to be around familiar acquaintances who are "tried and true." But we also need friendships that stretch us and make us grow.

Our church has a program called King's Men (K Men for short)—a simple but effective way for guys to build relationships. A group of six to eight men agree to read a series of books on the Christian life and meet together once a month for about eight months at the homes of the various men (or in a local restaurant). Each meeting lasts about two hours. After eating together, the guys discuss what they learned from the book and pray together. For a few years, I resisted being part of a K Men group because I already have a busy schedule and frankly, I didn't relish the idea of having assigned reading to do! But when I finally joined the program, I was surprised how much I liked it. Most of the guys I met with were young men in their twenties and thirties. I enjoyed visiting their homes, eating with them, learning from them, and getting to know the questions, stresses, and challenges they face.

It takes effort to build relationships across generational lines, but if we give them a chance, bold friendships will enrich our lives.

In addition to *old* friends and *bold* friends, there are what I call . . .

GOLD FRIENDS

Why do some people call old age our "golden years"? Some things about aging are not so golden. But senior adulthood will be truly golden if it becomes the season when we finally come to grips with life's true treasures.

Why did ancient kings and queens decorate their palaces with gold? Why are so many wedding rings made of gold? Why is the so-called gold standard considered a mark of economic stability for a nation's currency? The BBC published an article titled "Why Do We Value Gold?" that identified three main reasons gold is so precious: scarcity, stability, and beauty.

Gold is scarce. Experts estimate if you were to collect all the gold currently found in statues and jewelry in the world—gather up every earring and wedding ring, and every trace of gold found in computer chips—and melt it all down, you would have a cube that is only about 60 feet square.[7]

Gold is stable. It is hard, durable, nontoxic, and resists corrosion.

And obviously, gold is . . . well, golden! It is beautiful. The BBC article pointed out, "All the other metals in the periodic table are silvery-colored except for copper—and . . . copper corrodes, turning green when exposed to moist air. That makes gold very distinctive."[8]

Gold friendships are those rare ones we enjoy that prove to be stable, nontoxic, durable, and beautiful over the years.

I have known Dan Burton for more than half of my life. We became friends when I was in my thirties and he was in his twenties. Dan's degree in logistics management from Michigan State University and his experience serving in campus ministry made him the ideal person to partner with me in planting a new church near the University of Cincinnati. Later he and his wife, Sue, served as missionaries in Ethiopia, and I visited them there. Today we live in different cities and work in different ministries, but we have stayed in touch over the years. Whenever we see each other, we comfortably pick up the conversation as if we had not been apart. Dan's friendship is "gold" to me.

The directors of the Harvard Study of Adult Development compare deep friendships to a gold mine. They explain:

> We don't need to be with all of our good friends all of the time. In fact, some people who energize us and enhance our lives might do so specifically because we don't see them very often. Sometimes we are compatible with a person only to a point, and that point is good enough. But most of us have friends and relatives who energize us and who we don't see enough. A few adjustments to our most treasured relationships can have real effects on how we feel. We might be sitting on a gold mine of vitality that we are not paying attention to, because it is eclipsed by the shiny allure of smartphones or pushed to the side by work demands.[9]

If you are 40 years old, and you spend one hour each week having coffee with a special friend, by the time you turn 80 you will have spent the equivalent of 87 days together. By contrast, the average American spends about 11 hours every day interacting with television, radio, and smartphones. From the age of 40 to the age of 80, that adds up to 18 years of waking life.[10]

You are not too old for strong friendships—or to make some new ones. Don't isolate . . . relate! Don't be a hermit and go it alone . . . be a friend and stay connected. Get up, get out, and get going. Join a small group. Invest in other people. Get involved and stay involved in your local church.

Healthy relationships will turn your later years into greater years.

QUESTIONS FOR PERSONAL REFLECTION
AND GROUP DISCUSSION

1. Think of times when you have felt lonely.

   • What made you feel that way?

   • What positive steps helped you cope with your loneliness?

   • Who has been a friend to you during lonely times?

2. According to Exodus 33:11, "The Lord would speak to Moses face to face, as one speaks to a friend." Do you consider yourself a friend of God? Why, or why not?

3. Who comes to mind when you think of "old friends" you are comfortable being around? Who are some "gold friends" whose friendship you especially treasure?

   What traits or attributes make these friends especially valuable to you?

4. What steps will you take to build some "bold friendships" with . . . ?

   • someone from a religious, ethnic, or cultural background different from your own?

   • someone who is seeking the Lord or unsettled in their faith?

   • someone you don't like being around very much?

   • someone from a different generation than your own?

13 | Be Patient with the Patient— Embracing the Role of a Caregiver

"If I had it to do all over again . . . I think I would ask for help."
—Sign on an office desk

"Cast all your anxiety on him because he cares for you."
—1 Peter 5:7

Aristotle said, "Patience is bitter, but its fruit is sweet." According to another great philosopher, A. A. Milne's character Winnie the Pooh, "Rivers know this: there is no hurry. We shall get there some day."

Patient is an interesting word. We use it as an adjective to describe calm perseverance: "Mom is so patient, she never complains." And we use it as a noun when someone is injured or sick: "Dad was a patient in the hospital for two weeks."

Patience is an admirable attribute, but many of us find it elusive. Are you a "patient patient"? (I struggle with this because I hate being sick.) How patient are you when it's time for you to take care of others who are sick? (My wife, a retired registered nurse, is a better caregiver than I am.)

As we grow older, most of us will require some level of care, and many of us will serve as caregivers for others we love. Rosalynn Carter, the former first lady of the United States, was 12 years old when her father became ill with leukemia. As the oldest of four children, Rosalynn helped her mother care for him and her siblings until her dad died when she was 13. Less than a year later, her grandmother died unexpectedly, and her grieving grandfather moved into their home. Decades later, Mrs. Carter helped to care for her mother who died in 2000 at age 94. In 1987 she founded the Rosalynn Carter

Institute for Caregivers, headquartered in Americus, Georgia. According to Mrs. Carter, "There are only four kinds of people in this world—those who have been caregivers, those who are currently caregivers, those who will be caregivers, and those who will need caregivers."[1]

What does it take to be patient with the beloved patients who are part of our lives? Please keep reading as I introduce you to some senior adult couples whose stories teach valuable lessons about caregiving.

Dave and Valerie

In 2017, Candy and I led a Bible lands trip to Israel, Italy, Greece, Malta, and other locations in the Mediterranean area. When Dave and Valerie Reed heard about the trip, not only did they sign up to go with us, they recruited others to join our travel group as well. It was an exciting time for the Reeds because Dave and Valerie both had retired barely a year earlier, in 2016.

They married in 1976 on the day after they both graduated from college. By then, Dave was already loading trucks at UPS, and he continued working for the company for 43 years, driving little brown trucks and large semis. He also served as a union steward for six of those years, and he ended his career working in the company's Safety Compliance division. While working for UPS, Dave also served in part-time church ministry, and later he served as an elder and Sunday school teacher in his church.

After earning her master's degree in elementary education, Valerie taught fourth grade for one year, then stayed at home for 16 years to be a full-time mother for their three children. Later, she worked in a high school writing lab, earned her library media specialist license, and finally retired after 25 years of teaching. She also served on a local school board for eight years, taught Sunday school and VBS classes at her church, and served on the board of trustees when I was president of Cincinnati Christian University.

When Dave and Valerie retired in 2016, they had big goals for retirement. In their own words, they planned on "visiting the presidential libraries (we got about half done!), short-term mission trips (we got to volunteer at Haus Edelweiss, a training site for church leaders in Austria), traveling the world, taking up new sports and hobbies, and helping our children raise their families (like being a 'taxi driver' to ball games and helping with Girl Scouts)."

Everything changed, however, on February 6, 2019. While the Reeds were driving in heavy rain on an interstate highway in Kentucky, their car hydroplaned, slid off the road, and rolled over. Valerie was shaken up, but she was OK. Injuries from the accident, however, pinched Dave's spinal cord, causing paralysis that left him unable to move or feel anything below his neck. After the accident, he stayed in a hospital's intensive care unit for two weeks, supported by a feeding tube and a ventilator. After being released from the ICU, he entered an inpatient rehab program for 40 days, where specialists successfully removed the ventilator and feeding tube. The Reeds lived in Ohio near Cincinnati, but they spent over a year and half rehabbing in Louisville, Kentucky.

Today, Dave can move his left hand and left foot, and he has partial feeling in his limbs. Valerie says, "The good news is, the accident didn't affect his mind."

The bad news? Their lifestyle now is completely different from what they expected retirement to be.

Here's how Valerie explains their schedule. "Dave wakes up at 7:45 in the morning. An aide comes in for three hours to help bathe him, brush his teeth, dress him, put him in his wheelchair, feed him breakfast, and help with his exercises. He can use his computer and television with help from voice activation software. A specially equipped van allows us to get out and do things like going to the Kings Island amusement park with our grandkids. We also spend a few hours twice a week at a Cincinnati hospital using their therapy/wellness center, where Dave works out. We have family dinners every Saturday, when our children take care of dinner and anything we need done around the house."

Valerie wakes Dave up each morning, gives him his medications, and gets him ready for the aide's arrival. She runs errands, meets friends for breakfast, or takes a walk while the aide spends time with Dave. After the aide leaves, Valerie takes over and helps her husband with the rest of his day—making appointments, feeding him meals, and taking him places in their van.

The Reeds' experience reminds us not to take our health for granted, or to assume we know what the future holds. Well-laid plans can change in an instant.

What advice do the Reeds have for others who face unforeseen difficulties, and for those who find themselves in the role of caregivers?

"Look for God's hand in the process," they say. "We saw God working from the day we were in the accident."

Faced with the choice of Dave's hospitalization in either Louisville or Nashville, Valerie picked Louisville because it was closer to their home. Soon, she discovered, "Louisville had the number-one spinal cord hospital in the world. People from all over the world came there for their care."

"We saw God's hand in finding our aide," the Reeds say. "A friend introduced her to us three years earlier at a Cincinnati Reds ballgame. The aide—an experienced worker and a dedicated member of our church who loves what she does—lost her morning patient just a month before we needed her. We see God's hand in our friends as they visit us, bring us dinners, and help us in other ways. We see God's hand as he brings us into contact with other people we can influence with the gospel."

They add, "If the apostle Paul could spread the gospel from prison, we certainly can do it from a wheelchair!"

Dave and Valerie advise, "Accept that things are different. You never were in control to begin with! Take people up on their offers to help. For the caregiver: find time for yourself. Do things that make you feel 'normal,' like going out with a friend. Get plenty of help, both from paid workers and from friends who offer assistance. Find a support group and a counselor who can help you talk things out."

What Does It Mean to Be a Caregiver?

You might be a caregiver without realizing it.

According to Johns Hopkins researchers, "40 million Americans are providing care for an adult family member or friend, yet few of these identify themselves as caregivers. Often, the things that define being a caregiver, such as helping a parent purchase and organize their medications or taking a friend to their doctor's appointments, just seem like simply doing what needs to be done when someone needs help."[2]

The Centers for Disease Control and Prevention (CDC) acknowledges the important role of caregivers:

Caregiving is an important public health issue that affects the quality of life for millions of individuals. Caregivers provide assistance with another person's social or health needs. Caregiving may include help with one or more activities important for daily living such as bathing and dressing, paying bills, shopping, and providing transportation. It also may involve emotional support and help with managing a chronic disease or disability. Caregiving responsibilities can increase and change as the recipient's needs increase, which may result in additional strain on the caregiver.

Caregivers can be unpaid family members or friends or paid caregivers. Informal or unpaid caregivers are the backbone of long-term care provided in people's homes. In particular, middle-aged and older adults provide a substantial portion of this care in the U.S, as they care for children, parents or spouses.[3]

You are a caregiver if you help someone with activities like these:

- providing transportation to medical appointments, grocery shopping, and other errands;

- purchasing or organizing medicines;

- communicating with health-care providers or agencies, or advocating on your loved one's behalf;

- assisting with personal hygiene (bathing, showering, laundry, dressing);

- helping with meals, housework, and lawn care;

- managing finances.[4]

Caregiving takes different forms. Do you have some caregivers in your own circle of friends? When I think about caregivers I know, several situations come to mind:

- After Dad died, my mom continued to live in the house they had built on their farm. My brother Jim lives nearby. During the years before Mother died, Jim faithfully mowed her grass, checked on her daily needs, and drove her to lots of medical appointments.

- My friend Gayle assisted her husband, Herman, while he recovered from back surgery, but their roles reversed when she suffered a major stroke. Eight years later, they sold their house and Herman moved to a residence at a facility where Gayle was receiving care. He faithfully visited his wife in her room every day until she died.

- I know several families with beloved children whose disabilities require constant attention and special schooling. The parents, brothers, sisters, and grandparents of these children accept caregiving as a way of life.

- While attending a conference on grief and mourning, Candy and I met a new friend named Mosie, whose wife, Karla, died of ALS (amyotrophic lateral sclerosis, also known as Lou Gehrig's disease). She lived for two years after the disease was diagnosed. For the last year and a half of her life, she slept in a hospital bed in the living room of their house. When he got up to take care of her, she greeted him every morning with a smile. After she died, Mosie started a nonprofit organization called Karla's Smiles to encourage other caregivers.

In situations like these, caregivers need patience rooted not in human strength alone, but in the grace and power of God. This is especially true when you factor in the physical and emotional strain of caregiving. Studies show:

- 36.7 percent of caregivers report getting insufficient sleep.

- Over half of caregivers (53.4 percent) aged 65 years and older are dealing with two or more chronic diseases of their own, such as coronary heart disease, stroke, asthma, cancer, or diabetes.[5]

Furthermore, the need for caregiving is expected to increase in the future as the number of older adults continues to grow. Smaller families, plus an aging population, will create a shortage of people available to help. According to the CDC, "Currently, there are seven potential family caregivers per older adult. By 2030, it is estimated there will be only four potential family caregivers per older adult."[6] These statistics underscore the need for churches to step up and fill the void by making care a priority in our congregations and communities.

Henri Nouwen wrote:

> In the realm of the Spirit of God, living and caring are one. Our society suggests that caring and living are quite separate and that caring belongs primarily to professionals who have received special training. Although training is important, and although certain people need preparation to practice their *profession* with competence, caring is a privilege of every person and is at the heart of being human.[7]

Don and Judie

In 1960, when Don Ball began his career at Creative Packaging, a division of the Eli Lilly pharmaceutical company, his mother told him, "Be sure you contact our friends, Dot and Stan Baskwell, who live in Indianapolis." Don reached out to them, and they invited him to dinner.

Don remembers, "When I arrived, their daughter Judie answered the door. Wow, she was beautiful!" Judie and Don were married on May 5, 1961. For a few years his job took them to New York City, but eventually they returned to Indianapolis, where they have lived ever since.

One day in the mid-1970s, Don told Judie, "There is something missing in our lives." He recalls, "We were healthy and we had a good home, good kids, and lots of friends, but I just had this feeling that something was missing. About that time a friend invited us to go to a dinner where we heard Colonel Heath Bottomly, a decorated World War II fighter pilot, give a personal testimony about his faith. I related so much to what he said. After that dinner we went to our friend's house and my friend asked me, 'Did you ever feel there was something missing in your life?'"

Don accepted Christ as his Lord and Savior that night. Judie took a little while longer, but soon she also became a Christian.

"We started going to East 91st Street Christian Church," Don says, "where our minister Russ Blowers and others had a huge impact on our lives. We became very involved and started a young couples Bible class that grew to over 50 couples. Still today, many from that class continue to meet in small groups. It's wonderful to see how Christ has worked in their lives."

In January 2019, Judie was diagnosed with mild neurocognitive disorder, but before then, she already was experiencing memory difficulties and increasing levels of anxiety and depression (including hallucinations and delusions), and she was losing weight. Don continued caring for his wife at home, with help from two friends he calls his "extra hands" who stayed with Judie a few hours each week to give him a break. While he appreciated having time for himself, Don confessed, "To be honest, I felt guilty for doing that—having a good time while Judie was suffering."

Don began researching senior community placement options, and in time, he found a third aide who was available to spend time with Judie at their house. He also benefited from the counsel of a clinical social worker who knew Judie well and had experience in working with dementia patients.

"Many people have told me I should take care of myself," Don says. "Well, yes and no. This isn't about me; it's about Judie. Our marriage vows state that we are to remain together until death do us part. Biblically it is clear we are to remain together. My heart says we are to remain together, so that is what we are going to do. If our roles were reversed, Judie would do the same for me. If her condition worsens to a point where she must go to a memory care facility, or if I am unable to take care of her due to my own physical, mental, or emotional decline, then of course we will find the best place for her."

He continues, "We try not to worry about what we can't control. I know the future will be difficult, but I also know we have an awesome God. He doesn't promise us a life without difficulties, but he does promise to give us strength, wisdom, perseverance, and more to sustain us. So many friends and family members (including our children and grandchildren) love us and support us with their prayers, texts, phone calls, lunches, and other expressions of concern. It overwhelms me and I am grateful."

"Life is good even when it doesn't feel that way," Don insists.

Don's daily life is dramatically different than it was in the past. "I have to watch Judie 100 percent of the time," he explains. "There are so many things that we just can't do anymore. We can't go out for lunch, go to church, go to friends' homes, go for a ride, go together to the grocery store or any store, or even have friends over for any length of time. It feels like everything has been taken away."

A friend told Don, "Having a loved one with dementia leaves us with a physical presence that's a different version of the person we knew and still adore."

Don isn't a complainer, but he admits, "A couple of times I have gone to a restaurant by myself, and I felt horrible. There have been several times when I felt depressed and other times when I have just sobbed."

Yet, he finds reasons for gratitude. "Members of my family have been so helpful," he says, "and without them, I don't know what I would do. I am grateful for good health that allows me to care for Judie, but at the end of the day I am wiped out. Late in the day is by far the most difficult. Her condition worsens as the day goes on, and by then I'm mentally, physically, and emotionally drained."

Don has advice for others in similar situations.

"At the first sign of memory difficulties, get tested," he says. "Don't wait. Some medications are helpful in treating dementia in the early stages. Be grateful for those who offer to help and those who reach out to you. There will be people you think will call, text, email, mail, or visit, but they don't—which is disappointing, but don't let that discourage you. Find someone to stay with your loved one for even a short time so you can get away, and don't feel guilty about it.

"Many people have reached out," he continues, "but my brothers and sisters in Christ have gone the extra mile with phone calls, texts, handwritten notes, and visits. One of our daughters brings dinner regularly and helps Judie get a shower and wash her hair. I am unable to adequately express how much that means to me."

"Look for organizations that can help you cope." And Don stresses, "The most important thing for me has been my faith and knowing that God will give me the strength and wisdom to get through the day."

"Help Wanted"—What the Bible Says About Caregiving

You won't find the word *caregiver* in most translations of the Bible, but the concept weaves its way throughout the Scriptures. "Love your neighbor," says the Law of Moses in Leviticus 19:18, and that short sentence summarizes God's expectations for how we should treat one another (see Romans 13:8-10).

According to James 1:27, "Religion that God our Father accepts as pure and faultless is this: to look after orphans and widows in their distress and to keep oneself from being polluted by the world." Caring for vulnerable people appears to be at the very heart of what it means to walk with God.

At some point in life, almost every person could walk around carrying a "Help Wanted" sign. Accidental injuries, adverse financial circumstances, and unforeseen health problems can befall any of us. It's not surprising that numerous examples of caregiving appear in the Bible.

Do you ever think of King David as a caregiver? Consider how he provided for Mephibosheth, the son of his close friend Jonathan. Mephibosheth couldn't walk because his feet were injured in a childhood mishap when he was 5 years old (2 Samuel 4:4). Wanting to show kindness to Jonathan's descendants, David invited Mephibosheth to stay in his palace, where he "always ate at the king's table" (2 Samuel 9:1-13).

The supreme caregiver, of course, is Jesus himself. Although he was busy "proclaiming the good news of the kingdom," Jesus took time to care for people who suffered physical and spiritual hurts of all kinds (Matthew 4:23-24). His heart overflowed with compassion for all who were "harassed and helpless, like sheep without a shepherd" (Matthew 9:36). He paid attention to children and widows, healed the sick, wept with grieving friends, touched individuals who had leprosy (whom others scorned and avoided), and sought out long-term sufferers like a man who couldn't walk for 38 years and another who had been born blind (John 5:1-15; 9:1-7).

While the Bible doesn't provide all the details, other situations described in Scripture imply caregiving.

- Paul instructed first-century believers to "do good to all people, especially to those who belong to the family of believers" (Galatians 6:10). This included caring for "those widows who are really in need" (1 Timothy 5:16) and making sure their basic needs were provided. Caregiving was so important that the early church created a system for "the daily distribution of food" to those in need (Acts 6:1).

- Both the Old and New Testaments instruct God's people to care for the poor (Leviticus 25:35-36; Deuteronomy 15:7-11; Proverbs 19:17; 21:13; Isaiah 58:6-10; Luke 14:12-14; James 2:2-5; 1 John 3:16-18). More than merely providing financial support, God's instructions also required paying fairly and promptly for services rendered (Leviticus 19:13; Deuteronomy 24:14-15) and ensuring those who had minimal financial resources received fair treatment by the legal system (Proverbs 22:22-23). There was even a law that said if neighbors gave you their cloak as collateral for a loan, you had to return the cloak by sunset. Evidently the gracious heavenly Father didn't want anyone to sleep in the cold without a blanket (Exodus 22:25-27). Caregivers honor God when we assist our loved ones by providing financial support, serving as their advocates with medical professionals, helping them navigate legal tangles, or even tucking them into bed with a warm blanket at night.

- The Law of Moses required showing patience, kindness, and fairness to people with disabilities (Leviticus 19:14) and to people who migrated from other nations (Exodus 23:9), and it included special provisions to protect "the foreigner, the fatherless and the widow" who might tend to be overlooked (Deuteronomy 24:19-22).

- The psalmist wrote, "Defend the weak and the fatherless; uphold the cause of the poor and the oppressed" (Psalm 82:3).

- The New Testament encourages followers of Christ to love one another as brothers and sisters, "offer hospitality to one another without grumbling" (1 Peter 4:9), and visit prisoners (Hebrews 13:1-3).

- Jesus emphasized caregiving when he talked about helping people who need food, shelter, and clothing, caring for the sick, and visiting those in prison; and the Lord added, "Whatever you did for one of the least of these brothers and sisters of mine, you did for me" (Matthew 25:40).

When Jesus was dying on the cross, he looked at his mother and his friend John and told them, "Woman, here is your son," and "Here is your mother" (John 19:26-27). We don't know exactly how John took care of

Mary after Jesus died, but we do know the beloved disciple "took her into his home" (John 19:27). In his own dying moments, Jesus considered the care of his mother an important concern.

Throughout history, Christians have led the way in caring for the sick, vulnerable, poor, abandoned, and dying. Even an agnostic history expert expressed his admiration for the way Christians cared for others during the second and third centuries after Christ. He wrote:

> Love of one's neighbor is not an exclusively Christian virtue, but… the Christians appear to have practiced it much more effectively than any other group. The Church provided the essentials of social security: it cared for widows and orphans, the old, the unemployed, and the disabled; it provided a burial fund for the poor and a nursing service in the time of plague. But even more important, I suspect, than these material benefits was the sense of belonging which the Christian community could give.[8]

In his book, *Jesus Skeptic: A Journalist Explores the Credibility and Impact of Christianity,* John S. Dickerson describes the impact of Jesus Christ on hospitals and modern medicine. The author points out that in ancient cultures, many people "were so consumed with the difficulties of daily life that they did not go out of their way to care for the many lepers, diseased, injured, weak, or dying in society." Yet, history shows that "followers of Jesus sacrificed themselves in caring for the sick, the poor, the unwanted, and the outcasts of society" to such an extent that to this day, the phrase "Christian charity" describes orphanages, hospitals, and other care centers.[9]

Why Should We Care?

An impressive array of biblical values motivates us to pursue the ministry of caregiving.

Love. The Greek word *agape* has been defined as voluntary, committed, costly self-sacrifice, freely given. *Agape* is the word the New Testament uses when it says, "God so loved the world" (John 3:16) and "Husbands, love your wives, just as Christ loved the church and gave himself up for her" (Ephesians 5:25). Paul used this word when he wrote, "And now these three remain: faith, hope and love. But the greatest of these is love" (1

Corinthians 13:13). Caregiving is a way of expressing God's *agape* love.

Promise keeping. The Bible says, "When you make a vow to God, do not delay to fulfill it. He has no pleasure in fools; fulfill your vow. It is better not to make a vow than to make one and not fulfill it" (Ecclesiastes 5:4-5). Caregivers like Valerie Reed and Don Ball view caregiving as a way to fulfill the sacred promises they made on their wedding day.

Self-sacrifice. Scripture tells us to value others above our own interests (Philippians 2:3-4). Caregiving is a way of putting another's well-being above our own.

Kindness. The Holy Spirit can turn self-centered souls into tender-hearted servants, enabling caregivers to bear such fruits as love, peace, forbearance, kindness, and faithfulness (Galatians 5:22-23).

Compassion. Colossians 3:12 says, "Clothe yourselves with compassion, kindness, humility, gentleness and patience." Those words have special meaning for caregivers, because every day they apply the Golden Rule and do for others what they would want someone to do for them.

Boundaries. This point might surprise you, but the Bible illustrates the limits of what one person can do while caring for someone else. During his public ministry, Jesus didn't make himself available every moment; he often got away by himself. When he learned his friend Lazarus was sick, Jesus waited a couple of days before visiting (John 11:6). Evidently even the great apostle Paul found there are problems only God can solve and weaknesses only God can heal in his own way and in his own timing. Paul performed miracles of healing, yet he lived with his own unyielding "thorn in the flesh" (2 Corinthians 12:7-9), and at one point he left his friend "Trophimus sick at Miletus" (2 Timothy 4:20).

Prayer. Caregivers often find strength in prayer—but not the casual, run-of-the mill, Sunday school variety of prayer. They engage in raw, honest, heartfelt communication with God sometimes known as prayers of complaint. They offer impassioned intercession for their loved ones and pour out their hearts to God, expressing their own sorrow, physical exhaustion, emotional weariness, and spiritual questions. They understand why the prophet complained, "How long, Lord, must I call for help, but you do not listen?" (Habakkuk 1:2). Many caregivers can relate to prayers like this one:

Save me, O God, for the waters have come up to my neck. I sink in the miry depths, where there is no foothold. I have come into the deep waters; the floods engulf me. I am worn out calling for help; my throat is parched. My eyes fail, looking for my God" (Psalm 69:1-3).

But when they feel overwhelmed and on the brink of burnout, many caregivers also have learned to say bold, uplifting prayers like this one: "You, Lord, keep my lamp burning; my God turns my darkness into light" (Psalm 18:28).

WHAT ABOUT LONG-DISTANCE CAREGIVING?

If you live more than one hour's drive away from a family member or friend who needs your care, you still can make a difference. The National Institute on Aging (NIA.gov) offers these ideas:

- Learn all you can about the person's illness, medicines, and local resources and keep this information handy in a notebook or an online document.

- Connect with your loved one's primary caregivers and let them know what you can do to assist.

- Make the most of your visits by planning ahead and communicating with the primary caregiver. Could you assist with household tasks or trips to the doctor while you are in town? If possible, include something fun or interesting in your visits that is outside your loved one's normal routine. Take them to church, play a game, take a drive, go shopping, or watch a movie together.

Service. Jesus taught that to be great in the kingdom of God, you must be a servant. For Valerie Reed, serving others—even beyond caring for her husband, Dave—is part of her life. She says, "I can still make a meal for a friend who had surgery. I joined a group at church that sends cards and letters to encourage others, using names and addresses provided by a member of our church staff. I like to bake, so I make enough to share with our neighbors. We have several widows in our condo complex, and taking cookies to them gives me a chance to check on them. All these things bless me as well as the receiver. I don't tell about these things to brag, but to encourage others to continue to reach out, too."

Mark and Evelyn

Mark Taylor served as a senior editor and publisher at Standard Publishing when I worked for the company as a magazine editor under his leadership. Later, during the 12 years when I was president of Cincinnati Christian University, his wife, Evelyn, served on the college faculty, teaching English and other subjects. After her retirement in 2013, she continued serving as an adjunct instructor for a short time. Mark retired from Standard Publishing in 2017.

In 2019, the results of a spinal tap confirmed Evelyn's diagnosis of Alzheimer's disease.

"Looking back, I'm certain we were seeing some signs of slipping a couple of years before that," Mark recalls. "A different doctor used the word 'Alzheimer's' with us in 2018, but she never looked us in the eyes and said, 'Evelyn has Alzheimer's disease.' So, I was pretty much in denial, even though Evelyn was increasingly unable to make decisions or handle tasks.

"We were transferred to a new doctor in 2019—he's wonderful, I view the transfer as a gift from God—and he strongly urged the spinal tap so we could confirm the diagnosis. In retrospect, I'm glad we did it. No more denial. In 2021, the same doctor saw some very slight symptoms, which led him to order a brain scan looking for evidence of Parkinson's disease. The results were conclusive. Yes, Evelyn is afflicted with that disease, too. That year at Christmastime, we 'went public' because it felt right to tell the whole story to friends and family."

A year after letting the public know about Evelyn's condition, Mark started to write a blog called *Unchosen Journey* (www.unchosenjourney.com) to encourage others. As a result of the blog, Mark says, "I'm discovering a vast population of caregivers or former caregivers or relatives and friends of caregivers. Many seem to appreciate hearing someone express or describe feelings they haven't put into words or experiences similar to their own."

"Evelyn rests a lot now," Mark says. "[It's] such a contrast to the 'worker bee' I remember. She helps with some housework—folding laundry, emptying the dishwasher, making a bed—usually only after I've asked her. Many evenings she clears the dishes from the dinner table. We listen to music most days, and often sing along with a hymns playlist we found on YouTube. I try to take a walk with her every day in decent weather, but usually only for 10 or 15 minutes. Evelyn used to walk two miles in 30 minutes every day possible, even during the winter. With a history of Alzheimer's in her family, she was determined to prevent it in herself. Occasionally she will work on a jigsaw puzzle. I've been able to find several puzzles with fewer—sometimes much fewer—than 100 pieces that are still suitable for adults.

"She reads the daily newspaper and other magazines or maybe a book she finds lying around the house. She usually reads out loud and sometimes reads the same article or picture caption or headline several times in one sitting. It's fascinating to observe—and sometimes frustrating, if you're trying to do your own reading or writing in the same room at the same time. But I think it's a good thing, and I'm always happy to hear some news about something I don't understand or had never heard about, floating in from the living room to the kitchen where I may be working."

A loved one's safety is a common concern for caregivers, and that has been an issue for Mark and Evelyn.

"Three different times she has appeared at a neighbor's door while I was away or busy outside," Mark says. "As a result of her neighborly visits, I try not to leave her alone. The wandering has never happened at night, although she regularly gets out of bed and wanders around the house, sometimes visiting one of the other bedrooms. I know this has happened when the next morning I see the sheets turned down in one of the guest rooms. I hang a motion-sensitive door alarm on the front doorknob. A couple times during the day I've heard it going off and found her disabling it, and one morning I found it turned off on the coffee table. If the siren went off in the night, I didn't hear it."

Three half-day caregivers assist the Taylors every week: two paid workers and one volunteer. Mark says, "This allows me to get away, run errands, work uninterrupted in the library, or maybe see a movie. Friday mornings I volunteer at a ministry to under-resourced people, The Healing Center, sponsored by a local church."

Mark attends a weekly online support group where the facilitator says, "Remember, we're dealing with a disease of the brain." Another Alzheimer's caregiver advised Mark to keep in mind, "It's not her fault."

"When I see snippets of the woman I knew, a pretty smile or wry comment or a stack of perfectly folded dish towels, I am grateful," Mark observes. "When confronted with confusion or irritation or incontinence,

I try to remember I'm dealing with a disease, not a difficult person. This helps. Usually."

Mark has learned the importance of having the support of others. He insists, "Caregivers absolutely cannot do this alone. I regularly have breakfast or lunch with one of a half-dozen friends who stay in touch with me. Our daughter occasionally comes to stay so I can leave town for a few days. I'm investigating respite care for a similar purpose. The online support group is more helpful than I would have imagined. And in addition, I'm deeply grateful for a few other friends who will occasionally stop by to allow me to get out of the house. We have a small circle with whom we share meals, and they are patient—they act like they don't even notice—when Evelyn wanders instead of staying at the dinner table or uses a serving spoon to eat her own supper."

What have others done and said that Mark has found helpful?

"More than one friend has volunteered to come if I have an emergency need," Mark says. "One friend managed a big basement waterproofing project for us: finding contractors, getting estimates, advising about next steps, managing details. I never would have handled it by myself without feeling overwhelmed. Friends at church have treated Evelyn as much like normal as possible, and they help me keep our eyes on her as she wanders the lobby and halls on Sundays, greeting friends and admiring little children.

"A few have promised to get together with us without following through, but I understand. It takes an effort to be with us. One of my major points of grief is the inability now for the two of us to make new friends or nurture old relationships. I'm still fun to be around, I think; but this really isn't true for the two of us together."[10]

Some Humble Suggestions for Caregivers

My caregiving friends have taught me several lessons. And so, with deep respect for all my readers who are taking care of loved ones, I humbly offer the following words of encouragement.

Caregiving can be all-consuming and exhausting. Don't be surprised by your weariness. Feeling overwhelmed is a normal reaction to prolonged, unrelenting stress. Acknowledging this fact doesn't make the burdens any lighter, but it helps when you remember what the apostle Peter told his first-century friends who were suffering: "Do not be surprised at the fiery ordeal that has come on you to test you, as though something strange were happening to you," for "the family of believers throughout the world is undergoing the same kind of sufferings" (1 Peter 4:12; 5:9).

God is with you, and others care, too. Don't try to go it alone. Caring friends may relate to your circumstances more than you realize. "Come near to God, and he will come near to you" (James 4:8). "Cast all your anxiety on him because he cares for you" (1 Peter 5:7).

Don't try to do too much. Often, it's enough simply to be a companion. It's not your role to "fix" your loved ones or "treat" their condition. Most of all, they need you to be present with them.

Don't neglect your own needs. Self-care doesn't mean betrayal of your loved ones. To "love your neighbor as yourself," you must have a self to give. You can't wash someone else's feet if you are too tired to fill a basin and carry a towel. You can't bear someone else's burdens if your hands are already filled with heavy burdens. Caring for your own emotional, spiritual, and physical needs isn't selfish if it provides the strength you need to serve others.

Help your local church recognize the value of caregiving. Dynamic preaching, inspiring worship services, and interesting programs are important, but loving people must always be a priority for Christians. When I rejoined the staff of a local church at age 60, I decided to focus my personal ministry on two main priorities: *Teach the Bible, love the people.* (Candy made me a little plaque containing this simple message, which I keep in my office at work.) These two basic priorities sound simple, but they are quite profound. Unless we teach God's Word faithfully and love people consistently, the church isn't doing its job; but if we carry out these two responsibilities well, we will always have important work to do. Every person you encounter needs truth and love, and the ministry staff and elders can't meet every need. By your own example and involvement, you can help your congregation be an island of caring in a world of indifference.

It's good to be a caregiver, but remember this: the Lord alone is the cure-giver. There are problems only he can solve. That's why we must rely on Jesus Christ as the ultimate companion and healer. "For we do not have a high priest who is unable to empathize with our weaknesses, but we have one who has been tempted in every way, just as we are—yet he did not sin. Let us then approach God's throne of grace with confidence, so that we may receive mercy and find grace to help us in our time of need" (Hebrews 4:15-16).

QUESTIONS FOR PERSONAL REFLECTION AND GROUP DISCUSSION

1. Which would you rather be—a person giving care or a person receiving care? Why?

2. At this point in your life, where does your capacity as a caregiver fit on the following scale?

   • *Running on Empty*... I'm worn out and I don't have much more to give.

   • *Somewhere in the Middle* . . . I care about others, but I could be doing more.

   • *At Full Capacity*... I'm consistently engaged in caring for others in Jesus' name.

3. Think of people you know who are currently caring for a loved one. How could you encourage them? What can you do to lighten their load?

4. Is caregiving a priority in your local church? Is your congregation a body of believers where people demonstrate "equal concern for each other" (1 Corinthians 12:25) and care for the weak, vulnerable, and suffering in practical ways?

5. How can you help your church become the kind of caring community where the following statement is true? "If one part suffers, every part suffers with it; if one part is honored, every part rejoices with it" (1 Corinthians 12:26).

14 | Growing Through Grief—
Dealing with Loss When a Loved One Dies

"The greater the love the greater the grief,
and the stronger the faith the more savagely
will Satan storm its fortress."
—C. S. Lewis

"Blessed are those who mourn, for they will be comforted."
—Jesus, in Matthew 5:4

Our Messiah is "acquainted with grief" (Isaiah 53:3, *King James Version*), and that's good to know, because as we grow older, most of us become acquainted with it ourselves.

Grief affects all five senses.

You can see it when you watch lines of cars slowly proceeding toward a cemetery, when you read lines of an obituary describing a longtime friend, and when you observe the weary faces of a distraught family.

Grief has a sound. It's the voice of a friend who calls with shocking news, and it's the quiet whisper of the hospice worker who says, "She's gone."

Grief messes with your taste. It can steal your appetite and make your meals unappealing because it hurts to eat alone.

Grief even has an aroma. It smells like the flower arrangements in funeral homes.

Grief has a feel. Many would say it feels like hollowness—an enormous empty place in your heart. You can touch grief in the gentle hugs of mourners who stand in line to pay their respects. And for widows and widowers, it is the absence of touch, when they reach out in the night and find it empty and cold.

I am acquainted with grief for three main reasons. First, I'm human and, like it or not, grief is a normal part of life. Second, I have lived a long time, and in recent years, many of my friends, neighbors, and family members have grown old and died. Third, I have spent my entire adult life serving in church-related ministries. My pastoral roles have thrust me into more grief-producing situations than I can count, giving me up-close and personal encounters with a wide range of sorrows.

I have seen strong men weep when their parents died, and I have tried to comfort widows and widowers who struggled to tell their partners "goodbye."

I have stood with terrified families in hospital emergency rooms, waiting for good news but bracing ourselves for bad news. In one emergency room, I stood next to a woman while the doctor informed her that her husband, who seemed perfectly fine when he kissed her goodbye a few hours earlier, had suddenly died of a heart attack.

I have led memorial services for well-known individuals when thousands gathered to pay their respects, and I have presided over quiet, private funerals attended by a handful of mourners.

I have sobbed alongside young parents who held a dying baby in their arms.

I have looked into the downcast eyes of struggling believers who ask, "How do you explain this loss?" I have listened to distraught parents who demand to know, "Why did God allow my son to die?" while I silently prayed they will somehow understand that God's own Son died, too, so he knows how they feel.

I have learned that funerals make us confront not only the death of a loved one, but also our own mortality.

Ministers must deal with the sorrows and questions of others while we wrestle with our own griefs. I cried when my daughter had a miscarriage. I offered the eulogy at my dad's graveside. I stood by my mother's bedside stroking her hair while she took her last breath. I know firsthand the pain my son has faced throughout his life because he was born with cerebral palsy; and I am proud of the way he serves in ministry today. My son's best friend, a military veteran, died at age 39 from cancer resulting from exposure to radioactive materials in a war zone. One of my daughters is a registered nurse, and her husband is a skilled emergency room physician, but after he found a lump in his hip, he received a life-threatening cancer diagnosis. Our family has continued to walk through this dark valley together, and I rejoice that my son-in-law has not only survived but he continues to practice medicine to this day. My youngest daughter, an international adoptee, has helped me understand the unique form of grief that comes from not knowing one's birth parents. Today she is a therapist who specializes in assisting adoptive families.

Yes, I have learned a thing or two about grief. Live long enough, and we all become acquainted with it. The U.S. Constitution recognizes our rights to "life, liberty, and the pursuit of happiness," but how will we handle death and the pain of loneliness?

Old age brings lost youth, lost health, lost dreams, and other losses that can be difficult to bear. Our parents die, and at any age, it hurts to be an orphan. We attend an increasing number of funerals for lifelong friends. Gradually, married couples realize the time will come when one partner will say "goodbye" to the other, and the wedding vow that states "till death do us part" takes on new meaning.

Coming to Grips with Grief

Lest you get the wrong impression, Candy and I aren't somber, gloomy people. We don't sit around with frowns on our faces chatting about death and dying over the dinner table every night! But we do recognize the value of seeking further education so we can deal with our own grief and assist others in times of sorrow and loss.

Our expertise pales in comparison with the breadth of experience Dr. Alan Wolfelt possesses. As director of the Center for Loss and Life Transition headquartered in Fort Collins, Colorado, Dr. Wolfelt has authored dozens of books on death, grief, mourning, and loss, and he has provided counseling, instruction, and comfort to thousands.[1]

Candy and I became acquainted with Dr. Wolfelt during a workshop he led called "Tending to Your Broken Heart When Someone Dies: Hope for Your Healing." Later, we attended his four-day conference in Colorado on "Exploring the Spiritual Dimensions of Death, Grief, and Mourning." During that week, we interacted with three dozen participants, many of whom have faced losses of their own, and like us, they seek to serve as companions and comforters to others.

How will you handle grief and mourning in your senior adult years? I am neither a psychologist nor an expert on thanatology (the study of death and dying), but the losses I have experienced in my own life, along with my years of ministry and my access to insightful teachers, have taught me several lessons I want to share with you in this chapter.

My first observation is an unpleasant one.

FOR MOST OF US, GRIEF IS UNAVOIDABLE.

We shouldn't assume we can slide through life without dealing with sorrow. Job was right: We are "born to trouble as surely as sparks fly upward" (Job 5:7). Pain and loss eventually come our way, and it's important to acknowledge them, not deny them and pretend they don't hurt. This is a difficult lesson, especially for those of us who were taught to stifle our emotions rather than deal with them openly and honestly.

The only way to avoid suffering would be to avoid loving. C.S. Lewis rightly observed, "The greater the love the deeper the grief."

Candy and I have been married half a century—about three-fourths of our lives. We are partners in life and coworkers in ministry, glued together in faith, hope, and love. She is my best friend and my soulmate. People usually say our names together. It's not just "Dave," it's "Dave and Candy." If she were to die, I would have to wrestle with my own identity and ask the question, *Who am I without her?* If I die, she will have to deal with her own version of the same issue. But unless we happen to die at the same time, one of us eventually will face that profound loss.

During the conference on grief and mourning, Candy and I made a new friend, Dave Shank. One evening after class we ate dinner with him at a little restaurant where he shared his story over a bowl of pasta. Dave learned about death and dying by serving as a funeral director for 23 years and as a funeral service consultant for another 23 years, working in a total of 13 states. When he and his wife, Rhonda, retired in Arizona, he had nearly half a century of experience in the funeral business under his belt. But everything changed during Rhonda's 20-month battle with ovarian cancer that ended when she died on Sunday evening, September 26, 2021.

"In all those years working with funerals, I became very acquainted with *death*," Dave told us. "But with the loss of Rhonda, I realized I was unacquainted with *grief.* At the very least, I was unprepared and ill-equipped for the emptiness I have experienced in the wake of her absence." He admitted, "I felt like the Lord spoke to me through my wife, and now that she's gone, I sometimes find it hard to discern the voice of God."

Dave continued, "After knowing Rhonda for 50 years, her absence has left me feeling like a torn and ragged piece of fabric taken from a garment that once was so rich and beautiful. But she remains a part of me, at least the part of me that's better than what I'd be without having her in my life."

Dr. Wolfelt offers these encouraging words to widows and widowers: "If God has given you a heroic love, he can also help you have a heroic mourning."

GRIEF TAKES DIFFERENT FORMS.

It's not a matter of "one size fits all." The apostle Peter reminded first-century Christians, "you greatly rejoice, though now for a little while you may have had to suffer grief in all kinds of trials" (1 Peter 1:6). A form of the Greek word translated "grief" in that verse appears in Matthew 26:37, where Jesus was "sorrowful" and troubled while he prayed in the Garden of Gethsemane; and in Mark 14:19, where the disciples were "saddened" to hear that someone in their group was going to betray Jesus. In other words, Jesus grieved, and so did his original disciples. And notice: Peter says grief comes "in all kinds of trials." Losses come in many forms: illness, death, divorce, betrayal, job loss, physical separation, natural disasters, and relational estrangement, to name a few. But what loss feels more bitter (and more final) than the death of a loved one?

Here are some other ways to describe the kinds of loss that produce grief.

Real losses take away people and possessions we value, and *imaginary losses* can be painful, too. (Some of us spend a lot of energy grieving losses that never actually happen.)

Some losses are *concrete*, while others are *abstract*. If you lose the ability to walk or the freedom to drive, or if a loved one passes away, those are concrete losses. If retirement diminishes your self-esteem, it's an abstract loss, but it's still significant. The death of a spouse is a concrete loss, but adjusting to widowhood involves many abstract losses as well.

Immediate grief arises in the shocking moments when you first hear bad news. Sorrow hits you like a sledgehammer and leaves you reeling. Or maybe you have experienced *delayed grief*. At first you stayed calm and at the time of the loss, others commented, "You are handling things so well," but waves of profound sadness poured over you later.

Anticipatory grief refers to the sadness that comes before a loss occurs—like worrying about an expected downsizing at work, facing a pending divorce, or going through an extended illness while preparing for the inevitability of death.

The loss of a loved one also leads to *unfulfilled hopes and expectations.* You looked forward to having your dad walk you down the aisle when you married, or you thought your wife would get to enjoy your grandkids together with you, but death upended your plans and altered your expectations.

Dr. Wolfelt identifies five levels mourners go through as we adapt to significant losses and integrate them into our lives:

1. *Shock.* We are stunned and disoriented when we hear the difficult news about a loved one's death.

2. *Cognitive integration.* We know and begin to accept (at least intellectually) the reality that someone we loved has died.

3. *Affective or feeling.* Our emotions process how this loss is affecting us.

4. *Search for meaning and spiritual growth.* We might ask, "What does this loss mean for my life, and how can I cope and grow through it?"

5. *Behavior.* We begin to act in a way that remembers and honors our loved ones, while at the same time, we learn to shift from experiencing their presence to cherishing their memory.[2]

GRIEF HAS COMMON CHARACTERISTICS, BUT EACH INDIVIDUAL EXPERIENCES IT A LITTLE DIFFERENTLY.

Grief isn't the same as mourning. Dr. Wolfelt considers *grief* an internal response (the thoughts and feelings you experience after a loss) while *mourning* is "grief gone public" (an outward expression of grief). People who grieve on the inside need to mourn and express it on the outside by sharing their sadness with others. In his words, "Mourning is the public 'hello' we give to our grief."

Emotions are fickle and unpredictable. They come and go. About the time you conclude you are fine and the loss doesn't hurt anymore, you might be hit by a sudden "grief burst"—unexpected sadness triggered by something others might not even notice. A song reminds you of your deceased friend's singing voice. The aroma of homemade bread triggers memories of your mom. A whiff of aftershave from a passing stranger reminds you of your dad. The sight of a dog in the park reminds you how much you miss a favorite pet.

Grief stirs a variety of emotions, including depression, confusion, anger, and regret. In many cases, grief feels like numbness, emptiness, and disorientation. Mourners may ask questions like, "How can I go on?" or "Why didn't he take better care of himself?" or perhaps, "What could I have done differently to prevent this death from happening?"

Grief might generate feelings of protest, lethargy, guilt, fear, anxiety, panic—and perhaps even relief. It can cause physical symptoms ranging from exhaustion to hyperactivity, from loss of appetite to overeating, from insomnia that keeps mourners awake half the night to weariness that makes them want to stay in bed all day. Grief can lead a person to say, "I feel like part of me died." It is natural to want back familiar people and things you loved.

Maybe that's why God seems to show a special level of concern for widows.

While visiting Germany, Candy and I saw beautiful white swans swimming in lakes and rivers, and we learned that swans typically mate for life. According to news reports, one brokenhearted swan mourning its dead mate brought trains to a halt for almost an hour on a high-speed rail line in Germany. The sad swan refused to abandon the tracks after its companion flew into an overhead electric line and died. Twenty-three trains were delayed while the grieving fowl "sat beside the body in mourning, resisting attempts by officials to lure it away," according to reports.[3] One reporter summed up the story by writing, "Everyone needs some space when they're heartbroken."

My friends John and Joyce Samples married young and served together in church-related ministry for nearly 72 years. After Joyce died in 2022, their friends weren't used to seeing John without her. They asked him, "Do you have people to do things with, like going out to lunch?"

"Yes, I have plenty of people to do things with," John answered. "The problem is, I no longer have someone to do *nothing* with!" Many widows and widowers can relate to his words. Even when you are doing nothing in particular, there is security and comfort just in having your spouse around.

Bob Russell attended a reception honoring the fiftieth wedding anniversary for two of his friends. He congratulated the couple and remarked, "That's a long time!" and his friend responded simply, "Not as long as it would have been without her."[4]

GRIEF DOESN'T FOLLOW A SET TIMETABLE.

When a loved one dies, we might want to hurry through the sadness as quickly as possible, but the process cannot be rushed. Grieving requires a willingness to wait.

Abraham and Sarah waited for decades before the Lord kept his promise and gave them a son. Moses tended sheep in Midian for 40 years before leading the Hebrews out of Egypt, only to wander another 40 years in the wilderness before he finally arrived at the brink of the Promised Land. David was anointed as the eventual king of Israel, but he had to wait until King Saul's reign concluded before it was time for him to lead.

AN UNDERAPPRECIATED BIBLICAL DISCIPLINE

Waiting is a difficult but valuable part of life. Consider what the Scriptures tell us about waiting in passages like these.

- "But if we hope for what we do not yet have, we wait for it patiently" (Romans 8:25).

- "Wait for the Lord; be strong and take heart and wait for the Lord" (Psalm 27:14).

- "We wait in hope for the Lord; he is our help and our shield" (Psalm 33:20).

- "Be still before the Lord and wait patiently for him" (Psalm 37:7).

- "I wait for the Lord, my whole being waits, and in his word I put my hope" (Psalm 130:5).

- "Be patient, then, brothers and sisters, until the Lord's coming. See how the farmer waits for the land to yield its valuable crop, patiently waiting for the autumn and spring rains" (James 5:7).

Most of us are not good at waiting. As a culture, we even display impatience about the process of mourning. Sometimes at a ballgame, the players and crowd observe a moment of silence to honor someone who died—but it's quickly time to play ball again. It's good if your employer grants you bereavement leave, but if you go back to work after losing a loved one, it will take more than a few days to get over the loss.

Grief doesn't conform to a set timetable. After your loved one dies, will you feel better in time? Probably—but how much time is hard to say. Will your sadness diminish in a month? In a year? In five years? Perhaps. But will you ever have complete "closure" after the death of a loved one? Maybe not. (Dr. Wolfelt observes, "Closure is for windows and doors. Mourning goes on.") Don't assume you can quickly "let go" of your grief. Memorial services can help you deal with the loss, but instead of bringing closure, the visitation and funeral ceremony may indicate the grieving has only just begun.

During my doctoral studies years ago, I took a class called "The Minister's Personal Growth" taught by professor Dr. Archibald Hart. He has written several books about emotional health from a biblical and clinical standpoint, and at that time he also served as dean of the School of Psychology at Fuller Theological Seminary. As part of our class, Dr. Hart talked with our group of ministry students about dealing with our own losses and grief. I remember him saying, "If you minimize what you're going through or simply try to 'talk yourself out' of the depression, it will usually take you longer to get out of it." Instead of denying or minimizing your pain, Dr. Hart insisted, "The quicker you allow yourself to experience the depth of it, the sooner you may recover." As Dr. Wolfelt puts it, "You have to feel the loss to heal the loss." I have found this true in my own experiences with grief. If I lean into my sorrow, I tend to come out of it faster than if I try to ignore and suppress it.

Job's friends came and sat with him when they learned about his suffering. At first "they sat on the ground with him for seven days and seven nights. No one said a word to him, because they saw how great his suffering was" (Job 2:13). Sitting with him in silence for a whole week was a therapeutic response. Later, when they tried to figure out the reasons for Job's suffering, things seemed to get worse. They even pointed fingers of blame at Job himself; but by minimizing Job's losses, the friends aggravated his depression. It appears that the best help Job's friends provided was simply being present and keeping their mouths shut.

Dr. Alan Wolfelt recommends a grief counseling model he calls "companioning," which means "to walk alongside the grieving person—bearing witness, listening, affirming, and learning from them instead of the other way around."[5]

Grief is an ongoing journey. Someone who asks, "Will these bad feelings ever go away?" is looking for hope anchored in authenticity and honesty. I have found it helpful to say something like this: "Based on my personal experience and my interactions with other people who have experienced loss, you won't always feel like this. Things are going to be different. I can't predict how long the process will take. But you can't go around it; it's like a tunnel. You have to go through it to get to the other side."

EVEN DURING SEASONS OF GRIEF, YOU CAN STILL BE OF SERVICE TO GOD AND OTHERS.

It's OK to slow down and curtail normal activities during a season of mourning, but as we move through the tunnels of our own grief, we may find opportunities to comfort others who are "in the tunnel" as well. Dr. Wolfelt says, "If someone feels hopeless, give them some of your hope until they can find it on their own." Realistically, he admits, "When it comes to giving support, friends and family tend to break down into a 'law of thirds.' One third of the people offer support, another third remain neutral, and a final third are negative or hurtful. Be in the first third whenever you can."[6]

My friend Jennifer McGhee quotes Isaiah 61:3, where God promises to bestow on his people "a crown of beauty instead of ashes, the oil of joy instead of mourning." She says, "This verse came to life for me when, after losing most of my family (11 deaths in 18 months), I was in total despair and depression overtook me." Those 11 deaths included her father and her oldest brother. Later, her sister and brother-in-law were killed in a motorcycle accident, and their daughter who was pregnant at the time lost her baby. Jennifer's brother John died suddenly of a heart attack a short time later. In between, her best friend and her favorite uncle died, too.

Feeling overwhelmed, Jennifer decided to move to Indianapolis so she could be closer to her daughter and grandchildren. While attending her first worship service at her new church home, Connection Pointe Christian Church in Brownsburg, Indiana, she heard about a ministry called GriefShare (www.griefshare.org), which uses video messages and group discussions to serve mourners in what their website calls "a safe,

HOW TO HELP GRIEVING FRIENDS

Ralph Waldo Emerson said, "You cannot do a kindness too soon, for you never know how soon it will be too late." How can you show kindness to your grieving friends?

Be available. Don't abandon or avoid them because their sadness makes you uncomfortable and you don't know what to say. "Companion" them.

Be a listener. You don't have to answer all their questions, but you can help them keep the lines of communication open. Give them the gift of a listening ear. Shakespeare wrote, "Give sorrow words; the grief that does not speak knits up the o-er wrought heart and bids it break."

Be a learner. Don't try to "fix" your grieving friends. Show compassionate curiosity. Invite them to share their stories and talk about their loved ones. They are the experts about their own feelings, not you, so ask them to teach you. Speak the name of the person who died. Share your memories about the deceased and invite others to share their memories, too. Say things like, "Tell me about her—what was she like? What will you never forget about her? What do you hope others will remember about her?" Dr. Wolfelt advises, "Invite mourners to the dance—but let them lead."

Don't overidentify or be overly curious. Allow them to say what they are comfortable sharing. Don't say, "I know how you feel," because you probably don't; and don't seek more details than you need to know.

Don't minimize their grief. Dr. Wolfelt recommends that we should avoid saying things that are "true, but not helpful," like "You had him for 50 years" or "Well, he lived to be 89." Use words that lift people up instead of pushing them down.

Don't compare one person's grief with another's. "Each heart knows its own bitterness" (Proverbs 14:10). Even if another person's sorrow looks mild to you, remember that you haven't walked in their shoes. Another piece of ancient wisdom says, "Like one who takes away a garment on a cold day, or like vinegar poured on a wound, is one who sings songs to a heavy heart" (Proverbs 25:20). If you have a casual attitude about someone's heavy heart, you will add to their burden instead of easing their pain.

Don't tell a grieving person to "let go." The instinct of a mourner is not to let go, but to hold on. As Dr. Wolfelt puts it, over time, "You can help them shift the relationship from one of interactive presence to one of appropriate memory."

Encourage them to identify "linking objects"—items that help them remember and honor their loves. A linking object might be a photo, a piece of jewelry, a book, or some other memento that stirs positive memories.

welcoming place where people understand the difficult emotions of grief."
Jennifer says:

> I knew GriefShare was what I desperately needed! I attended
> that first 13-week session and felt God was calling me to be the
> leader. Now, 14 years later, I have been blessed to see how God
> has met all my needs and I have had the privilege to see God
> work in other people's lives as well. During the first GriefShare
> gathering, the people come in so broken, but after meeting
> each week they see God is there and walking beside them to
> give them the strength to face each new day. As we meet each
> week, we laugh and cry together and share our thoughts and
> struggles, and one added thing makes a big difference: *Jesus!*

Jennifer believes God has used her own grief to help others. "I'm a
simple senior citizen," she says, "who sometimes has nothing to offer."
But after years of facilitating group discussions for mourners, she quickly
adds, "I now have a much closer relationship with Jesus and a purpose.
An added blessing is forming new friendships with others as they navigate
their journey of grief." Jennifer appreciates another Bible verse, which says,
"Return to your rest, my soul, for the Lord has been good to you" (Psalm
116:7). She asks, "Who knew that God had something more for me in the
later years of life?"

GRIEF COMPELS US TO ASK IMPORTANT QUESTIONS.

Grief exercises emotional muscles that otherwise go unused, and
losses cannot always be explained rationally. But grief has an intellectual,
logical component as well. In times of loss, it's not uncommon to ask, *What
do I believe about life after death? Where is God in this situation? How can I pray
when I feel sad? Where can I find comfort?*

Pain and sorrow raise the classic question, *How do we reconcile God's
power and goodness with the existence of evil in the world?* I have addressed this
question at length in my books, *Honest Questions, Honest Answers* and *Faith
Under Fire* (a study of 1 and 2 Peter). Here's how I summarize my answer in
Faith Under Fire.

> There's no "ouchless" answer to the problem of suffering. Pain is
> real, but so is God's concern. No matter how well we understand

the problem intellectually, we struggle to deal with it emotionally when we, or others we love, writhe in pain.

A satisfying answer to the problem of evil can be found only in Jesus. He shows that God indeed is good, for Christ lived on this planet in perfect innocence. And Jesus shows us that God indeed is all-powerful—even able to overcome death. . . .

The cross holds the answer to the problem of evil. When all has been said and done, the answer isn't in how we handle suffering, but in how God handled it.[7]

Caregivers can "companion" our grieving friends and come alongside them in their search, even if we can't answer every question they ask. It's been said, "Pain can make us bitter, or it can make us better." Pain makes us better when it causes us to pursue a stronger relationship with God.

GRIEF ISN'T A BETRAYAL OF FAITH; IT CAN AND SHOULD BE COMPATIBLE WITH FAITH.

Did anyone ever give you the impression that if you have enough faith, you will never grieve? Actually, the Bible tells about numerous strong believers who dealt with sorrow and loss. Don't shame yourself for being human. When you experience grief, you are in good company.

The shepherd boy David had enough faith to defeat Goliath; but when sorrow overwhelmed him, the brave warrior sounded like a drowning victim crying out for a lifeguard. He prayed, "Save me, O God, for the waters have come up to my neck. I sink in the miry depths, where there is no foothold. I have come into the deep waters; the floods engulf me" (Psalm 69:1-2). Grief can feel like that—as if you're sinking in sorrow so deep you can hardly breathe. And David wasn't finished. He went on to confess his weariness and frustration: "I am worn out calling for help; my throat is parched. My eyes fail, looking for my God" (Psalm 69:3).

Was David betraying his faith in God by saying such hard-hitting prayers? No! Faith moved him to be honest with the Lord. His faith was under stress. It was faith suffering, faith questioning, faith wondering, faith weeping—but it was still faith. In that very same Psalm, David's faith moved him to cry out to the Lord, "Rescue me from the mire, do not let me sink; . . . Do not let the floodwaters engulf me or the depths swallow me up or the pit close its mouth over me. Answer me, Lord, out of the goodness of your love; in your great mercy turn to me" (Psalm 69:14-16).

Jeremiah had great faith, but he grieved so much for the Jewish people that he has been nicknamed the weeping prophet. Believers known for their strong faith faced torture, jeers, flogging, chains, imprisonment, poverty, persecution, and other forms of mistreatment, yet they "were all commended for their faith" (Hebrews 11:35-39). For now, at least, God doesn't eliminate all sorrow from our lives, but he promises a great day is coming when he will "wipe every tear from [our] eyes" (Revelation 21:4).

Instead of being a betrayal of faith, grief can generate in us the gutsy kind of faith that trusts God even when we go through the fire.

GRIEF DOESN'T HAVE THE LAST WORD.

After a loved one dies, sorrow can close in like a cold wind on a dark February day when it seems like spring will never come. In comparison with eternity, our griefs last only "for a little while" (1 Peter 1:6); but when you're in the throes of grief, it's not unusual to go through what many believers call a "dark night of the soul." The death of a loved one can trigger sadness so profound, it feels like it will never end.

Dr. Wolfelt points out, "As long as you love the person who died, you will continue to grieve them." He goes on, however, to offer these words of encouragement:

> But thank goodness, grief *does* change over time. It softens. The intense early pain grows duller [and] then eventually settles into the background—especially if you've been actively mourning along the way. Like a serious but healed wound on your body, it's always there, but it no longer demands your daily (or hourly or minute-by-minute) attention. Nor does it hurt so much.
>
> Love doesn't end. It learns to live with the absence. I promise you, you will feel better. Your life will feel normal again, even though it will be a new normal.[8]

Even if grief accompanies you for the rest of your life, the Lord is willing to be your companion, too.

Grief doesn't have the last word; Jesus has the last word! When the apostle John beheld the risen Christ, the Lord's glory was almost more than he could bear. John wrote, "When I saw him, I fell at his feet as though dead. Then he placed his right hand on me and said, 'Do not be afraid. I am the First and the Last. I am the Living One; I was dead, and now look. I am alive for ever and ever. And I hold the keys of death and Hades'" (Revelation 1:17-18). When you are overwhelmed by grief, can you picture Jesus reaching out and placing his right hand on you? Can you hear him assuring you that he himself went through death—but now he is alive forever?

Joseph Scriven was acquainted with grief. Raised and educated in Ireland, Scriven dreamed of serving in the military, but health problems prevented him from achieving his goal. Tragically, his fiancée drowned on the night before their wedding, and to cope with his grief, Scriven left Ireland and moved to Canada to start a new life. There he earned a modest salary by teaching school, and he met and courted another woman; but the woman he loved fell ill and died before they could marry, leaving him to grieve once again. In 1855, Scriven wrote a poem and sent it to comfort his mother back in Ireland. Later, a songwriter used the poem to compose a much-loved hymn that begins with Scriven's words: "What a friend we have in Jesus, all our sins and griefs to bear!"[9] Scriven indeed was well-acquainted with grief. As the song reminds us, Christ not only bears all our sins; he bears our griefs as well.

The Master Teacher said, "Blessed are those who mourn, for they will be comforted" (Matthew 5:4). Let's not overlook the fact this famous Beatitude contains two parts. Part one states, "Blessed are those who mourn," which is a counterintuitive statement. Jesus' original listeners must have been stunned to hear him pronounce a special blessing on those who endure sadness. It's tempting to assume mourning is incompatible with happiness and well-being. But to experience the blessedness Jesus speaks about, we can't skip the mourning part. We must go through the mourning to get to the second part: "For they will be comforted." Instead of sugarcoating grief, Jesus made it plain that for comfort to occur, mourning comes first.

Will mourners receive the comfort Jesus spoke about in this lifetime or the next? The answer isn't "either/or," it's "both/and." In the present, followers of Jesus receive comfort from the Holy Spirit, whom Jesus called "the Comforter" or *Paraklete,* the one "called alongside" to encourage and strengthen us. We also receive comfort from other believers who understand what it means to "mourn with those who mourn" (Romans 12:15). And we find comfort in Scriptures like Psalm 46:1, which assures us, "God is our refuge and strength, an ever-present help in trouble."

Our ultimate healing, however, won't happen here, but in the hereafter. Grief is inevitable on this side of heaven; but the reality of grief doesn't obliterate the authenticity of hope. That's why the apostle Paul told the Thessalonian believers, "you do not grieve like the rest of mankind, who have no hope" (1 Thessalonians 4:13).

Even in the face of death, we have hope! This is the message of the gospel. God is forever. Heaven is forever. Love abides forever. While the hollowness, loneliness, and sadness of grief may not fade with time, the Lord offers us a "living hope through the resurrection of Jesus Christ from the dead" and "an inheritance that can never perish, spoil or fade" (1 Peter 1:3-4).

Years ago, in his class on "The Minister's Personal Growth," Professor Archibald Hart discussed how to handle depression and loss. He had a lot to say about this subject, but I particularly remember Dr. Hart reading from Philippians 3:7-9, where the apostle Paul wrote:

> But whatever were gains to me I now consider loss for the sake of Christ. What is more, I consider everything a loss because of the surpassing worth of knowing Christ Jesus my Lord, for whose sake I have lost all things. I consider them garbage, that I may gain Christ and be found in him, not having a righteousness of my own that comes from the law, but that which is through faith in Christ—the righteousness that comes from God on the basis of faith.

Reflecting on that Scripture, Dr. Hart pointed out, "All of life is loss. The sooner we accept this, the healthier we will be." Speaking to a classroom full of ministry leaders, our professor advised us, "Do your grieving ahead of time! As Paul did, go ahead and accept the loss of all worldly things—but then recognize Christ's victory."

Like a baseball team with a won-lost record, Paul wrote a long list of achievements he had accumulated in the "Win" column of his life (Philippians 3:4-6)—and then he declared his willingness to move them all over to the "Loss" column. As long as he had Christ in the "Win" column, that was enough.

To follow Christ, we give up things that don't last forever, but in the process, we find hope that never goes away. The late missionary Jim Elliot famously said, "He is no fool who gives what he cannot keep to gain what he cannot lose."

The risen Lord can change the sadness of mourning into the bright hope of morning. He can turn long dark nights into bright new days. In times of pain and disappointment, he can be your comfort, your companion, and your hope.

MORE THAN YOU CAN ASK OR IMAGINE

When I was in my early thirties, I wrote a short list of places I hoped to visit before I die. It included some predictable destinations (Alaska, Hawaii) and some not-so-predictable places (England, Maine). For some reason, my list also included Switzerland. I don't know why. Maybe it's because I like the food: Swiss cheese, Swiss steak, and Swiss chocolate. When we were closing in on age 70, Candy and I finally traveled to Switzerland.

After a couple of days in Basel and Zurich, we took a six-hour train ride called the Glacier Express to the town of Zermatt, located near the famous Matterhorn. The long train ride gave me time to create a corny joke that I gladly shared with my fellow travelers: "What is Switzerland's least popular attraction? *The 'Doesn't Matterhorn.'*"

The morning air was cool and clear, and the sun shone brightly as we boarded another train that took us up the steep incline to the Gornergrat Glacier near some of the Alps' highest peaks. The blue skies continued all afternoon while we hiked down a trail surrounded by evergreen forests, snow-capped mountains, picturesque Swiss chalets, and meadows filled with wildflowers. For good measure, there was even a flock of sheep grazing nearby.

We took dozens of photos that day with our cell phones. Candy took a picture that shows me walking alone on the mountain trail with the sun shining on the Alps in the background. For some reason, that particular picture makes me tear up whenever I see it. I told Candy, "Please be sure to include that photo in my funeral service someday!"

But whenever we look at the photos from that memorable afternoon, Candy and I agree: "Our pictures don't do it justice!" No matter how powerful the camera or skillful the photographer, there was no way a cell phone camera could capture the beauty we saw that day. You had to be there! The colorful scenes we enjoyed on the mountainside are etched on our minds but difficult to put into words. Even though our pictures bring happy memories, they cannot fully express what we saw and shared together that day in the shadow of the Matterhorn.

Likewise, there is a lot I don't know about heaven. But here is what I do know. The Lord our God "is able to do immeasurably more than all we ask or imagine" (Ephesians 3:20-21). And that is an amazing statement, because when it comes to heaven, I can "ask or imagine" a lot!

I don't picture heaven as a dull, bland place where people sit around on clouds strumming harps. I prefer to think God will give the physical universe a complete do-over, creating a "new heaven and a new earth" where we can dwell with him forever (Revelation 21:1). I suspect that glorious place will be like the Garden of Eden—an environment untainted by pollution and unstained by sin—a place where humans reflect God's undistorted image as he originally intended. Finally, we will relate to God and to each other in harmony as we were designed to do.

Since the Creator chose to fill the earth with fascinating animals, it's easy for me to imagine animals inhabiting the new heaven and new earth. After all, the prophet Isaiah described the messianic age by saying, "The wolf will live with the lamb, the leopard will lie down with the goat, the calf and the lion and the yearling together; and a little child will lead them. The cow will feed with the bear, their young will lie down together, and the lion will eat straw like the ox" (Isaiah 11:6-7). I picture heaven as a peaceful, purposeful place filled with meaningful work, glorious colors, and soul-satisfying worship that far surpass the sights, sounds, feelings, tastes, and smells our current earth has to offer. And remember, God can do far more than we imagine!

I believe heaven will be a place of unbridled joy where loved ones reunite, like the time Jesus resurrected a young man and "gave him back to his mother" (Luke 7:15). I am convinced we will recognize each other there. No name tags will be needed! During the Lord's transfiguration, his disciples watched and listened while Jesus engaged in conversation with Moses and Elijah, two great faith figures who had died centuries before. They were still identifiable; they retained their names and evidently their unique personalities; and no one needed to wear a name tag. Paul urged the Thessalonians to look forward to a grand time ahead when the Lord will gather his followers from the past and the present and "we will be with the Lord forever. Therefore encourage one another with these words" (1 Thessalonians 4:17-18). To me, that sounds like the best family reunion ever. And remember, God can do even more than we can imagine!

When John wrote the book of Revelation, the Holy Spirit guided him to use human words to describe divine realities. John's grand vision portrays heaven with glorious imagery: streets paved with gold, city gates made of single pearls, a river flowing with crystal clear water, a tree that never stops bearing fruit. John exhausted the limits of human language with artful descriptions of heavenly glory that include gemstones and bright lights, vibrant colors, and multitudes of angels praising God. And yet, although John faithfully executed his mission and painted a beautiful picture of heaven, just as Candy and I learned on that mountainside in the Alps, sometimes even the best pictures cannot fully capture a scene that is beyond our ability to comprehend. When you're there in person, the reality of heaven's glory will be even greater than you can imagine.

God has prepared for his people "what no eye has seen, what no ear has heard, and what no human mind has conceived" (1 Corinthians 2:9). Grief hurts. It can seem unbearable. But our hope in Christ compels us to "fix our eyes not on what is seen, but on what is unseen, since what is seen is temporary, but what is unseen is eternal" (2 Corinthians 4:18).

If you want your later years to be greater years, prepare to get acquainted with grief. And as the next two chapters show, you're not too old to face your own mortality. In fact, now is the perfect time to prepare for your own approaching death.

QUESTIONS FOR PERSONAL REFLECTION AND GROUP DISCUSSION

1. When have you gone through a season of sorrow or grief? What helped you through it? What did you learn from it?

2. Based on your own personal experiences, how would you describe what grief feels like?

3. Who (or what) has given you comfort in your times of grief? When and how have you given comfort to someone else in their times of grief?

4. How does your faith in God affect the way you grieve?

   a. My faith hasn't been a factor because . . .

   b. My faith gives me comfort because . . .

   c. My faith is struggling because . . .

   d. My faith has grown because . . .

5. What is your reaction to this quote from Dr. Archibald Hart? "Do your grieving ahead of time! As Paul did, go ahead and accept the loss of all worldly things—but then recognize Christ's victory."

6. How do you picture heaven? Are your ideas about heaven based on Scripture, or do they come from other sources? What is your favorite biblical description of heaven? Explain.

15 | Live Until You Die— What Wise Leaders Can Teach Us About Aging

"The wise listen to advice."
Proverbs 12:15

*"The older I get, the more I want to say, 'Why has it taken
me so long to find out there is nothing to worry about?'"*
—**Elisabeth Elliot,** missionary and author

*"I incorporated my faith into football in my preparation, my intensity, and
my performance. I wanted it all to be for his glory. Since God gave me that gift,
it was my goal to make every single play a worship performance. I decided to take
someone or something in my life and thank God for it in every game."*
—**Anthony Munoz,** offensive lineman for the Cincinnati Bengals;
NFL Hall of Fame, Class of 1998

"I want to live until I die—I mean, be fully alive."
—**Bill Gaither,** poet and songwriter

I don't want to merely grow older. I want to keep growing! That's why I
need to seek wisdom by listening to wise leaders God puts in my path. King
Solomon noted long ago, "The heart of the discerning acquires knowledge,
for the ears of the wise seek it out" (Proverbs 18:15).

In 1996, I started writing a weekly magazine column about how the
Bible applies to life. One blessing of my work as a writer has been the

opportunity to interview a number of interesting people who have served the Lord productively over the long haul.

Three interviewees stand out because, although they came from different walks of life with very different careers, all three have made a positive and lasting difference. Elisabeth Elliot was a missionary widow, Anthony Munoz is one of professional football's all-time greats, and Bill Gaither is a well-known musician and songwriter.

Elisabeth Elliot

Life magazine and numerous other publications have chronicled the story of Elisabeth Elliot and her martyred husband, Jim. Their lives inspired movies, including the 2002 documentary *Beyond the Gates of Splendor* and the 2006 film *End of the Spear*.

Elisabeth authored more than 20 books and hosted a radio program for 13 years called *Gateway to Joy*. "The deepest things that I have learned in my own life have come from the deepest suffering," she wrote. "And out of the deepest waters and the hottest fires have come the deepest things I know about God."

After she died in 2015, her family donated many of her personal effects and collections, which are now on display in the Elisabeth Elliot Collection at the Museum of the Bible in Washington, D.C. The museum's website offers this biography:

> In 1958, Christian missionary Elisabeth Elliot returned to the Ecuadorian rainforest to live with the Waodäni, the tribe who had killed her husband [Jim] only two years earlier. Her choice to forgive, rather than retaliate, sparked a change in the Waodäni, who left behind a cycle of violence to embrace a life of love. This remarkable story rippled across the globe, inspiring millions to serve God through missions. In the years that followed, Elliot created a writing system for the Waodäni language, advocated for their education, and paved the way for a New Testament translation finished in 1992. She eventually returned to the United States, becoming an active and vocal advocate for the gospel, for missions, for families, and for women. Her best-selling book, *Through Gates of Splendor*, began a writing and speaking career that lasted four decades.[1]

I met Mrs. Elliot in 1998, when she was in St. Louis to speak at the North American Christian Convention. At that time, I was editor of *The Lookout* magazine, and she agreed to sit down with me in the convention's exhibit area for an interview that we published a few weeks later. We discussed what it means to live by faith over the long haul. Here are some excerpts from our interview.

Someone has said that you are one of the few people saying the hard things anymore. You talk a lot about sacrifice and commitment. Do you think those themes are overlooked in the church today?

Elisabeth: Yes. . . . [And] I think they were overlooked way back when Jesus articulated them. . . . He made it perfectly clear that if you want to be his disciple you must give up your right to yourself. That has to be the hardest thing God asks of us. And he put it right up-front. No ifs, ands, or buts. You must give up your right to yourself, or "deny yourself."

You are known for your faith. But even people who live by faith have their down times when it's difficult to hang on. Have there been times when God seemed distant to you?

Elisabeth: As I look back over more than seven decades, I can see how there is nothing to worry about. [But] I'm a worrywart by nature. My parents were worrywarts. We come from a long line of champion worriers! And yet the Bible says not to worry about anything whatever. So even when God is being silent and doesn't seem to be giving any direction, we can rest assured that he is working his purposes out.

Have you found it more difficult or a little simpler to live by faith as you've gotten older?

Elisabeth: It is much, much simpler. It is so simple really. I don't mean *easy* when I say *simple*. But what God tells us to do is simple. Often, it's very hard to do because we're recalcitrant and we don't want to do it. Or we're saying, "Wait a minute, God, you can't really expect me to do that." Obedience always leads to joy. The older I get, the more I want to say, "Why has it taken me so long to find out there is nothing to worry about?" God is totally in charge even when the worst happens.

As you probably know, I've lost two husbands. *[Her first husband, Jim, was killed as a missionary martyr in Ecuador. Her second husband, Addison, died of cancer four years after they were married.]* In both cases, I was desperately praying for God's protection and healing. Each day I was saying to the Lord, "Could you just give me a little hint if, for example, my (second) husband is going to be cured of his cancer?" And the Lord never said yes. He just said, "I want you to trust me." I hope I've learned those lessons for good. But I don't worry nearly the way I used to. I don't think you could find a more contented and happy woman than God has finally made me.[2]

Anthony Munoz

As a lifelong sports fan, I enjoyed conversing with Anthony Munoz, one of the top offensive linemen ever to play in the NFL. He grew up near Los Angeles, where he excelled in football, basketball, and baseball. At the University of Southern California, he earned All-American honors and helped lead the Trojans to the NCAA football National Championship in 1978. He was selected by the Cincinnati Bengals as the third overall pick of the 1980 NFL Draft.

During his 13-year career, Anthony was selected to play in 11 consecutive Pro Bowls and was named the NFL Offensive Lineman of the Year multiple times. He started all but one of 186 straight games from 1980 to 1990, while battling through a number of injuries that could have ended his career. In 1991, he was honored as the Walter Payton NFL Man of the Year, and in 1998 he was enshrined in the Pro Football Hall of Fame in Canton, Ohio.

Anthony sat down with me in a coffee shop to talk about football, family, and faith. Here are some of the questions I asked, along with his responses.

What was it like for you growing up?

Anthony: I never met my dad. He was in and out of prison. I have two older brothers and two younger sisters. Mom raised the five of us by herself, working two or three jobs. We didn't have a lot financially, but we had a lot of support and encouragement. Because Mom worked so much, we had to learn how to clean the house, cook, and wash clothes. We never had a car. We rode bicycles a lot.

At what point did you realize God had blessed you with unique athletic ability?

Anthony: When I was about 7 or 8. Baseball was my first love. I was big for my age and I was already very competitive. They couldn't start the games until the coach showed my birth certificate to prove my age because I was so big. My childhood dream was to be a Major League Baseball player. I played in high school, mostly third base, and I pitched. But at six foot six and 280 pounds by my junior year in high school, it looked like the football uniforms were going to fit a little better! I always wanted to go to USC, and they offered me the opportunity to play both baseball and football.

What life-lessons did you learn from playing football?

Anthony: It's not about being a tough guy. It's about being disciplined physically and mentally. I learned that I could take myself beyond the threshold of where I thought I could go in my weightlifting and conditioning. Every year as I got older, I stepped up the intensity of my preseason conditioning. I learned to be on time. I still do that now. I learned that if you need to be somewhere at a certain time, you get up a little earlier so you can be there ahead of time. I learned how to complete tasks, and how to work together with my teammates—black, white, brown—whatever your cultural or socioeconomic background, you could work together for the same goal. I learned the importance of remaining teachable and coachable. During my twelfth and thirteenth year in the NFL, I was still learning. I've seen guys get to the point where they say, "Don't worry about it, Coach, I've got it." The slippery slope starts right away and they start to decline. You have to be able to accept constructive criticism and correct what you are doing wrong.

You endured several injuries throughout your career. What did you learn from dealing with pain and hardship?

Anthony: Injury is part of the game. It's going to happen. Three out of my four years at USC I was under the knife. I've had 15 or 16 football-related surgeries. But after missing more than half of my college games because of injuries, I didn't miss a pro game until week 14 of my eleventh year. There were questions about my durability, so that motivated me. That's why you have to do your preparation, conditioning, and weight training. You have to learn to overcome adversity. I've met a lot of successful people, and I can't remember one who hasn't gone through some tough times and obstacles. I learned from Mom and from my mentors to work hard and never give up.

How did you integrate your Christian faith with athletics?

Anthony: My wife, DeDe, and I got involved in Bible studies during our last couple years of college. After I was drafted and started playing in the NFL, God showed me that worship isn't just about Sunday morning. Colossians 3:23 says, "Whatever you do, work at it with all your heart, as working for the Lord." I incorporated my faith into football in my preparation, my intensity, and my performance. I wanted it all to be for his glory. Since God gave me that gift, it was my goal to make every single play a worship performance. I decided to take someone or something in my life and thank God for it in every game. It was natural for me to lift up my mom, and see every play as a worship performance for the glory of God, and do it to honor my mom. But the games could get very intense, and I needed a couple of focal points. I drank a lot of water during the games, so I chose the water jug and the cross bar on the goal post. Every time I took a drink of water or looked at the cross bar, they reminded me, "Lord, I'm playing for you."

Now that your playing days in the NFL are over, how do you spend your time?

Anthony: Football gives me an instant connection with young people. I started the Anthony Munoz Foundation to impact youth mentally, physically, and spiritually. The Foundation gives us a chance to mentor young people, hold character camps, and provide scholarships to help young people go to college the way others helped me.[3]

Bill Gaither

For over 50 years, no one has done more to impact Christian music than Bill and Gloria Gaither. Married since 1962, this husband-wife team has collaborated to create more than 700 gospel songs, including favorites like "Because He Lives" and "He Touched Me." They have garnered eight Grammy Awards and received over 40 Gospel Music Association (GMA) Dove Awards, earning the title "Songwriter of the Year" eight times.

A mutual friend, Ed Simcox, drove with me to the Gaithers' studio near their home in Indiana, where we sat down for an extended conversation with Bill (who was accompanied by his beloved dog Windsor). At the time of the interview, Bill was 87 years old.

Psalm 92:14 talks about how God's people "will still bear fruit in old age, they will stay fresh and green." What comes to mind when you and Gloria think about bearing fruit in this season of your life?

Bill: One word is *perspective*. I learned this from my own father. I would come to him, drained and worried about something that was going to happen, or a creative new idea I was excited about, and he would say, "Bill, I don't think this is quite as serious as you think it is." Then he would pause, and with a twinkle in his eye he would add, "and probably not as good an idea as you thought it was." He helped me get things in the right perspective. That was a good model for me. As you get older, some people think the problems are less. But if you have kids and grandkids, challenges come to you every day. If you live long enough, people will come to you and ask, "Is there hope beyond my problems?" They need someone who can help them keep things in perspective.

You also need to think about your *priorities*. Sometimes others make requests that fit within your priorities, and sometimes they don't. Gloria and I often have to discuss and decide, why are we doing this or that? What you say "yes" to and what you say "no" to will determine your effectiveness. We should set our priorities when we are young and choose to live outwardly. We're here to bless others. It's the call of the New Testament to say, "We are here to serve."

250 | NOT TOO OLD
David Faust

In 1965, you and Gloria wrote a song called, "The Longer I Serve Him, the Sweeter He Grows." The title of that song makes me want to protest and say, "Wait a minute. Life doesn't necessarily get sweeter as we get older." But you didn't say "life" gets sweeter and easier. You were talking about the Lord.

Bill: Yes, even when our circumstances are not getting sweeter, the Lord is bigger than any of this. To get the gas—the fuel—to keep going, we need to go back to the Source—the Lord.

In the New Testament, Jesus says, "Come, follow me." If you're going to follow Christ, you have to embrace the mystery and say, "There are things I can't understand." Too many times, philosophers worship at the shrine of the mind. But our minds can only take us so far.

Gloria wrote a song that quotes Jesus' words on the cross, "It is finished," where he was talking about salvation's plan—what he had come to live and die for. However, for us personally, those words, "It is finished," also describe the work of grace God does in our lives. Near the end of the song, Gloria wrote these lyrics:

Yet in my heart the battle was raging;
Not all prisoners of war have come home.
These were battlefields of my own making;
I didn't know that the war had been won.

Then I heard that the King of the Ages
Had fought all my battles for me.
And the victory was mine for the claiming,
And now, praise His name, I am free!
It is finished!⁴

In other words, you surrender and say, "I'm tired of fighting a battle that's already been won 2,000 years ago on the cross." Gloria and I like to say that when we surrender to the Lord, it's the one time when surrender means victory! We addressed some of those same ideas in another song we wrote called "I Am Loved." We met Christians who knew the Lord, but they seemed so unhappy and angry, and we wondered, "Do they know how much they are loved?" The lyrics of that song say:

I am loved! I am loved!
I can risk loving you,
For the One who knows me best loves me most.⁵

In 1971, you co-wrote with Gloria what may be your most famous song, "Because He Lives." You were young (in your thirties) when you wrote those lyrics. What do they mean to you now, in this later season of your life?

Bill: When we wrote "Because He Lives," at first I didn't think it was as good as some of our other songs. But in hindsight, when I look back on more than 50 years of that song, I feel like I'm analyzing a gift that was given to Gloria and me. God has used that song in a special way. It has been translated into hundreds of different languages and sung all over the world.

A great old hymn called "He Lives" talks about the fact of Jesus' resurrection. But we added the adverb *because*, which answers the question, "OK, this happened, but why does it make a difference to me on Monday and Tuesday, Wednesday and Thursday? How is it going to make any difference to me tomorrow when I go back to the house and "she's gone" or "he's gone" and they are not coming back? In our song, the lyrics say, "Because he lives, I can face tomorrow . . . all fear is gone . . . and life is worth the living."

People today have a huge hole in their hearts. There's a lot of anger and toxicity—an epidemic of loneliness. What makes life worth living? It's what Solomon talks about in Ecclesiastes. We search for the answer in sports, food, entertainment, sex—even through our ministries in church. People are searching for intimacy, and Hollywood has distorted what that means. I think you really begin to figure out what intimacy is when you're in your eighties. Gloria and I would say that intimacy is coming into the room and looking into the other person's eyes, and you both know what the other person is thinking.

In the first of the Ten Commandments, God says to have "no other gods before me." God comes first. If you get that wrong, you'll get life wrong. We wrote another song called, "I'll Worship Only at the Feet of Jesus." The lyrics say:

> I went to visit the shrine of plenty,
> But found its stores all filled with dust,
> I bowed at altars of gold and silver,
> But as I knelt there, they turned to rust.

So I'll worship only at the feet of Jesus,
His cup alone, my holy grail,
There'll be no other gods before Him,
Just Jesus only will never fail.[6]

Is the pressure real? Yes, but because the resurrection of Jesus is true, I can relax. I don't have to live in toxicity. Ira Stanphill wrote a song called "I Know Who Holds Tomorrow." It says, "Many things about tomorrow I don't seem to understand, but I know who holds tomorrow, and I know who holds my hand." By faith I say, "I know God holds the future, so things may not always turn out the way I want, but I know I'm in good hands."

What goes through your mind when you think about dying?

Bill: I want to live until I die—I mean, be fully alive. It's good to keep your mind going and take care of your health. You can't give in to the aches and pains. But until that hole in your heart is filled with the Lord—until you go back to the Source—you will be scared about death.

Common Themes

The three unique individuals interviewed in this chapter have had vastly different careers, but they all have borne fruit for the Lord over the long haul. Some common themes emerge from their observations.

They all found a way to focus on the Lord rather than themselves. For Anthony Munoz, a literal goal post reminded him to pursue a higher purpose. Bill and Gloria Gaither have written hundreds of songs and performed before millions, but they insist that only the Lord can fill the emptiness of the human heart. Elisabeth Elliot endured moments of profound personal loss, but she trusted and obeyed the Lord anyway.

All of them persevered through times of hardship. Anthony wisely observed, "I've met a lot of successful people, and I can't remember one who hasn't gone through some tough times and obstacles."

They exemplify what it means to "live until you die." In his late eighties, Bill Gaither continues to keep a demanding concert and recording schedule. He keeps looking ahead to the next album or performance, with no end in

GLORIA GAITHER'S INSIGHTS ABOUT THE SONG, "BECAUSE HE LIVES"

In 1998, when I was editor of The Lookout *magazine, I interviewed Gloria Gaither and she related some of her own memories about the writing of the Gaithers' best-known song, "Because He Lives." She said:*

We looked at what was happening in the '60s and said, "It's crazy for us to bring children into a world like this! If it's like this now, what will it be when [our] babies grow up to face the world?" It was a time of deep depression for us.

A few months before, we had paved the parking lot behind our office. The workmen had put down layer after layer of crushed stone, pea gravel, sand, and then blacktop. But that spring, Bill's dad took us out in the parking lot and pointed out something amazing: a little blade of grass sticking up through all those layers of pavement—a reminder of hope and persistence. In the summer I gave birth to a precious baby boy. After our winter of discontent, our baby seemed like the blade of grass pushing up through the pavement. So we wrote:

How sweet to hold our newborn baby
And feel the pride and joy he gives;
But greater still the calm assurance—
This child can face uncertain days because He lives.

I couldn't get the visual image of that blade of grass out of my mind.[7]

sight. What drives him to keep going? For that matter, what motivates any of us to get up in the morning and face a new day with energy and purpose? We can find a certain level of satisfaction by using our talents, coaching next-generation talent, and finding outlets for our creative energy. But my conversation with Bill led me to conclude he is motivated by something more. He believes God has called him to use music to inspire, encourage, and lift up others. He reminds me of the apostle Paul's words to a group of elders, "I consider my life worth nothing to me; my only aim is to finish the race and complete the task the Lord Jesus has given me—the task of testifying to the good news of God's grace" (Acts 20:24).

If we want to truly "live until we die," we must faithfully obey God's call and keep serving in the kingdom until the King calls us home. Acts 13:36 describes the death of David by saying, "Now when David had served God's purpose in his own generation, he fell asleep." That's what I want to do: serve God's purpose in my generation until I fall asleep in the arms of the Lord.

When I talk with seasoned believers whose faith has stood the test of time, they remind me that our later years will be greater years if we devote ourselves to bearing fruit for the Lord, not merely pursuing our own happiness.

Henry Wadsworth Longfellow declared, "A single conversation across the table with a wise man is better than 10 years mere study of books." As you grow older, who is sitting across the table offering you wise advice?

QUESTIONS FOR PERSONAL REFLECTION
AND GROUP DISCUSSION

1. Proverbs 12:15 says, "The way of fools seems right to them, but the wise listen to advice." Do you readily accept critique, counsel, encouragement, and advice from others? Why, or why not?

2. What lessons can you learn from this chapter's interviews with Elisabeth Elliot, Anthony Munoz, and Bill Gaither? Which of their comments stand out to you? Why?

3. What older, wiser individuals are giving you advice and speaking into your life to help you keep "growing," not just "growing old"?

4. Bill Gaither mentioned the importance of having the right *perspective* and *priorities* as you age. How has growing older shaped your perspective about life and altered your priorities?

16 | Rounding Third and Heading for Home— Preparing Yourself to Die Well

"Death is like the distant roll of thunder at a picnic.
We're aware of its impending approach,
but we'd rather not think about it."
—William H. Auden

"Show me, Lord, my life's end and the number of my days;
let me know how fleeting my life is."
—Psalm 39:4

"Pillow my head on no guesses when I die."
—Sir Joseph Cook, former prime minister of Australia

"For you have delivered me from death and my feet from stumbling,
that I may walk before God in the light of life."
—Psalm 56:13

Candy and I sat pondering an important decision. We were considering buying a piece of property, and Adrienne, the seller's representative who sat across the table from us, politely answered our questions and explained the costs. During half a century of married life, Candy and I have made a lot of purchases together. I still remember how nervous we felt when we signed the papers to buy our first house—a little two-bedroom home in a crowded Long Island neighborhood. Over the years we have bought cars, furniture, and clothes together.

But this purchase was different. We were at Oaklawn Memorial

Gardens. Adrienne works for a mortuary. The property we were buying consisted of two cemetery plots where our earthly remains will be buried someday.

To be clear, our conversation that day wasn't morbid or depressing. Although it's uncomfortable to think about death, it's wise to do so. The Bible says, "It is better to go to a house of mourning than to go to a house of feasting, for death is the destiny of everyone; the living should take this to heart" (Ecclesiastes 7:2). It's wise for senior adults to preplan our funerals, engage in estate planning, and discuss end-of-life issues with our friends and adult children. Candy and I decided to make our funeral arrangements and pay for them in advance because we hoped to lift a burden from our kids and grandkids.

On the day Dad died, my brother and I sat in another funeral home office while the director pulled a folder out of a file cabinet. He showed us a form, filled out in Dad's handwriting. Years before, our parents had prepaid for their funeral. I remarked to my brother, "This is one more way Dad and Mother showed their love for us."

As a minister, I have led many funerals over the years—including quite a few at the Oaklawn cemetery, which is located only about half a mile from our home. I drive past it every day. A sign over the front gate says, "Est. 1954" (the year I was born).

"Do you have a special gravesite in mind?" Adrienne asked. "Is anyone else buried here at Oaklawn that you want to be near?"

"The only place that comes to mind," I replied, "is the spot near some trees where Russ and Marian Blowers are buried."

Russ Blowers served more than 45 years as senior minister of East 91st Street Christian Church. I succeeded him in that role in 1999. After his wife, Marian, was diagnosed with Alzheimer's disease, Russ cared for her at home as long as he could, then he visited her regularly in the Alzheimer's unit of a nearby care center. In an article called "Good-Byes," Russ wrote:

> Good-bye is so terminal. Jesus never once said it. He said things like, "I'm leaving, but I'll be back." He said, "Peace I leave with you," but he never said good-bye.
>
> All the language groups use some word that is more in line with, "I'll see you again." *Hasta la vista. Arrivederci. Aloha. Auf Wiedersehen. Au revoir.* Humanity is not into good-byes. Good-bye can be a painful separation that lasts for a long time.

My Marian says good-bye a dozen times a day. In her lonely Alzheimer's world she repeats her litany: "I want to die. Jesus, let me die today. Good-bye." I know there will come a day when she will go Home where she wants to be. I read and read the precious promises about being where Jesus is, where there are no more tears, no more death, no more mourning, no more pain, no more "long good-byes."

And I rejoice that "good-bye" is just an old Anglo-Saxon term meaning "God be with ye." He is, and he will be, and that is enough to soften the sweet sorrow of parting.[1]

Russ and Marian's young daughter, Mindy, had Down syndrome. Russ remembered how, after Mindy died, the hospital staff left him alone with her body in a small room with curtains around it. "I took 10 minutes to talk to her and God," Russ wrote, but "I never said good-bye, because I knew she was even then 'beholding the face of my Father in heaven' [as Jesus mentions in Matthew 18:10], and I would see her again. In the winter of my weeping I said, 'See you, Mindy. See you in the morning.'"[2]

Candy and I bought two burial plots at Oaklawn, right next to Russ and Marian's graves. Someday our family and friends will gather on that lovely piece of ground to say, "God be with you till we meet again."

Facing the Reality of Death

Tombstones typically include two dates: the day people were born and the day they died. We know our birthdays, but we don't know our death days. Henri Nouwen wrote:

> We will all die one day. That is one of the few things we can be sure of. But will we die well? That is less certain. Dying well means dying for others, making our lives fruitful for those we leave behind. The big question, therefore, is not, "What can I still do in the years I have left to live?" but "How can I prepare myself for my death so my life can continue to bear fruit in the generations that will follow me?"[3]

Have you come to grips with your own mortality? You are neither too old nor too young to face the reality of your own death. Life's timeline is short. You could illustrate it with a short line contained inside two brackets, like this:

Birthday [_____] Death Day

Even if you live to be 100, your life will pass by quickly. (Almost all older people will attest to this!) But Scripture clearly indicates that your earthly death will not end your existence. Your timeline extends far beyond this earthly life and into eternity. We could illustrate it like this:

Birthday [_____] Death Day

Here's another way to think of it. Take a tape measure and imagine each inch represents a year of your life. If you are now 48 years old, pull the tape measure out to inch 48. If you are 70, pull it out to the 70-inch mark. (If you are 90 or older, you may need a longer tape measure!) When you step back and look at your life as a whole, it's amazing how much is behind you—and how little still appears to be ahead.

But it will change your perspective if you live with eternity in mind. Paul wrote:

> Though outwardly we are wasting away, yet inwardly we are being renewed day by day. For our light and momentary troubles are achieving for us an eternal glory that far outweighs them all. So we fix our eyes not on what is seen, but on what is unseen, since what is seen is temporary, but what is unseen is eternal (2 Corinthians 4:16-18).

Peter wrote:

> Praise be to the God and Father of our Lord Jesus Christ! In his great mercy he has given us new birth into a living hope through the resurrection of Jesus Christ from the dead, and into an inheritance that can never perish, spoil or fade. This inheritance is kept in heaven for you, who through faith are shielded by God's power until the coming of the salvation that is ready to be revealed in the last time. In all this you greatly rejoice, though now for a little while you may have had to suffer grief in all kinds of trials (1 Peter 1:3-6).

KEEPING YOUR APPOINTMENTS WITH GOD

You had an appointment with God when you were born. The Lord told Jeremiah, "Before I formed you in the womb, I knew you" (Jeremiah 1:5).

You have an appointment with God when you are reborn. Jesus told the aging leader Nicodemus, "Very truly I tell you, no one can see the kingdom of God unless they are born again" (John 3:3-8). Your soul gets a do-over when you accept Christ as your Savior and Lord and your sins are forgiven (John 3:16; Acts 2:38; Colossians 2:9-14; Titus 3:3-7; 1 Peter 1:3).

You have an appointment with God when you die, for "people are destined to die once, and after that to face judgment" (Hebrews 9:27).

God always keeps his appointments. If your soul is secure with him, you won't be "disappointed" when you die!

Nyna looked serene as she walked into my office. She had requested an appointment without specifying what she wanted to discuss. Though our paths had crossed at church, I didn't know her well, and my ministerial instincts told me to brace myself to hear a challenging question or a complaint about something happening in our congregation.

"I'm 81 years old," she began, "and I want to let you know a little about my story." Her smile and peaceful demeanor put me at ease. Getting right to the point, she said, "I have cancer and I have been under hospice care for the last nine months."

Surprised, I blurted out, "But you look like the picture of health."

She nodded and smiled. "So far, I have surprised the doctors and I'm doing very well. Caregivers come to my house each week, but I don't need much from them. Mostly we just sit and talk."

She seems sincere, I thought, *but is she in denial?*

"I want to talk with you about who will lead my funeral," she continued. "My health is holding up for now, but the cancer eventually will end things. In the meantime, I choose to enjoy my life."

We talked about how her faith in Christ affected the way she handled her illness. Earnestly she said, "This has been one of the best seasons of my entire life. Once you finally accept that you are going to die, you are free."

She's not in denial, I realized. *She's demonstrating a profound kind of acceptance.* About two years after that conversation in my office, I presided at Nyna's funeral service.

How could her faith be so resilient and steadfast in the presence of crushing sorrow?

Faith has many faces. You see it in the wide-eyed wonder of a child in Sunday school who hears about Jesus' miracles for the first time, and on the face of a new believer who stands in the baptistery and confesses, "I believe that Jesus is the Christ, the Son of the living God." You can see faith in idealistic teenagers who want to change the world, and in seasoned believers who trust God even though they recognize how little of the world they can change. You can see faith in the wrinkled brows of deep thinkers whose souls bear the scars of intellectual questions and emotional wounds, yet they cling to the cross and the empty tomb because with Simon Peter they ask, "Lord, to whom shall we go? You have the words of eternal life" (John 6:68).

That day when I met with Nyna in my office, I saw faith on the face of a woman in her eighties who was not afraid to die. And as a result, she was free to live.

Preparing Yourself to Die

In Scripture, the Lord is called "the living God" (for example, in Matthew 16:16, Peter calls Jesus "the Messiah, the Son of the living God"). God is very much alive and he is the source of all life. God breathed into Adam's nostrils "the breath of life, and the man became a living being" (Genesis 2:7), and throughout history it has been God who "gives everyone life and breath and everything else" (Acts 17:25). We all can join with the psalmist who praised God by saying, "You created my inmost being; you knit me together in my mother's womb" (Psalm 139:13). Life is a precious gift to be respected, enjoyed, and protected.

That's why the Bible portrays death as an intruder—a violation of God's original intent for his perfect creation. Scripture calls death "the last enemy to be destroyed" (1 Corinthians 15:26). One author sums up biblical teaching about death by saying, "The theme of death is expressed descriptively (as history), poetically (as lamentation and complaint), theologically (as the outcome of sin), and eschatologically (as overcome through the resurrection of Jesus Christ)."[4] Another writer refers to death as "the Great Interruption, tearing loved ones away from us, or us from

BIBLICAL ANSWERS TO THREE COMMON QUESTIONS ABOUT DEATH

1. **Why do we die?**

    "And the Lord God commanded the man, 'You are free to eat from any tree in the garden; but you must not eat from the tree of the knowledge of good and evil, for when you eat from it you will certainly die'" (Genesis 2:16-17; see also Genesis 3:17-19).

    "Therefore, . . . sin entered the world through one man, and death through sin, and in this way death came to all people, because all sinned" (Romans 5:12).

    "Then, after desire has conceived, it gives birth to sin; and sin, when it is full-grown, gives birth to death" (James 1:15).

2. **"If someone dies, will they live again?" (Job 14:14).**

    "Multitudes who sleep in the dust of the earth will awake: some to everlasting life, others to shame and everlasting contempt. Those who are wise will shine like the brightness of the heavens, and those who lead many to righteousness, like the stars for ever and ever" (Daniel 12:2-3).

    "Jesus said to her, 'I am the resurrection and the life. The one who believes in me will live, even though they die'" (John 11:25).

3. **Are heaven and hell real?**

    "The Son of Man will send out his angels, and they will weed out of his kingdom everything that causes sin and all who do evil. They will throw them into the blazing furnace, where there will be weeping and gnashing of teeth. Then the righteous will shine like the sun in the kingdom of their Father. Whoever has ears, let them hear" (Jesus, in Matthew 13:41-43).

    "A time is coming when all who are in their graves will hear his voice and come out— those who have done what is good will rise to live, and those who have done what is evil will rise to be condemned" (Jesus, in John 5:28-29).

    "Then I saw a great white throne and him who was seated on it. . . . And I saw the dead, great and small, standing before the throne, and books were opened. Another book was opened, which is the book of life. The dead were judged according to what they had done as recorded in the books. . . . The lake of fire is the second death. Anyone whose name was not found written in the book of life was thrown into the lake of fire" (Revelation 20:11-15).

    "Then I saw 'a new heaven and a new earth,' for the first heaven and the first earth had passed away, and . . . . And I heard a loud voice from the throne saying, 'Look! God's dwelling place is now among the people, and he will dwell with them. They will be his people, and God himself will be with them and be their God. "He will wipe every tear from their eyes. There will be no more death" or mourning or crying or pain, for the old order of things has passed away'" (Revelation 21:1-4).

them. . . . the Great Schism, ripping apart the material and immaterial parts of our being . . . [and] the Great Insult, because it reminds us, as Shakespeare said, that we are worm food."[5]

Yet, many of us approach life with an assumption of invulnerability as if we are invincible. We try not to think about death. We dismiss it, downplay it, and pretend it doesn't apply to us—as if only the most aged should ponder their own mortality. Terminal cancer? A sudden heart attack? A fatal traffic accident? Slow physical decline in old age? Surely those things won't happen to me—or will they? Someone observed that we don't like going to other people's funerals because we sense those services are role rehearsals for our *own* funerals!

Cultural anthropologist Ernest Becker argued in his book, *The Denial of Death*, that most human activity comes from attempts to ignore or avoid the inevitability of death. Although we may be unconscious of it, the underlying fear of death motivates us to do all kinds of things. On the positive side, it spurs us to search for significance in our professions, to create works of art that express our ideas and passions, to construct buildings that will outlast us, and to give money to causes we hope will benefit others after we are gone. However, Becker glumly observed, "Man is literally split in two: he has an awareness of his own splendid uniqueness in that he sticks out of nature with a towering majesty, and yet he goes back into the ground a few feet in order blindly and dumbly to rot and disappear forever."[6] According to Becker, as humans desperately try to circumvent the painful reality of death, "Modern man is drinking and drugging himself out of awareness, or he spends his time shopping, which is the same thing."[7]

Ironically, *The Denial of Death* was published in 1973, and the book won a Pulitzer Prize in 1974—two months after Becker died of colon cancer at the age of 49.

Psychologists use the word *thanatophobia* (from the Greek *thanatos*, "death," and *phobia*, "fear") to describe a fearful obsession with death. Though most of us will never be diagnosed with thanatophobia, it's not unusual to struggle with death anxiety. Author/columnist Jonathan Merritt spoke for many of us when he confessed, "I worry a lot about when I'll die, how I'll die, and what waits for me on the other side of the veil that separates this world from the next."[8]

From a pastoral perspective, I believe there are three main issues to consider as you prepare yourself for death: (1) *Prepare your soul.* Make sure you have personally accepted God's gift of eternal life in Jesus Christ. (2) *Prepare your possessions.* Take practical steps to "get your house in order." (3) *Prepare your loved ones.* Do whatever you can to make things a little easier for your family and friends after you are gone.

Let's take a closer look at these three preparation steps.

PREPARE YOUR SOUL.
Accept God's gift of eternal life in Jesus Christ.

A friend of mine owns a drone—one of those small, remotely-operated flying devices—that he uses for photography and videography. One day he thought he had lost the drone because it flew out of his sight. Fortunately, on the drone's controls there is a "Home" button. He pushed the button, and before long he heard a whirring sound. The drone responded to the beacon from its owner, and soon it landed right at his feet.

We wandered off like that drone and lost our way. We all have sinned against God. We are like lost sheep that have strayed away from the flock. But something (actually Someone) calls us back home. Because of his love for us, the Good Shepherd came to earth on a search and rescue mission.

There is one place our wandering souls can find security. "Even in death the righteous seek refuge" (Proverbs 14:32)—and that refuge has a name. Jesus Christ says, "I am the Living One; I was dead, and now look, I am alive for ever and ever! And I hold the keys of death and Hades" (Revelation 1:18).

In a section of Scripture labeled, "the last words of David," the great king and psalmist said, "If my house were not right with God, surely he would not have made with me an everlasting covenant, arranged and secured in every part; surely he would not bring to fruition my salvation and grant me my every desire" (2 Samuel 23:5). Are you sure your "house is right with God"?

Eternal life isn't something we can earn or buy. It is a gift we receive, based not on our good deeds or personal accomplishments, but on the finished work of Christ. "For the wages of sin is death, but the gift of God is eternal life in Christ Jesus our Lord" (Romans 6:23). We receive this gift by faith and confirm our commitment to the Lord in baptism (Acts 2:36-41; 8:12, 26-39; 16:31-34; Romans 6:1-4). Death still hurts, yet because of the risen Christ, we can face death with confidence and say, "But thanks be to God! He gives us the victory through our Lord Jesus Christ" (1 Corinthians 15:57). John assured his readers, "I write these things to you who believe in the name of the Son of God so that you may know that you have eternal life" (1 John 5:13).

In his book, *The Cross of Christ*, British scholar John R. W. Stott wrote:

> Since the law clamors for my death as a law-breaker, how can I possibly be justified? Only by meeting the law's requirement and dying the death it demands. If I were to do this myself, however, that would be the finish of me. So God has provided another way. Christ has borne the penalty of my law-breaking, and the blessing of what he has done has become mine because I am united with him. Being one with Christ, I am able to say, 'I died to the law' (Galatians 2:19), meeting its demands, because "I have been crucified with Christ" and now he lives in me (Galatians 2:20).[9]

At 112 years old, Richard Overton was the oldest man in the United States when he died in Texas in December 2018. An Army veteran, Richard served his country during World War II. On Veterans Day in 2013, President Barack Obama honored him during a ceremony at Arlington National Cemetery. Mr. Overton accepted Christ and was baptized when he was 107. He said "it was about time" to make that decision![10]

The Bible says, "Now is the time of God's favor, now is the day of salvation" (2 Corinthians 6:2). The most important decision you will ever make is the choice to accept God's gracious gift of eternal life. Why put it off? There's no guarantee you will live to be 112.

One day I was pondering my own mortality when suddenly I remembered, "I died when I was 9!" (That's how old I was when I confessed my faith in Christ and was baptized.) I thought, *I've been a walking dead man ever since!* Colossians 2:12 says, "Having been buried with him in baptism, in which you were also raised with him through your faith in the working of God, who raised him from the dead." What a relief! Through faith in Christ, I already "died" long ago. Mercifully, God has allowed me to live on this earth for another 60-plus bonus years. He has blessed me with the joy of a long, happy marriage. He has given me the privilege of being a brother, a dad, a grandpa, and a friend to others. He has helped me carry burdens that seemed too heavy to bear alone.

But I don't need to worry about dying, for spiritually speaking I died long ago, when I was 9. If you have accepted Christ as your Savior and Lord, the Bible says, "You [have] died, and your life is now hidden with Christ in God. When Christ, who is your life, appears, then you also will appear with him in glory" (Colossians 3:3-4).

PREPARE YOUR POSSESSIONS.
Take practical steps to "get your house in order."

King Hezekiah became ill and was near death. The prophet Isaiah told him, "This is what the Lord says: Put your house in order, because you are going to die; you will not recover" (2 Kings 20:1). Have you "put your house in order"? Senior adulthood is a logical time to get organized. Since you can't take your possessions with you when you die, it makes sense to downsize them, not supersize them.

As Candy and I grow older, we are learning to live more simply. This means giving things away and decluttering the garage, the basement, and the bookshelves. (It's especially difficult for me to part with the hundreds of books that have been my literary friends through the years!) Jesus said not to store up treasures on earth (Matthew 6:19-21). It's OK to enjoy God's blessings, but we shouldn't hoard them. Why accumulate unnecessary possessions that collect dust, knowing our adult children will have to deal with all the clutter after we are gone?

You don't have to be wealthy to engage in long-range financial planning, make an estate plan, have a will, and clarify your end-of-life wishes. God alone knows the future; but it honors him when we prepare faithfully for what is ahead. The Bible says:

- "A good person leaves an inheritance for their children's children" (Proverbs 13:22).

- "Commit to the Lord whatever you do, and he will establish your plans" (Proverbs 16:3).

- "In their hearts humans plan their course, but the Lord establishes their steps" (Proverbs 16:9).

PREPARING YOUR "WHEN I DIE" BOX

As you grow older, one way to "put your house in order" is to make sure your financial records and end-of-life documents are accessible in a safe, secure location known to your loved ones. Here are some items your "When I Die" Box might contain:

- Will
- Financial records, including passwords for online accounts and financial advisors' contact information
- Estate plan
- Advance health care directive and living will
- Safety deposit box location and a list of its contents
- Trust
- Guardianship
- Funeral plans, wishes, and instructions
- Farewell letter

Consult an attorney to draft important end-of-life legal documents. Your financial planner, a local funeral home, or online resources like https://simplysquaredaway.com/10-important-documents/ and https://www.rd.com/list/how-prepare-for-death/ may provide additional suggestions.

PREPARE YOUR LOVED ONES: Do whatever you can to make things a little easier for your family and friends after you are gone.

Have you talked with your children, grandchildren, and close friends about your end-of-life wishes? You don't need to belabor this conversation, but it's wise to remind your loved ones, "There is a time for everything," including "a time to be born and a time to die" (Ecclesiastes 3:1-2).

Before Jacob died, he called together his sons, spoke a special blessing over each of them, and gave them specific instructions about where he wanted to be buried (Genesis 49:1-33). And consider the example of King David:

> When the time drew near for David to die, he gave a charge to Solomon his son. "I am about to go the way of all the earth," he said. "So be strong, act like a man, and observe what the Lord your God requires: Walk in obedience to him, and keep his decrees and commands, his laws and regulations, as written in the Law of Moses. Do this so that you may prosper in all you do and wherever you go" (1 Kings 2:1-3).

Jesus prepared his disciples for his approaching death (for example, see Matthew 16:21-23 and John 12:32-33). He assured them, "In a little while you will see me no more, and then after a little while you will see me" (John 16:16). Perhaps you want to say something similar to your loved ones: "I'll be gone when I die, but because of God's grace, soon we'll be together again."

Jesus spoke frankly about the pain of death's separation and the hope of future resurrection. He told his disciples, "You will grieve, but your grief will turn to joy" (John 16:20). As Peter prepared to die, he told his friends, "I will make every effort to see that after my departure you will always be able to remember these things" (2 Peter 1:15).

What Will Happen at Your Funeral?

I was in my twenties when I was ordained as a minister. As an ordination gift, my in-laws gave me a hardcover volume entitled *My Pastoral Record Book*. Over the decades since, in that book I have recorded the dates, titles, and Scripture texts of hundreds of sermons I have preached, and I have jotted down a long list of handwritten names in the sections labeled "Baptisms," "Weddings," and "Funerals."

Over the years, I have walked with church members and neighbors through many kinds of losses. The oldest person for whom I have performed a funeral died at age 104, but my book also reminds me of funerals I led for young adults and infants who died before or shortly after childbirth. Some of those funeral services were for individuals whose deaths were sudden and unexpected (accidents, heart attacks, and suicides), while others died after years of prolonged illness. Some were large, well-attended gatherings, while others were quiet, sparsely attended funerals for precious souls known by God but little-known in the world. During the COVID pandemic in 2020, I led socially distanced funerals, livestreamed and videotaped funerals, and private graveside services. Grief is always difficult, and it's even more difficult to face it in isolation.

No funeral is commonplace. Every person matters to God, and every death is a sacred moment that generates far-reaching ripples of grief. I have led a lot of funerals, but they are never routine to me. After being

HOW SHOULD WE TALK ABOUT DEATH?

Did you hear about the physician whose patient died? The doctor wrote on the patient's chart, "He failed to fulfill his wellness potential." That kind of understatement reminds me of the workers who were fired from their jobs and their employer explained, "They were placed on non-duty, non-pay status."

Discomfort with death leads people to use some strange and insensitive euphemisms. "He kicked the bucket." (And died from a toe injury?) "He bought the farm." (And died from buyer's remorse?) "She expired." (Like a parking meter?) "He croaked." (Don't compare me to a frog when I die.) By contrast, the Bible uses meaningful and comforting word pictures to describe a believer's death and resurrection.

Gathered. Abraham, Isaac, and Jacob were "gathered to [their] people," which makes death sound less lonely and more like a family reunion (Genesis 25:8; 35:29; 49:33).

Rested. When King David died, he "rested with his ancestors" (1 Kings 2:10) and he expected to "dwell in the house of the Lord forever" (Psalm 23:6).

Dismissed. Devout old Simeon waited faithfully because the Holy Spirit had revealed that he wouldn't die before he had seen the Messiah (Luke 2:26). When Mary and Joseph brought baby Jesus into the temple courts, "Simeon took him in his arms and praised God, saying: 'Sovereign Lord, as you have promised, you may now dismiss your servant in peace. For my eyes have seen your salvation . . .'" (Luke 2:28-30). Dismissed—what a vivid way to describe Simeon's approaching death! It's like a teacher saying, "Class dismissed," or a commanding officer giving the order, "At ease, soldier!"

Departed. Heavenly light surrounded Jesus as he talked with Moses and Elijah on the Mount of Transfiguration. "They spoke about his departure, which he was about to bring to fulfillment at Jerusalem" (Luke 9:31). Peter used the same term in reference to his own death. "I will make every effort," he wrote, "to see that after my departure you will always be able to remember these things" (2 Peter 1:15). Departure translates the Greek word exodos, literally the "way out," bringing to mind the way God led the Israelites out of Egypt and into the Promised Land. For a Christian, death isn't an inescapable trap. Christ is the way out! Death is our "exodus," our departure—an exit, not extermination. Someone has said, "Earth's exodus is Heaven's genesis."

Changed. A believer's death and resurrection will lead to glorious transformation. "Listen, I tell you a mystery: We will not all sleep, but we will all be changed—in a flash, in the twinkling of an eye, at the last trumpet. For the trumpet will sound, the dead will be raised imperishable, and we will be changed" (1 Corinthians 15:51-52).

Blessed. The final book of the Bible offers this beatitude: "'Blessed are the dead who die in the Lord from now on.' 'Yes,' says the Spirit, 'they will rest from their labor, for their deeds will follow them'" (Revelation 14:13).

One popular euphemism for death, however, never appears in the Bible in reference to a Christian. First John 2:17 says, "The world and its desires pass away, but whoever does the will of God lives forever." When believers in Christ die, it's not accurate to say they "passed away," for in Christ we will live forever!

notified about a death, normally I meet with relatives of the deceased and take several hours to plan the services, giving families personal attention as they mourn their loved ones. In my opinion, a proper funeral service has two main parts: honoring the deceased and anchoring our hope in the Lord. Funerals should acknowledge the loss, comfort the family, honor the person who died, and most of all, point to the living Christ as the source of our hope.

Funerals often provide teaching moments—opportunities to learn from the examples of departed loved ones. I once led a funeral for a man who spent his career working for the telephone company, and during the visitation, tables in the church lobby displayed several phones he had invented or helped to engineer. Another time I presided at the memorial service for a woman who had been a florist, and the funeral home was filled with flowers, like the ones she had prepared for others so many times before.

Some funerals contain humorous moments. Years ago, I wrote an article called, "Who Puts the Fun in the Funeral?" (found at the end of this chapter.) We should never take death lightly, but it's good to recall a loved one's sense of humor, and it's OK if happy memories make us smile. After all, we're not only supposed to "mourn with those who mourn," but also to "rejoice with those who rejoice" (Romans 12:15).

During a visit to Jordan, I stood atop Mount Nebo, the place where God gave Moses one last sweeping view of the Promised Land before the great lawgiver died. Near that place, "The Israelites grieved for Moses in the plains of Moab thirty days" (Deuteronomy 34:8). Funerals help bring closure, but for many of us, mourning takes far more than 30 days. There is no need to rush. It's tempting to try to hurry the grief process—because it hurts. Instead, we should take whatever time is required—because it matters. Grief is painful, but followers of the risen Christ "do not grieve like the rest of mankind, who have no hope. For we believe that Jesus died and rose again" (1 Thessalonians 4:13-14).

Have you written down (and shared with your loved ones) your preferences about your own funeral? Are there Bible verses or songs you would like the service to include? Are there friends or family members you would want to say a few words? Is there a minister you want to lead the service? Be careful, though, not to be overly prescriptive about your funeral plans. It's enough to write down a few ideas to guide your loved ones after you are gone, and trust others to handle the details.

In biblical times, some "young men" (the original pallbearers!) took care of burying the dead (Acts 5:6, 10), and someone will be there to take care of your funeral arrangements when the time comes. While it's good to plan ahead, we should trust our friends and family to do the right things. Theologian Ray S. Anderson reminded us that others "will have the last look, the last touch and the last word. I do not need to speak in my own death, [for] I am spoken for."[11]

Where Can We Find Hope?

When faced with the reality of death, we have three choices: (1) hard-hearted cynicism, (2) untethered optimism, or (3) gutsy faith.

Hard-hearted cynicism is the gloomy perspective that says, "This life is all there is. When we die, that's the end. Heaven is a religious delusion—a myth we use to make ourselves feel better." The author of the book of Ecclesiastes expressed this rather depressing approach when he wrote, "The same destiny overtakes all. The hearts of people, moreover, are full of evil and there is madness in their hearts while they live, and afterward they join the dead" (Ecclesiastes 9:3). As the apostle Paul pointed out, "If the dead are not raised," we may as well just live it up and "eat and drink, for tomorrow we die" (1 Corinthians 15:32).

At the other end of the spectrum, *untethered optimism* responds to the reality of death with well-meaning, cheery statements like, "She's in a better place" or "He's up there smiling down on us," but can the people making those statements point to clear evidence that supports their view? Universalism is a popular viewpoint today—the idea that everyone will be saved and go to heaven, no matter what they believe or what they have done. The problem is, this widespread belief has little to support it except our own wishes. We know that God is incredibly gracious, and we don't want anyone to die without hope. Indeed, God himself doesn't want anyone to be lost (1 Timothy 2:3-4; 2 Peter 3:9); that's why he has gone to great lengths to make our salvation possible. But the idea that everyone will be saved, even in the absence of personal faith and repentance, contradicts plain biblical teaching about the reality of sin and our need to accept God's gift of salvation. Our view about death and the afterlife must take into account Jesus' warnings about God's judgment and our individual responsibility to repent and believe.

Instead of approaching death with hard-hearted cynicism or untethered optimism, I recommend *gutsy faith*—the kind of determined faith that says with Job, "I know that my redeemer lives" (Job 19:25) and with Paul, "For to

---

EVIDENCE OF JESUS' RESURRECTION

The resurrection of Jesus Christ is central to the Christian faith and it is the basis of our hope. Does it make sense to believe it really happened? What evidence indicates that Jesus truly rose from the dead?

- The eyewitnesses were numerous. They saw the risen Lord over a period of 40 days while he provided "many convincing proofs that he was alive" (Acts 1:3). After his resurrection, more than 500 people saw Jesus alive at the same time (1 Corinthians 15:6). His resurrection appearances were not merely private visions or hallucinations.

- The eyewitnesses were skeptical at first, and Thomas wasn't the only doubter. When the women came running with news of the resurrection, at first the apostles considered the report "nonsense" (Luke 24:11). Even when the risen Christ showed them his hands and feet, "they still did not believe it because of joy and amazement" (Luke 24:41). They were thrilled to see Jesus alive again, but it seemed almost too good to be true. As any reasonable investigators would do, they reacted cautiously and required compelling evidence before they were persuaded. After the resurrection, Jesus ate broiled fish (Luke 24:42-43)—evidence that Jesus' resurrected body was real. Saul of Tarsus was no friend of Jesus until his encounter with the risen Lord on the road to Damascus and his subsequent conversation with a disciple named Ananias changed Saul the persecutor into Paul the apostle (see Acts 9:1-19). Jesus' brother James didn't believe in him at first, but he turned to faith after encountering the risen Lord (compare John 7:5 and 1 Corinthians 15:7).

- The eyewitnesses were credible. Commonsense fishermen like Peter and John were convinced that Jesus arose. So were highly trained scholars like Paul and ordinary women like Mary Magdalene. Critics like to highlight discrepancies in the resurrection narratives, but viewed another way, the witnesses' varying accounts provide independent testimony about the fact of the resurrection while providing different perspectives on the details.

- The eyewitnesses put their own lives on the line. They had little to gain by believing in Jesus' resurrection. Why should the apostles lie and die for a crucified leader they knew was rotting in the grave? As Paul put it, "If I fought wild beasts in Ephesus with no more than human hopes, what have I gained? If the dead are not raised, 'Let us eat and drink, for tomorrow we die'" (1 Corinthians 15:32). The resurrection changed Jesus' disciples from fearful huddlers in an upper room to bold witnesses in Jerusalem's streets.

For more evidence of Jesus' resurrection, I recommend Lee Strobel's book, *The Case for Christ* (Zondervan, 1998).

me, to live is Christ and to die is gain" (Philippians 1:21). Gutsy faith tethers us to the rock-solid promises of Jesus, who said, "I am the resurrection and the life. The one who believes in me will live, even though they die" (John 11:25). As the hymn "The Solid Rock" puts it, "My hope is built on nothing less than Jesus' blood and righteousness. I dare not trust the sweetest frame, but wholly lean on Jesus' name."

This kind of hope isn't vague optimism or merely wishing on a star; it is confident expectation rooted in the real, historical fact that "Christ has indeed been raised from the dead" (1 Corinthians 15:20).

Your later years will be greater years if "the Spirit of him who raised Jesus from the dead is living in you, [for] he who raised Christ from the dead will also give life to your mortal bodies because of his Spirit who lives in you" (Romans 8:11).

Remarkably, Jesus said, "Do not be afraid of those who kill the body but cannot kill the soul" (Matthew 10:28). What a statement! Who isn't afraid of "those who kill the body"? All kinds of things can cause us physical harm: illnesses, accidents, violent crime, and pandemics—in addition to the normal aging process. But bad as they are, those things cannot kill our souls. In the face of death, we can remain spiritually strong and courageous if we know the Lord.

Physical death separates the human spirit from our bodies (James 2:26), but in the coming resurrection, God's people will receive new bodies that are imperishable, powerful, immortal, and glorious (1 Corinthians 15:42-54). Spiritual death separates us from God, but the grace of God restores our souls and raises us up to new life (Ephesians 2:1-10). Bob Russell uses the analogy of a gloved hand to illustrate what happens at death. He says, "When the hand is removed from a glove, the form of the hand remains in the limp glove, but the substance that gave it life is gone. And when one dies, the body retains the form, but the spirit that animated it has departed. After the departure from the body comes the immediate presence with God."[12] That's why Scripture describes the death of a believer as being "away from the body and at home with the Lord" (2 Corinthians 5:8). Shortly after celebrating his eightieth birthday, Bob wrote in a blog:

> Jesus Christ promises me that the best is yet to be! . . . . Because of that promise, I am more joyful at 80 years of age than I was at 40.

Who is the most joyful person on an airplane? Is it the passenger who is just 15 minutes into a 16-hour flight or the passenger who is 15 minutes from landing at home? The passenger who is almost home may not look as good or feel as fresh, but they are more joyful because the long journey is almost over.[13]

Candy and I traveled to Sedona, Arizona, arriving late at night. We had never been to Sedona before, although we had heard others describe it as a beautiful place. Weary after our long flight, we drove through the dark on an unfamiliar highway, navigating our rental car through narrow construction zones and winding our way through hills and valleys we had never driven before. We finally arrived at our hotel at 1:00 a.m. and dove into bed exhausted.

We woke up the next morning and walked outside in the bright morning sunshine, amazed to find ourselves surrounded by breathtaking views of Arizona's unique red-stone mountains. The night before, it had been too dark to see the beauty, and we were distracted by the difficulties of the journey. But when darkness gave way to sunrise, we realized we had arrived in a place of spectacular, almost indescribable beauty.

I imagine death will be something like that. When the long, hard journey ends, believers will open our eyes to the glorious presence of God and exclaim with amazement and joy, "I once was blind, but now I see."

QUESTIONS FOR PERSONAL REFLECTION AND GROUP DISCUSSION

1. Which of the following best describes your feelings about death and dying?
   a. *Denial.* I avoid thinking about it.
   b. *Fear.* Death really worries me.
   c. *Hope.* My faith gives me peace.
   d. *Other:*

2. Which of the following best describes your *beliefs* about death?
   a. *Hard-hearted cynicism.* I have no real hope beyond the grave. I believe death will simply end my existence.
   b. *Untethered optimism.* I have a vague hope that I will live on and go to heaven, but I can cite no solid evidence to back up my belief.
   c. *Gutsy faith.* I am relying on God's grace to save me because his Son, Jesus, died and rose again for me, and I have accepted him as my personal Savior and Lord.

3. When you think about your approaching death, what step(s) do you need to take to prepare your soul? To prepare your possessions and finances? To prepare your loved ones?

4. What would you want your own funeral service to include? What do you hope others will say about you on that occasion?

5. For further reading on the subject of death, here are some suggested resources:
   • Erwin W. Lutzer, *One Minute After You Die* (Moody, 2015)
   • Lee Strobel, *The Case for Heaven* (Zondervan, 2021)
   • Randy Alcorn, *Heaven* (Tyndale House, 2004)
   • Timothy Keller, *Hope in Times of Fear: The Resurrection and the Meaning of Easter* (Penguin, 2022)

WHO PUTS THE FUN IN THE FUNERAL?

I hope people laugh at my funeral.

Don't get me wrong. I know the serious side of grief. I've attended more funerals than I can count, and I've officiated at quite a few. I've felt the pain of loss that comes when there's nothing left to do but say "goodbye." When my friends and relatives gather to mourn my passing, I hope they shed some tears. It would be a shame if no one missed me.

But I hope they laugh, too. Smiles, chuckles, and belly laughs will be welcome. I hope they tell stories about funny things we did together and jokes we enjoyed. I hope my children recount pleasant memories about the way we tossed the ball together in the backyard and wrestled on the family room floor. Maybe they'll laugh about my cooking and recall how they groaned when I served my dreaded "Daddy casseroles." Or my daughter will tell about the time I baked her a birthday cake that resembled a one-inch slab of strawberry flavored shoe leather.

Most of all, I hope someone preaches the gospel at my funeral. I hope the preacher tells how Jesus died on the cross and rose from the grave. I hope the service reminds the gathered mourners that in Christ we do not "grieve like the rest of mankind, who have no hope" (1 Thessalonians 4:13). I hope the preacher mentions Jesus' reassuring promise, "I am the resurrection and the life. The one who believes in me will live, even though they die; and whoever lives and believes in me will never die" (John 11:25-26). I want those who attend my funeral to know I really believed this, and that they can believe it too.

I want them to understand that, for those who belong to Christ, death doesn't mean leaving the fun behind. It means the fun has just begun— and the wonder, the blessedness, the joy of being "away from the body and at home with the Lord" (2 Corinthians 5:8).

For Christians, death means relocation, not termination—it's a change of address marking our move to a far better place.

Dwight L. Moody quipped that Jesus broke up every funeral he ever attended by raising the dead! I hope the people who attend my funeral realize that Jesus will do the same for me, and for all of us "who have longed for his appearing" (2 Timothy 4:8). It's just a matter of being patient till "the trumpet of the Lord shall sound, and time shall be no more."

Now, I admit, *fun* probably isn't the right word to describe the blissful joys of Heaven. To most of us, fun means something shallow and fleeting—a good time that doesn't last. That's why it's foolish to make personal pleasure our main goal in life. When will we learn that "the world and its desires pass away, but whoever does the will of God lives forever" (1 John 2:17)?

When will we learn that the purpose of life is not merely to store up treasures on earth that quickly fade away?

There's a lot I don't know about heaven, but I know the Lord is there. I know spectacular light and color and beauty and worship are there. And I know what's *not* there: no frightening darkness, no tears, no death, no mourning or crying or pain. Sorry if the word offends you, but that sounds *fun* to me!

Years ago, after publishing an article about the humor of Christ, I received a letter of rebuke from a Christian brother who insisted that Jesus never laughed or smiled. I phoned the letter-writer and spent about a half-hour trying to show him that, since Jesus was "full of joy through the Holy Spirit" (Luke 10:21), it's highly probable that the Lord occasionally expressed joy on his face. I didn't convince my critical friend, but ironically, whenever I think about our conversation, it makes me smile!

Jesus spoke about joy in heaven. He said there is joy "in the presence of the angels of God over one sinner who repents" (Luke 15:10). Joy *in the presence* of the angels? That makes me wonder if the Lord himself joins their rejoicing. I think he does.

So, I hope there's rejoicing at my funeral—rejoicing that celebrates another forgiven sinner's graduation to glory. I hope my loved ones who say "goodbye" understand we'll see each other again someday around the throne of God. When they think about their own graduation to glory, I hope they smile.

I'm pretty sure that I'll be smiling too.

Father, when it's time for me to die, let me rely completely on your grace to lead me safely through the valley. And since I don't know when that time may come, let me live each day in confident anticipation of the day you welcome me home. Replace my fear of death with the hope and the joy that come from knowing the power of Jesus' resurrection. Everyone I meet this week will face death also someday, so make me a hope-giver and an encourager for their sake. I pray in the name of Christ. Amen.

This article by David Faust first appeared in *The Lookout* magazine, November 9, 2003, and was reprinted in the book, *Monday Morning Insights* (CCU Resources, 2011), 29-30.

17 | Finishing Well— Staying Faithful Till It's Time to Go

"I have a lot to accomplish.
I don't have anything left to prove."
—Steph Curry, NBA basketball star

"I have brought you glory on earth by
completing the work you gave me to do."
—Jesus in John 17:4

"Don't stop."
—Fred Schmid, national cycling champion in the 80+ category,
when asked his secret to racing into his eighties

My friend Fadi and his family live in the ancient city of Bethlehem, a few blocks from the famous Church of the Nativity. One evening, Fadi and I were standing outside his house while dinner was being prepared. Olives had fallen from the limbs of an olive tree next to the fence. Noticing a dry, withered olive on the concrete patio, I picked it up and casually tossed it over the fence.

"What are you doing?" Fadi asked.

"It was just an old, shriveled-up olive," I said with a shrug.

A disapproving frown covered my friend's usually smiling face. It turns out, I had a lot to learn about olives.

Fadi took me to the basement of the house and showed me a large pile of olives his family was collecting. "We use them all," he insisted. "The young green ones, the ones that are perfectly ripe, even the old ones. You'd be surprised how much oil can be found in an old, shriveled-up olive!" Once the olives are all collected, he explained, the family takes them to a large olive press in town and turns them into delicious homemade olive oil.

I learned a valuable lesson that day: *Even if you're old, you still have some juice left in you!*

Have you seen a football team get off to a bad start, but come roaring back in the fourth quarter and win the game? Have you heard a musician stumble over a few notes, but end the song on a beautiful high note? Have you met someone with a rough past who became a productive citizen and a faithful follower of Jesus? These examples remind us: *Mistakes don't matter much if you finish well.*

But on the other hand . . .

Have you heard about a promising movie star whose career quickly crashed and burned? Have you known of a company that started strong but faded fast? Have you seen someone quickly move up the career ladder only to fall flat? These examples remind us of another important truth: *A good start isn't enough if you finish poorly.*

Jesus' dying words on the cross, "It is finished" (John 19:30), were uttered in triumph, not in despair. His death and resurrection fulfilled ancient prophecies and opened salvation's door for all who believe.

How can you finish well? Your later years won't be greater years if old age makes you grumpy, grouchy, and graceless. What does it take to stay fruitful and faithful until it's time to go home and be with the Lord? It has been said, "You can't go back and change the beginning, but you can start where you are and change the ending."

Three Crucial Commitments if You Want to Finish Well

My daughter bought me a Fitbit, so now if someone asks, "Are you fit?" I can say, "Just a bit!" The device measures my heart rate and the number of miles and steps I walk each day, but it can't measure my walk with God. Only the Lord can do that.

Noah "walked faithfully with God" for a long time (Genesis 6:9). Enoch "walked faithfully with God for 300 years" before "God took him away" (Genesis 5:22-24).

My friend Michael Mack, editor of *Christian Standard* magazine, died suddenly of a blood clot on his 63rd birthday while mountain-biking in Colorado. A couple of weeks before he died, he agreed to do some editing work on this book. I was deeply saddened by his sudden death, but it led me to read some words he published a decade before he died. Mike referenced Enoch and wrote, "No, I don't want to live another 300 years! But I do want to live in close fellowship with God throughout what's left of my life, and then for God to take me when he's ready."

My walk with God isn't finished yet, but I like the way the apostle Paul described his own approach to the end of his time on earth. He wrote, "For I am already being poured out like a drink offering, and the time for my departure is near. I have fought the good fight, I have finished the race, I have kept the faith" (2 Timothy 4:6-7).

What does it look like to finish well? Fight the good fight. Continue running the race till you reach the finish line. Keep the faith. I want to make those three crucial commitments my own . . . and I assume you want to do the same.

FIGHT THE GOOD FIGHT

As long as I live . . .

I will fight to guard my heart. "Above all else, guard your heart, for everything you do flows from it" (Proverbs 4:23).

I will fight to control my tongue. With age, it becomes more important than ever to pray, "Lord, keep your arm around my shoulder and your hand over my mouth." Let's determine that we will not harm others, dishonor God, or damage our reputations by being careless with our words. "Those who guard their mouths and their tongues keep themselves from calamity" (Proverbs 21:23).

I will fight against sinful pride. Old age is humbling—but that's a good thing. Proverbs 11:2 reminds us, "When pride comes, then comes disgrace, but with humility comes wisdom." (*The Message* version of the Bible translates that verse, "The stuck-up fall flat on their faces, but down-to-earth people stand firm.") Old age is a time to relinquish the limelight and serve others humbly, without fanfare. Someone has said, "Doing great things for God might mean simply doing tiny things over and over for years with no recognition." Senior adulthood is a good time to heed the words of Paul, who wrote, "Do nothing out of selfish ambition or vain conceit. Rather, in humility value others above yourselves" (Philippians 2:3). Peter urged, "Humble yourselves, therefore, under God's mighty hand, that he may lift you up in due time" (1 Peter 5:6).

I will fight against apathy and complacency. I will not just count my years; I will make my years count. Romans 12:11 urges, "Never be lacking in zeal, but keep your spiritual fervor, serving the Lord." Paul instructed Archippus, a friend who led the church at Colossae, "See to it that you complete the work you have received in the Lord" (Colossians 4:17).

I will fight against idealizing or idolizing the past. There's a lot to learn from history, but we can't live there. Someone defined *nostalgia* as "longing for the place you wouldn't move back to." Senior adults have a choice to make: Will we follow the Lord cheerfully into the future, or will he have to drag us into the future against our will? Scripture admonishes, "Do not say, 'Why were the old days better than these?' For it is not wise to ask such questions" (Ecclesiastes 7:10).

I will fight against resentment. Old age is hard enough; why carry around the added burden of unresolved conflicts? *Resentment* has been called the "poison we drink expecting our enemy to die." Scripture warns us not to allow a "root of bitterness" to grow in our hearts (Hebrews 12:15, *English Standard Version*). Our later years will be greater years if we "get rid of all bitterness, rage and anger, brawling and slander, along with every form of malice. Be kind and compassionate to one another, forgiving each other, just as in Christ God forgave you" (Ephesians 4:31-32). According to preacher and author Tony Evans, "Forgiveness is not pretending like it didn't happen or like it didn't hurt. That's called lying. Forgiveness is a decision to release a debt regardless of how you feel."

The Japanese people have refined an art form called kintsugi, which repairs broken pottery using lacquer and gold powder. Kintsugi treats breakage and repair as part of an object's story, not as something to hide. If we open our hearts to his leading, God can take the broken pieces of our lives and make them into something beautiful.

FINISH THE RACE

I was a speedy runner when I was young—a member of my high school track and cross-country teams. Although I still like to walk, my pace has slowed with age and I don't run much anymore. But as a follower of Christ, I'm still running the race that matters most—and I won't stop until I reach the finish line.

If you are a senior adult, are you willing to agree with the apostle Paul and say, I will not "run like someone running aimlessly" or fight like a boxer who is merely "beating the air" (1 Corinthians 9:26)? With God's help, will you forget what is behind, strain toward what is ahead, and make it your goal to "press on toward the goal to win the prize" (Philippians 3:13-14)?

Sometimes we must keep running even when we're hurt. During the 2012 Olympic Games in London, Manteo Mitchell, a member of the United States' track and field team, was running the leadoff leg of a 4 x 400 relay race when he broke a bone in his leg. He felt his fibula snap, and thought at first it might just be a cramp.

"I wanted to just lie down," Mitchell said later. "It felt like somebody literally just snapped my leg in half." The problem was, he still had 200 more meters to run, and if he didn't finish his part of the race, the U.S. relay squad would be eliminated from the event. Despite excruciating pain, he kept running the last half-lap until he handed off the baton to his teammate. Amazingly, the American team finished second in that heat, qualified for the final round, and ended up winning a silver medal in the event.[1]

During every season of life, including senior adulthood, we must take to heart the biblical passage that says:

> Therefore, since we are surrounded by such a great cloud of witnesses, let us throw off everything that hinders and the sin that so easily entangles. And let us run with perseverance the race marked out for us, fixing our eyes on Jesus, the pioneer and perfecter of faith. For the joy set before him he endured the cross, scorning its shame, and sat down at the right hand of the throne of God. Consider him who endured such opposition from sinners, so that you will not grow weary and lose heart (Hebrews 12:1-3).

KEEP THE FAITH

During a visit to Turkey, our guide pointed out a kind of stone the ancient Romans used for their building projects. It's called *tuff*—an igneous rock formed by the ash, magma, and other materials that fall to earth after an explosive volcanic eruption. Compacted and cemented together, tuff is hard enough to use for building, but soft enough that it can be carved and shaped.

AVOIDING CHAPTER 11
(Life Lessons About Perseverance
from the Book of First Kings)

Chapter 11 is a well-known section of the United States Bankruptcy Code that permits businesses or individuals to reorganize their finances. When a company goes bankrupt, it's common to hear it "filed Chapter 11." But another kind of bankruptcy is even more heartbreaking.

King Solomon faced a spiritual Chapter 11—although, ironically, during the first 10 chapters of First Kings, he enjoyed one success after another. His father, David, installed him as king (chapter 1) with words of affirmation and blessing (chapter 2). In chapter 3, God gave Solomon a special gift of wisdom. Chapter 4 says that under Solomon's leadership the people "ate, they drank and they were happy" (4:20).

God blessed him with extraordinary knowledge in science and art. Solomon wrote 3,000 proverbs and 1,005 songs, and he taught about plants, animals, birds, reptiles, and fish (4:32-33). He oversaw the construction of elaborate buildings, including a temple for the Lord and a palace for his own residence (chapters 5-7). He led worship, dedicating the temple with a long and beautiful prayer (chapter 8). He sent ships to faraway lands to bring back cargoes of gold (chapter 9). His fame spread around the world, and the visiting Queen of Sheba gushed with admiration, "Not even half was told me; in wisdom and wealth you have far exceeded the report I heard" (10:7). Solomon accumulated enormous quantities of gold, silver, ivory, robes, weapons, spices, horses, and chariots. He even collected apes and baboons (10:22).

Then came Solomon's spiritual "Chapter 11." After 10 chapters describing the king's prosperity, 1 Kings 11:1 bluntly interrupts the narrative about his success with these words: "King Solomon, however, loved many foreign women" (11:1). Chapter 11 goes on to say, "As Solomon grew old, his wives turned his heart after other gods, and his heart was not fully devoted to the Lord his God" (11:4). How could Solomon turn to other gods after the Lord had blessed him so abundantly? Chapter 11 marked a sad turning point. Solomon's life took a downward turn, and so did the nation he led. Israel's prosperity gave way to spiritual decline and political controversy, ending with the people in exile far from home.

We must remain steady in our walk with God through every chapter of life. George Bernard Shaw observed, "Life is no 'brief candle.'" Instead, it is a "splendid torch which I have to hold for the moment, and I want to make it burn as brightly as possible before handing it on to future generations."

First Kings 11 warns about unfaithfulness, but there's a different story in Hebrews chapter 11, which lists one person after another who lived by faith because they were sure of what they hoped for and certain of what they could not see (Hebrews 11:1). Instead of turning our hearts from God, let's pave the road with faithfulness for the generations yet to come.

Senior adults need to be *tuff!* As I age, I want to be flexible and pliable enough to keep growing, but remain firm about what I believe.

I am determined to stay "rooted and built up in him, strengthened in the faith" (Colossians 2:7).

I will be accountable to others who help me "say 'no' to ungodliness and worldly passions" and encourage me to adopt a lifestyle that is "self-controlled, upright and godly" (Titus 2:12).

I will not cower before Satan's bullying or be deceived by his lies, nor will I adopt unbiblical ideas because they are easy and popular. I will take seriously Paul's instructions: "Be on your guard; stand firm in the faith; be courageous; be strong. Do everything in love" (1 Corinthians 16:13-14).

Someone asked G. K. Chesterton, "If you were stranded on a desert island and could have only one book, which one would you choose?" Most people in the group answered, "The Bible." Chesterton wryly replied, "Thomas's Book of Ship Building." In fact, there is no better book to consult for guidance than the Bible. God's Word remains true ("All Scripture is God-breathed) and relevant ("useful for teaching, rebuking, correcting and training in righteousness") in every season of life (2 Timothy 3:16).

I will continue believing, learning, and applying biblical truth as long as I live, and I will respect the wisdom of faithful followers of Christ from past generations. The hymn, "Faith of Our Fathers," exhorts us to say:

> Faith of our fathers, we will love
> Both friend and foe in all our strife;
> And preach Thee, too, as love knows how
> By kindly words and virtuous life.[2]

I asked poet and songwriter Bill Gaither, "What do you think it means for a person to finish well?"

His answer? "For us, it means to actually believe and live out the songs we have written."

Your Later Years Can Be Greater Years

One "tuff" senior adult who stayed the course and finished well was Polycarp. He had been a disciple of the apostle John. At age 86, he led the church in Smyrna (now called Izmir) in Asia Minor. Persecution against Christians broke out. When a search party came to arrest Polycarp, he treated the arresting officers like friends, and he directed that food and drink should be served to them. His only request? A little extra time to spend in prayer.

The authorities had second thoughts about arresting such an old man, and when Polycarp was led into the arena to face death, the proconsul pleaded with him: "Curse Christ, and I will release you." But Polycarp bravely replied, "Eighty-six years I have served him. He has never done me wrong. How then can I blaspheme my King who has saved me?"

The proconsul threatened to burn him alive, but Polycarp said in response, "You threaten fire that burns for an hour and is over. But the judgment on the ungodly is forever."

Polycarp died in February of AD 155. According to one historian, "His followers gathered his remains like precious jewels," and though his martyrdom was an example of painful injustice, when viewed through the eyes of faith, "it was as much a day of triumph as it was a day of tragedy."[3] Polycarp finished well.

Jacob tangled with the Lord in a wrestling match that left the aging patriarch limping with a dislocated hip. But as the old man limped away the next morning, "the sun rose above him" (Genesis 32:31). Even if you walk with a limp—or you must use a walker or a cane—you will finish well if you keep walking with God.

My mother finished well. She was a quiet, humble woman with strong, secure faith. She died one month short of her ninetieth birthday, soon after suffering a severe stroke. Candy and I stayed in the hospital room with her for a couple of nights to keep her company, but the stroke limited her ability to speak. A group of doctors came into the room. They told us, in no uncertain terms, that she didn't have long to live, and if we put her on life support, she might survive a few more days but she wouldn't be able to communicate with us.

After the doctors left, I took her hand and asked, "Mother, did you hear what those doctors said?"

She nodded.

"Do you want the doctors to put you on a ventilator?"

Her lips spoke no words, but she shook her head back and forth emphatically to say "No."

"Are you at peace?" I asked.

She nodded, managing a slight smile.

Candy and I tried to smile, too. But tears filled our eyes.

"Thank you for being such a wonderful mother to us," Candy told her, speaking for both of us.

Mother looked directly at Candy and summoned the strength to speak. With a husky voice, she said, "Thank *you*."

Those were the last words I heard her say, and my mother's sweet whisper still echoes in my ears: "Thank you." I cannot imagine any better words to say as our earthly lives come to a close—especially for all who trust the Lord's promise: "They will still bear fruit in old age" (Psalm 92:14).

Our later years will be greater years if they are *grateful* years, for when we die, the journey isn't over. It's only just begun.

QUESTIONS FOR PERSONAL REFLECTION
AND GROUP DISCUSSION

1. As you think about growing older, what does the phrase "finishing well" mean to you?

2. Read Hebrews 12:1-3.

    a. Who are some believers in the "great cloud of witnesses" who set a positive example for you during their final season of life?

    b. What hinders your walk with God? What sin "easily entangles" you and holds you back?

    c. Practically speaking, what does it mean to "fix your eyes on Jesus"? How does focusing on Christ help you to persevere?

3. Which of the following goals seems the most challenging to you? Why?

    a. Fighting the good fight

    b. Finishing the race

    c. Keeping the faith

4. As you conclude your study of this book, what ideas stand out most from what you have read? Has your view of aging changed? If so, how?

END NOTES

1

[1] "The New Map of Life," Stanford Center On Longevity, https://longevity.stanford.edu/the-new-map-of-life-report/.

[2] "Life Expectancy in the U.S. Dropped for the Second Year in a Row in 2021," Centers for Disease Control and Prevention, August 31, 2022, https://www.cdc.gov/nchs/pressroom/nchs_press_releases/2022/20220831.htm.

[3] "Senior Report 2022," America's Health Rankings (website), accessed April 2023, https://www.americashealthrankings.org/explore/senior/measure/pct_65plus/state/ALL.

[4] For example, see Phil Cooke, "Mind Blowing Facts About People Over 50," https://www.philcooke.com/mind-blowing-facts-about-people-over-50/.

[5] "Senior Report 2022," America's Health Rankings.

[6] For example, see https://www.pewresearch.org/religion/religious-landscape-study/generational-cohort/baby-boomer/. See also "A Snapshot of Faith Practice Across Age Groups," July 23, 2019, accessed April 2023, https://www.barna.com/research/faithview-on-faith-practice/.

[7] John 4:35, *King James Version*.

2

[1] David and Candy Faust, *Puppet Plays with a Point* (Standard Publishing, 1995), pp. 56-57.

[2] Julia Vitale, "A Look at the United States' Aging Prison Population Problem," Interrogating Justice (website), April 7, 2021, https://interrogatingjustice.org/ending-mass-incarceration/aging-prison-population/. See also Meredith Greene, et al., "Older Adults in Jail: High Rates and Early Onset of Geriatric Conditions," *Health and Justice Journal*, February 17, 2018, https://healthandjusticejournal.biomedcentral.com/articles/10.1186/s40352-018-0062-9.

3

[1] Adrienne Tyler, "The Simpsons: How Old Is Mr. Burns? Every Change to His Age Explained," Screen Rant (website), March 27, 2020, https://screenrant.com/simpsons-show-mr-burns-age-old-changes-explained/.

[2] Jeffrey M. Jones, "In U.S., Childhood Churchgoing Habits Fade in Adulthood," Gallup, December 21, 2022, https://news.gallup.com/poll/467354/childhood-churchgoing-habits-fade-adulthood.aspx?utm_source=alert&utm_medium=email&utm_content=morelink&utm_campaign=syndication.

[3] Tracy Munsil, "Biblical Worldview Among U.S. Adults Drops 33% Since Start of COVID-19 Pandemic," Arizona Christian University (website), February 28, 2023, https://www.arizonachristian.edu/2023/02/28/biblical-worldview-among-u-s-adults-drops-33-since-start-of-covid-19-pandemic/.

[4] J. Warner Wallace, "The Reasonable, Evidential Nature of Christian Faith," Cold-Case Christianity (website), February 23, 2018, https://coldcasechristianity.com/writings/the-reasonable-evidential-nature-of-christian-faith/.

4

[1] Robert Tinsky, *Jump for Joy* (CreateSpace, 2017), 7.

[2] Rod Huron, *Love, Laughter, and Leadership: The Ministry of Wayne B. Smith* (Host Communications, 2005), 100.

[3] Robin Gallaher Branch, "Laughter in the Bible? Absolutely!" Biblical Archaeology Society (website), November 20, 2022, https://www.biblicalarchaeology.org/daily/biblical-topics/bible-interpretation/laughter-in-the-bible-absolutely/.

[4] Robert Wolgemuth, *Daddy @ Work* (Zondervan, 1999), 141.

[5] Derek Prime, *A Good Old Age* (10 Publishing, 2017), 74.

[6] Dexter Louie, BA, Karolina Brook, MD, and Elizabeth Frates, MD, "The Laughter Prescription," *American Journal of Lifestyle Medicine*, July-August 2016, 262-267.

[7] Mandy Smith, *Life Is Too Important to Be Taken Seriously: Kite-Flying Lessons from Ecclesiastes* (College Press Publishing, 2004), 94-95.

5

[1] Norman L. Geisler, *A Popular Survey of the Old Testament* (Baker Books, 1977), 21-22.

[2] Bill and Judy Norris, *What the Bible Says About Growing Old* (College Press, 1988), 141.

[3] Ibid., 153.

6

[1] Nicholas Weiler, "Menopausal Killer Whales Are Family Leaders: The Wisdom of Elders May Help Whales Survive Years of Famine," *Science*, March 5, 2015, https://www.science.org/content/article/menopausal-killer-whales-are-family-leaders.

[2] Lisa Esposito, "The Health Benefits of Having (and Being) Grandparents," *U.S. News & World Report*, September 13, 2017, https://health.usnews.com/wellness/articles/2017-09-13/the-health-benefits-of-having-and-being-grandparents.

[3] Gary Smalley and John Trent, *The Blessing* (Thomas Nelson, 1986), 24. [This book has since been updated.]

7

[1] Robert Tinsky, *I'm Not Old, I've Just Lived a Long Time* (CreateSpace, 2016), 70.

[2] Tyler Huckabee, "Is There Actually a Link Between Physical Health and Spiritual Health?" *Relevant Magazine* (relevantmagazine.com), March 6, 2023.

[3] J. I. Marais, "Body," *International Bible Encyclopedia* (Eerdmans, 1939), 492.

[4] Michael Schirber, "The Chemistry of Life: The Human Body," *Live Science*, April 16, 2009, https://www.livescience.com/3505-chemistry-life-human-body.html.

[5] Bob Russell, *Take Comfort: Encouraging Words from Second Corinthians* (Standard Publishing, 1991), 86-87.

[6] Waneen W. Spirduso, *Physical Dimensions of Aging* (Human Kinetics, 1995). See also "Older and Wiser," *Athletic Business*, September 30, 2003, https://www.athleticbusiness.com/home/article/15140609/older-and-wiser.

[7] "Older and Wiser," *Athletic Business*, September 30, 2003.

[8] Michelle Crouch, "The #1 Exercise to Do as You Get Older," *AARP*, December 27, 2022, https://www.aarp.org/health/healthy-living/info-2022/squats-best-exercise-for-strength.html.

[9] Chris Crowley, Henry S. Lodge, M.D., and Allan J. Hamilton, M.D., *Younger Next Year: Live Strong, Fit, and Sexy—Until You're 80 and Beyond* (Workman Publishing, 2019), 29, 49, 296-298.

[10] "Using the Nutrition Facts Label: For Older Adults," https://www.fda.gov/food/new-nutrition-facts-label/using-nutrition-facts-label-older-adults.

[11] Crowley, Lodge, and Hamilton, *Younger Next Year*, 205.

[12] Class notes from Dr. Archibald Hart's Doctor of Ministry course, "The Minister's Personal Growth," Fuller Theological Seminary, May 7, 1992.

[13] "A Good Night's Sleep," National Institute on Aging, November 3, 2020, accessed via www.nia.nih.gov.

[14] Matthew Sleeth, M.D., *24/6: A Prescription for a Healthier, Happier Life* (Tyndale House, 2012), 8-9.

[15] Joe Leech, "Seven Science-Based Health Benefits of Drinking Enough Water," *Healthline*, March 8, 2023, https://www.healthline.com/nutrition/7-health-benefits-of-water.

[16] Ben Cachiaras, "What Should the Church Do About the Mental Health Crisis?" *Christian Standard*, July 1, 2022, https://christianstandard.com/2022/07/what-should-the-church-do-about-the-mental-health-crisis/.

8

[1] David Brooks, *The Second Mountain: The Quest for a Moral Life* (Random House, 2019), 215.

[2] Sermon by Jeffrey A. Johnson Sr., Eastern Star Church, Indianapolis, Indiana, June 25, 2023.

9

[1] "The Chumps Who Had to Move the Tabernacle," SabbathThoughts. com, April 5, 2019, https://sabbaththoughts.com/the-chumps-who-had-to-move-the-tabernacle/.

[2] Lynn Hulsey, "Baby Boomers Driven to Retirement by COVID-19 Return to Work Amid Labor Shortage and High Inflation," *Dayton Daily News*, June 12, 2022.

[3] Alan Spector and Keith Lawrence, *Your Retirement Quest: 10 Secrets for Creating and Living a Fulfilling Retirement* (Cincinnati Book Publishers, 2010), 72.

[4] Fay Vincent, "Old Age Is Like a Debenture," *The Wall Street Journal*, January 18, 2023.

[5] Bob Russell, "A Time to Retire," Bob Russell Ministries, February 5, 2023, http://www.BobRussell.org.

[6] Spector and Lawrence, *Your Retirement Quest*, 75.

[7] Joe Hernandez, "Woodpeckers Went Nuts, Stashing 700 Pounds of Acorns in the Wall of a California Home," NPR [website], https://www.npr.org/2023/02/08/1155458695/.

[8] "Is Long-term Care Insurance Worth the Price?" ReJoyce Financial [website], https://rejoycefinancial.com/long-term-care-insurance/, accessed April 17, 2023.

[9] Spector and Lawrence, *Your Retirement Quest*, 56-58.

[10] Bob Russell, "A Time to Retire."

10

[1] "Haydn Shaw: Churches Need to Improve Their Generational IQ," *Faith & Leadership*, January 26, 2016, https://faithandleadership.com/haydn-shaw-churches-need-improve-their-generational-iq.

[2] Melissa DeWitte, "Gen Z Are Not 'Coddled.'" Stanford News Service, January 3, 2022, https://news.stanford.edu/2022/01/03/know-gen-z/.

[3] "Haydn Shaw: Churches Need to Improve Their Generational IQ."

[4] Dallas Willard, *The Spirit of the Disciplines* (HarperCollins, 1988), 221.

[5] Ibid.

[6] Haydn Shaw, *Generational IQ: Christianity Isn't Dying, Millennials Aren't the Problem, and the Future Is Bright* (Tyndale Momentum, 2015), 13-14.

[7] "Haydn Shaw: Churches Need to Improve Their Generational IQ."

[8] Kara Powell, Jake Mulder, and Brad Griffin, *Growing Young: Six Essential Strategies to Help Young People Discover and Love Your Church* (Baker Books, 2016), 53.

11

[1] Fifties Web, https://fiftiesweb.com/pop/prices-1954/.

[2] Bob Russell, *Money: A User's Manual* (Multnomah Books, 1997), 154.

12

[1] Leonard Sweet, *I Am a Follower* (Thomas Nelson, 2012), 216.

[2] "Where Is Point Nemo?" National Oceanic and Atmospheric Administration, https://oceanservice.noaa.gov/facts/nemo.html; also see, "Eerie Facts About Point Nemo, the Most Remote Location on Planet Earth," All That's Interesting [website], https://allthatsinteresting.com/point-nemo.

[3] Carl Zimmer, "Friends with Benefits," *Time*, February 20, 2012.

[4] Chris Crowley and Henry S. Lodge, MD, with Allan J. Hamilton, MD, *Younger Next Year* (Workman Publishing, 2019), 338-339.

[5] Robert Waldinger and Marc Schulz, "The Lifelong Power of Close Relationships," *The Wall Street Journal*, January 13, 2023, https://www.wsj.com/articles/the-lifelong-power-of-close-relationships-11673625450.

[6] Ibid.

[7] Justin Rowlatt, "Why Do We Value Gold?" BBC, December 8, 2013, https://www.bbc.com/news/magazine-25255957.

[8] Ibid.

[9] Waldinger and Schulz, "The Lifelong Power of Close Relationships."

[10] Ibid.

13

[1] "Written Testimony of Former First Lady Rosalynn Carter Before the Senate Special Committee on Aging," May 26, 2011, https://www.cartercenter.org/news/editorials_speeches/rosalynn-carter-committee-on-aging-testimony.html.

[2] "What Is a Caregiver?" Johns Hopkins Medicine [website], https://www.hopkinsmedicine.org/about/community_health/johns-hopkins-bayview/services/called_to_care/what_is_a_caregiver.

[3] "Caregiving for Family and Friends—A Public Health Issue," Centers for Disease Control and Prevention, https://www.cdc.gov/aging/caregiving/caregiver-brief.html.

[4] "What Is a Caregiver?" Johns Hopkins Medicine.

[5] "Caregiving for Family and Friends—A Public Health Issue," CDC.

[6] Ibid.

[7] *Hope for Caregivers: A 42-Day Devotional in Company with Henri J. M. Nouwen,* edited by Susan Martins Miller (InterVarsity Press, 2022), 17.

[8] E. R. Dodds, *Pagan and Christian in an Age of Anxiety* (W. W. Norton & Company, 1965), 136-137.

[9] John S. Dickerson, *Jesus Skeptic: A Journalist Explores the Credibility and Impact of Christianity* (Baker Books, 2019), 109-110.

[10] In addition to his blog, found at www.unchosenjourney.com, Mark Taylor wrote an article published in the July/August 2023 edition of *Christian Standard* magazine called "Learning About Alzheimer's, Myself, and God," https://christianstandard.com/learning-about-alzheimers-myself-and-god/. Mark also recommends an online support network for caregivers, accessible at https://www.hilarityforcharity.org/caregivers.

14

[1] For further information and to see a full list of publications authored by Dr. Alan Wolfelt, contact The Center for Loss and Life Transition, 3735 Broken Bow Road, Fort Collins, CO 80526; https://www.centerforloss.com; 970.226.6050.

[2] Dr. Alan Wolfelt, "Exploring the Spiritual Dimensions of Death, Grief, and Mourning," May 15-18, 2023, Fort Collins, Colorado.

[3] David Meyer, "Swan in Mourning Brings German Trains to a Halt for Nearly an Hour," *New York Post*, December 29, 2020.

[4] Bob Russell, "Marriage—A Basic Building Block of Society," Bob Russell Ministries, July 25, 2021, http://www.bobrussell.org.

[5] Alan D. Wolfelt, PhD, *You're Not Crazy—You're Grieving: 6 Steps for Surviving Loss* (Companion Press, 2023), 5.

[6] Alan D. Wolfelt, PhD, and Kirby J. Duvall, MD, *Healing Your Grief About Aging: 100 Practical Ideas on Growing Older with Confidence, Meaning and Grace* (Companion Press, 2012), 83.

[7] David Faust, *Faith Under Fire: Studies from 1 and 2 Peter* (College Press, 2008), 120.

[8] Wolfelt, *You're Not Crazy—You're Grieving*, 108.

[9] "'What a Friend We Have in Jesus' Was Written by Port Hope Man," *Lakeshore Summer* (Ontario, Canada), June 20, 1983.

15

[1] "Through Gates of Splendor: The Elisabeth Elliot Story," Museum of the Bible, https://www.museumofthebible.org/magazine/exhibitions/through-gates-of-splendor-the-elisabeth-elliot-story.

[2] David Faust, "Trust and Obey: An Interview with Elisabeth Elliot," *The Lookout*, October 4, 1998, 7-8.

[3] David Faust, "Anthony Munoz: Eyes on the Goal," *The Lookout*, February 3, 2017, https://lookoutmag.com/anthony-munoz-eyes-on-the-goal/. For more information about the Anthony Munoz Foundation, go to https://www.munozfoundation.org.

[4] "It Is Finished," by Gloria Gaither. The lyrics appear in Gloria's book, *Something Beautiful* (Gaither Music Group, 2007), 89-90. Used by permission.

[5] "I Am Loved," by Gloria Gaither and William Gaither. The lyrics appear in Gloria's book, *Something Beautiful* (Gaither Music Group, 2007), 106. Used by permission.

[6] "I'll Worship Only at the Feet of Jesus," by Gloria Gaither. The lyrics appear in Gloria's book, *Something Beautiful* (Gaither Music Group, 2007), 34-35. Used by permission.

[7] David Faust, "Because He Lives: An Interview with Gloria Gaither," *The Lookout*, April 26, 1998, 5-7.

16

[1] Russ Blowers, "Good-Byes," *The Lookout*, November 15, 1998, 13.

[2] Ibid.

[3] Henri Nouwen, "Dying Well," Henri Nouwen Society, February 10, 2018, https://henrinouwen.org/meditations/dying-well/.

[4] Ray S. Anderson, *Theology, Death, and Dying* (Fuller Seminary Press, 1986), 38.

[5] Timothy Keller, *On Death* (Penguin Books, 2020), 1-2.

[6] Ernest Becker, *The Denial of Death* (The Free Press, 1973), 26.

[7] Ibid., 284.

[8] Jonathan Merritt, "An Ash Wednesday Reflection," @JonathanMerritt on X (formerly Twitter), February 22, 2023.

[9] John R. W. Stott, *The Cross of Christ* (InterVarsity, 1986), 341.

[10] "Richard Overton, 109th Birthday," *The Christian Chronicle*, June 10, 2015, https://christianchronicle.org/richard-overton-109th-birthday/; and "Oldest WWII Vet—and Member of a Church of Christ—Dies at 112," *The Christian Chronicle*, December 28, 2018, https://christianchronicle.org/oldest-wwii-vet-and-member-of-a-church-of-christ-dies-at-112/.

[11] Ray S. Anderson, *Theology, Death, and Dying*, 157.

[12] Bob Russell, *Take Comfort: Encouraging Words from Second Corinthians* (Standard Publishing, 1991), 88.

[13] Bob Russell, "Eighty Years Old and Close to Home," Bob Russell Ministries, October 8, 2023, http://www.bobrussell.org/eighty-years-old-and-close-to-home/.

17

[1] Steve Almasy, "U.S. Runner Finishes Relay on Broken Leg," CNN, August 9, 2012, https://www.cnn.com/2012/08/09/sport/olympics-runner-broken-leg/.

[2] Frederick W. Faber, "Faith of Our Fathers," first published in 1849, public domain.

[3] Ken Curtis, "Who Was Polycarp?" Christianity.com, May 3, 2010, https://www.christianity.com/church/church-history/timeline/1-300/polycarp-11629601.html.

OTHER BOOKS
by DAVID FAUST

Embracing the Truth:
Becoming a Believer

Faith Under Fire:
Studies from First and Second Peter

Growing Gracefully:
How to Lead a Growing Church
and Live a Balanced Life

Honest Questions/Honest Answers:
How to Engage in Compelling Conversations
About Your Christian Faith

Lifted by Love:
Stepping up When Life Knocks You Down

Married for Good:
31 Devotions and Discussion Starters
for Engaged and Married Couples

Monday Morning Prayers:
Starting Your Work-Week with God
(also *Monday Morning Insights*
and *Monday Morning Proverbs*)

Praise Under Pressure:
A New Look at David
(Shepherd, Psalmist, King, Sinner)

The Life of Moses:
Blueprints for 30 Messages Built Upon God's Word

Unquenchable Faith:
Studies in 1 and 2 Thessalonians

Made in United States
Orlando, FL
15 April 2024